CHILDREN IN CONFLICT:
A CASEBOOK

CHILDREN IN CONFLICT: A CASEBOOK

ANTHONY DAVIDS

Brown University

with contributions by
SPENCER DE VAULT *and* **JOHN J. LAFFEY**
Rhode Island College

John Wiley & Sons, Inc.
New York · *London* · *Sydney* · *Toronto*

Copyright © 1974, by John Wiley & Sons, Inc.

All rights reserved. Published simultaneously in Canada.

No part of this book may be reproduced by any means, nor transmitted, nor translated into a machine language without the written permission of the publisher.

Library of Congress Cataloging in Publication Data:

Davids, Anthony.
    Children in conflict.

    1. Child psychiatry—Cases clinical reports, statistics.   I. Title. [DNLM: 1. Child psychiatry—Case studies.   WS350 D251c 1974]

RJ499.D383   618.9′28′909   73-20108
ISBN 0-471-19697-5
ISBN 0-471-19699-1 (pbk.)

Printed in the United States of America

10 9 8 7 6 5 4

PREFACE

This book deals with cases of emotionally disturbed children who were studied and treated in a variety of child-treatment settings. A knowledge of these cases will be helpful to students in child psychology, personality, abnormal psychology, special education, and psychiatry. The collection also will be interesting for school teachers, psychiatric nurses, physicians, social workers, psychologists, and paraprofessionals who work with abnormal children and youth.

Following a general introduction to the field of childhood psychopathology, there are fifteen case studies under five categories: psychosomatic disorders, behavior disorders, learning disorders, neurotic disorders, and psychotic disorders. The specific introductions to the sections describe significant problems and issues related to the particular type of disorder, and provide the necessary background and setting for considering the cases within the sections. A final section discusses critical problems that require an increased understanding in this field.

The troubled children came from a variety of family backgrounds; some children were culturally deprived and terribly neglected (including one boy who was abandoned in infancy), and some came from intact, stable, and upper middle-class families. Some children were privately treated by child psychiatrists and pediatricians. Others were treated in outpatient child guidance clinics. But the majority of them were patients in a residential treatment center. The methods of treatment varied, including psychotherapy, behavior therapy, drug therapy, milieu therapy, and special education.

The theoretical orientation is eclectic, as the variety of treatment approaches implies. With several of the cases, there is predominantly a psychodynamic orientation, utilizing Freud's concepts, interpretations, and techniques. But there are also many instances in which the attempts at understanding and treatment are guided by a learning theory orientation, employing concepts and procedures derived from Dollard and Miller's stimulus-response theory, and from Skinner's operant conditioning theory. With many of the children in residential treatment, heavy reliance was placed on the techniques of modeling and observational learning as emphasized in Bandura's social learning theory. In addition to this combination of psychodynamic and behavioral therapy, some children who were diagnosed as suffering from the hyperkinetic impulse disorder (with its related learning difficulties) were also treated by medication. Thus, this collection of cases presents the various types of childhood disorders and different approaches to the treatment of them.

This casebook examines normal and abnormal personality development in children. It will be informative to the educated layman, who does not have a background of formal academic courses in psychology, and will serve as an introduction to the field of childhood psychopathology. It is primarily intended, however, to be a supplementary reading in college and university courses ranging from introductory psychology to personality and abnormal psychology.

The book has profited greatly from contributions by two of my colleagues, Dr. Spencer DeVault and Dr. John J. Laffey. We first worked together at the Emma Pendleton Bradley Hospital in 1957. Although our professional affiliations and duties have changed somewhat, we have spent many years collaborating in the study of emotionally disturbed children. Dr. DeVault is now Professor of Psychology and Director of the School Psychology Program at Rhode Island College. Dr. Laffey is Associate Professor of Psychology and Director of the Learning Center at Rhode Island College. I have continued to serve as Professor of Psychology at Brown University and Director of Psychology at Bradley Hospital.

Dr. DeVault wrote four case studies (Ricky, Robby, Donny, and the twins); Dr. Laffey wrote two (Roger and Jerry); and I wrote the remaining nine case studies. Since I formulated and organized the book, and wrote all other material in it, I assume the sole responsibility for any of its shortcomings.

Anthony Davids

CONTENTS

CONTENTS

CHILDREN IN CONFLICT:
A CASEBOOK

1

INTRODUCTION

There are many ways in which psychological conflicts and emotional disturbance can affect children. The case studies presented here reveal the major types of psychopathology found in children. Some children "act out" their difficulties, displaying socially unacceptable behaviors that get them into trouble with their parents, school authorities, or the law.

Other children take out their emotional conflicts on themselves, becoming frightened, anxious, depressed, and generally unable to function up to their potential. They sometimes show specific neurotic disorders such as phobias and compulsions. Moreover, they may develop physical ailments, known as psychosomatic disorders. In these cases, emotional conflicts gain expression through abnormal physiological functioning of the body.

A very broad and inclusive category of disability is the category of learning disorders. They can be caused by emotional conflicts, neurological impairments or, in many cases, by a combination of psychological and physical factors. In keeping with the diversity of causes of learning disorders are the varied types of treatments used with these child cases, including psychotherapy, special education, and drug therapy.

Of all the psychopathological disorders of childhood, psychosis is the most intriguing and bewildering. Although the specific symptoms are many and varied, all psychotic children show a break with reality and are unable to cope with the demands of ordinary social living. To date, clinicians and investigators have been unable to agree on the etiology (causes) or methods of treatment, and current controversies are often heated and far from being resolved. However, with the great surge of interest being evidenced in childhood psychosis, significant advances should be forthcoming.

Emotionally disturbed children come from all types of family backgrounds. Some of the children studied started life in environ-

1

ments that were almost certain to lead to psychopathology—with broken homes and alcoholic, psychotic, or criminal parents who neglected and abused them. Others have come from perfectly respectable home settings, with intact families, normal siblings, and parents who truly cared about the child's well-being. It is somewhat surprising that the most seriously disturbed children do not always come from the most pathological backgrounds. In fact, more of the psychotic children have parents who are hard-working, effective members of society, while more of the children with conduct disorders (acting-out, delinquent behaviors) come from the pathological early environments.

The professionals who work with disturbed children and their families include child psychiatrists, pediatricians, psychiatric nurses, clinical psychologists, psychiatric social workers, and special educators. All of these "helping professions" require graduate education, professional degrees, and years of supervised clinical experience before recognizing one's ability and competence to treat children in conflict. These children are viewed in varied treatment settings such as private practice, public schools, outpatient child guidance clinics, residential treatment centers for children, and locked wards in state mental hospitals. Where the children are living away from home, in residential centers and psychiatric hospitals, much of the therapeutic work may be performed by nonprofessionals such as attendants, aides, and childcare workers. These people serve as parental substitutes for the children away from home, and they often have much more influence on the course of treatment than the professional therapists who spend much less time in daily interactions with the child patients.

The cases presented reveal the wide range of disorders found in troubled children; they show how much and how little is known about the causes of these disorders; and they indicate the kinds of treatments employed and results obtained with children treated in different therapeutic settings. In most instances, the case study covers the youngster's development and life experience from birth to the time of a follow-up assessment at some point after therapeutic treatment in childhood. While the names, dates, places, and other sources of identifying information have been changed to guard against revealing the personal identity of these children and their families, the essence of each case has not been altered. Therapeutic failures have been included along with successful cases. There is no attempt to provide a prolonged commentary on these cases. Although various theoretical orientations are described in the introductory sections, the intent is to encourage the reader or instructor to use his own preferred theoretical framework in interpreting the case findings.

In contemporary society the number of children in conflict seems to be increasing steadily, yet advances in methods of treatment come very slowly, if at all. The long-range outcomes attained with certain cases may cause concern about the effectiveness and value of treatments currently available to disturbed children. Other cases, however, reveal an impressive degree of success, and thus provide evidence of having done something worthwhile for a child in conflict.

If in studying these cases the reader personally experiences feelings of doubt and pessimism, mingled with occasional joy and hope, he will be reacting emotionally in a similar fashion to most clinicians who do their daily work in child treatment settings. A great deal of the work with disturbed children is frustrating, anxiety producing, and depressing. Actually, most of us harbor remnants from our own childhood conflicts; many of us would like to be miracle workers and, somehow, change troubled children into happy ones. But this is not the way it is. There are no easy victories, as the reader will realize when he gets to know the children whose early lives are portrayed in these case studies.

SUGGESTED READING ON CHILDHOOD PSYCHOPATHOLOGY

Although this casebook can be read and understood without recourse to other written works, the serious student of childhood psychopathology should also read other books that provide a more comprehensive coverage of this field. Some of the major and most recent works that serve this purpose are listed below. In addition to these general abnormal child psychology texts, more specific lists of recommended reading are provided at the end of the introduction to each of the five sections.

Clarizio, H. F., & McCoy, G. F. *Behavior disorders in school-aged children.* Scranton, Penna.: Chandler, 1970.

Davids, A. *Abnormal children and youth: Therapy and research.* New York: Wiley-Interscience, 1972.

Davids, A. *Issues in abnormal child psychology.* Monterey, Calif.: Brooks/Cole, 1973.

Engel, M. *Psychopathology in childhood.* New York: Harcourt Brace Jovanovich, 1972.

Harrison, S. I., & McDermott, J. F. (Eds.) *Childhood psychopathology: An anthology of basic readings.* New York: International Universities Press, 1972.

Kessler, J. W. *Psychopathology of childhood.* Englewood Cliffs, N.J.: Prentice-Hall, 1966.

Quay, H. C. & Werry, J. S. (Eds.) *Psychopathological disorders of childhood.* New York: Wiley, 1972.

Rie, H. E. (Ed.) *Perspectives in child psychopathology.* Chicago: Aldine-Atherton, 1971.

Ross, A. *Psychological disorders of children: A behavioral approach to theory, research, and therapy.* New York: McGraw-Hill, 1974.

Wolman, B. B. *Manual of child psychopathology.* New York: McGraw-Hill, 1972.

2

PSYCHOSOMATIC DISORDERS

Psychosomatic disorders (sometimes called psychophysiologic disorders) consist of physical ailments that presumably possess a fundamental psychological component. These disorders are not hypochondriacal or merely imaginary; they are very real. The person with a psychosomatic illness is just as sick and incapacitated as one whose illness resulted from a purely organic cause. For example, a man with a bleeding ulcer in his stomach or a child suffering a severe attack of bronchial asthma are equally sick, whether their physical abnormalities result from unresolved emotional conflicts or from an organic disease process. Thus, psychosomatic disorders are (1) very different from neurotically imagined ailments, (2) produce true physical damage and illness, and (3) are presumed to result from psychological conflicts.

There are different theories of psychosomatic disorders, but most of them can be classified as *specific* or *nonspecific*. According to specific theories, certain psychodynamic conflicts are specific for a given psychosomatic disorder; thus all people who show the disorder should have the same underlying conflicts. These specific theories maintain that the type of personality problem determines the choice of symptoms. For example, frustrated dependency needs lead to stomach ulcers; unfulfilled needs for tactile stimulation and affection lead to dermatitis; and repressed rage against the mother leads to asthma. From the psychodynamic position, asthmatic wheezing is viewed as suppressed crying. The child fears separation from the mother and is angry toward her, but fears rejection and therefore cannot express these emotions directly. Thus emotions gain expression in the form of asthma attacks.

Nonspecific theories hypothesize that psychosomatic symptoms occur in response to any stress (nonspecific), with the choice of symptoms or the organ breakdown being determined by individual sensitivities or physical vulnerability perhaps based on heredity or previous physical disease. Thus, according to these nonspecific theories, the association is *not* between a specific emotional constellation and a particular type of bodily upset, but between general psychological stress resulting from any form of environmental stimulation and a malfunctioning of whatever bodily organ is most susceptible.

In addition to these psychodynamically oriented theories, attempts have been made to account for psychosomatic disorders in terms of stimulus-response learning theory. According to this view, a basic affect (for instance rage, dependency, and anxiety) and its physiological component (stomach contractions) become associated with certain stimuli (the mother). This process of conditioning occurs in interpersonal relations within the first years of life, with the psychological aspect becoming repressed while the specific physiological symptom continues in a maladaptive fashion. Thus, early learning determines affective arousal patterns that are specific to the individual, and the specific symptoms or disease are related to the learned arousal patterns.

Today, these various viewpoints and explanations are strictly hypothetical. We need further empirical work devoted to increased understanding of both the etiology (causes) of psychosomatic disorders and the choice of psychophysiological symptoms. All psychosomatic theories agree, however, that unpleasant emotions resulting from negative psychological experiences (usually repressed from consciousness) cause normally adaptive psychophysiological mechanisms to malfunction, culminating in organic pathology and bodily upset.

In the various types of psychosomatic disorder, some prevalent adult disorders are rarely, if ever, seen in children. For example, peptic ulcers, essential hypertension, and migraine headaches are psychosomatic ailments found almost exclusively in adults. On the other hand, some forms of psychosomatic problems are found either primarily, or at least quite frequently, in children. Among these are feeding difficulties, bowel and bladder problems, bronchial asthma, and skin conditions. Bowel and bladder problems take such forms as chronic constipation, ulcerative colitis (inflamed colon and rectum, with bloody diarrhea) encopresis (uncontrolled bowel movements), and enuresis (uncontrolled urination, while awake or asleep). Since in some of the cases described in other sections, bowel and bladder problems play a prominent role in the psychopathology, the cases in the present section were selected to show other types of psychosomatic disorders.

The focus in two of these cases is on pathological feeding behavior—in one instance on overeating and in the other on refusal to eat. In the case of Todd, we see a boy suffering from bulimia, which is "an abnormal craving for food." As a result of his insatiable appetite, Todd had become obese when he was 11 years old, and was getting more so as time went on. It was hypothesized that Todd felt unloved, worthless, and guilty, and that his insatiable appetite somehow represented an attempt to prove to himself that he was worth caring for. Along with his abnormal food intake, Todd engaged in self-mutilating activities such as sticking pins in himself and cutting off strips of flesh with a razor blade. Moreover, he constantly got himself into situations where he would be hurt by other children or punished by adult authority figures. Thus, Todd's psychopathology and psychosomatic disorder seemed to be greatly influenced by his feelings of rejection and sense of guilt.

Debbie is a most unusual case—a very young child who absolutely refused to take any solid food or liquid into her mouth. Consequently, she was literally starving to death when she was less than one year old. There had been some serious physical and metabolical problems at birth, and Debbie's earliest feeding experiences were not pleasant. During the later stages of infancy, Debbie and her mother encountered increasing difficulties in the feeding process. By eight months of age, feeding experiences had become so traumatic that Debbie would no longer swallow any form of food; it became necessary to insert a tube into her stomach in order to tube-feed her on a regular and continuing basis.

Medical treatment had been ineffective and Debbie was much too young for psychotherapy (which relies on verbal communication), but something had to be done to motivate her to eat normally. Therefore this seemed like an ideal situation in which to apply behavior therapy. This procedure, also known as behavior modification, uses psychological principles derived from learning theory and techniques developed in laboratory work with animals to treat abnormal behavior in humans. Behavior therapy focuses on the specific problem or symptom that is in need of modification and is not concerned with the underlying cause of the behavioral abnormality. This approach is quite different from psychodynamically oriented therapy, which believes that it is essential to help the troubled individual understand the cause and meaning of his abnormality. Starting from a firm scientific base, these experimentally derived procedures are now being used widely, and with impressive success, in modifying the behavior of children with a variety of educational and psychological problems.

We refer to Debbie's case as an eating phobia, but older children or adults who refuse to eat as a result of psychological conflicts are usually said to suffer from "anorexia nervosa." This form of psychosomatic disorder is found much more frequently in females than in males and usually afflicts girls in late adolescence or early adulthood. The psychodynamic interpretation of anorexia nervosa is that the girl does not want to leave childhood and become an adult—the refusal to eat signifies a refusal to grow up. There are more sexualized interpretations of this form of psychopathology, hypothesizing that through a distortion of reasoning the maturing female child unconsciously fears oral impregnation and thus ceases to take in food. True cases of anorexia nervosa are pathetic to see and, for the nonprofessional, are difficult to understand. The patients' body weight drops to dangerously low levels; they look like the emaciated people who were released from Nazi concentration camps, and they willingly submit to daily intravenous feedings rather than eat a morsel of food in a normal manner. Although we have presented the case of Debbie, a 15-month-old girl who cannot be considered as a case of anorexia nervosa, her psychosomatic symptomatology shows, at an exceptionally early age, what is more often seen in somewhat older children and adolescents.

In the course of normal human development, one learns to desire certain foods and to enjoy eating when hungry. Experiencing insatiable cravings, eating indiscriminantly, or starving oneself are forms of seriously maladaptive behavior. Here, we will study two children (Todd and Debbie) in whom the eating process had gone awry. However, other than the fact their psychosomatic disorders centered around the intake of food, there is no similarity between the two cases, their treatment, or their outcomes.

The third case, Donny, suffered from two different psychophysiological disorders that are believed to contain a large psychological element—asthma and eczema. While this case may not provide clear-cut evidence supporting one theoretical model of psychosomatic disorders and disconfirming others, it vividly shows an association between emotional conflicts and psychophysiological malfunctioning. This youngster endured repeated separations from his seriously disturbed mother and must certainly have feared rejection and desertion, while also being very resentful of this treatment. Thus his asthmatic attacks could have symbolically represented a cry for affection. His skin condition (eczema) could similarly represent a psychosomatic expression of his desire for close physical contact with the mother. Both physical ailments became more pronounced when Donny experienced increased frustration, threat, and loneliness.

These three cases and several others give convincing evidence that emotional upset and bodily dysfunction are often intimately related in children. It is difficult to ignore the 'facts" presented here. But it is obvious that an understanding of these phenomena is far from adequate, and many areas need clarification. For example, there remains the perplexing problem of symptom placement. Why does an individual develop a certain type of psychosomatic disorder instead of some other form of expressing his conflicts? Answers to this and other questions about psychosomatic disorders very likely will come from research studies of children in the process of developing neurotic conflicts and their solutions.

RECOMMENDED READING

Alexander, F. *Psychosomatic medicine: Its principles and applications.* New York: Norton, 1950.

Apley, J., & McKeith, R. *The child and his symptoms: A psychosomatic approach.* Philadelphia: Davis, 1962.

Costello, C. (Ed.) *Symptoms of psychopathology.* New York: Wiley, 1970.

Garner, A. M., & Wenar, C. W. *The mother-child interaction in psychosomatic disorders.* Urbana, Ill.: University of Illinois Press, 1959.

Grinker, R. *Psychosomatic research.* New York: Norton, 1953.

1. THE CASE OF TODD:
Obesity from a Sense of Guilt

When 11-year-old Todd was admitted to the residential treatment center he was very much overweight (5 feet, 1 inch in height and weighed 155 pounds). He had gained more than 50 pounds in less than a year. The primary reason for his institutionalization, however, was not his tremendous appetite nor his pathological overeating. Among the chief complaints mentioned at the time of his admission were:

1. Low frustration tolerance with frequent aggressive and destructive outbursts.
2. Stealing—usually in such a way that he got caught.
3. Sticking pins and sharp objects into various parts of his body and removing strips of flesh with razor blades.
4. Poor school adjustment.
5. Fairly mild stuttering.

With this constellation of socially undesirable behaviors, Todd entered residential psychiatric treatment.

BACKGROUND HISTORY

Todd was born from his mother's first pregnancy. She had mild morning sickness during the first three months and during the fourth month, she said that the gynecologist told her that there was no fetal heartbeat and that the baby was dead. She became extremely disturbed and visited another doctor who did not confirm these findings. She gained 25 pounds during her pregnancy. Todd was born on schedule with a labor of 12 hours and low forceps delivery. His birth weight was 7 pounds. He was breast-fed for 4 months, and weaning was completed by 18 months. Toilet-training was instituted at 18 months of age and completed by the time he was 30 months old.

A sister was born when Todd was two years old, and a brother was born when he was four. A third sibling, another boy, was born when Todd was eight. Until this time, Todd had made a good adjustment at home and at school.

Shortly after the birth of the youngest sibling, Todd went to visit a male cousin who had previously lived with Todd's family. During this visit, Todd pushed this boy through a glass door (presumably accidentally) and, severely cut, he was rushed to the hospital. The boy almost bled to death and Todd became extremely upset and hysterical at the time of the accident. He was unable to state that he had pushed his cousin through the door until about two years after the event had occurred. At that time, Todd blamed himself for the accident. Soon after this, Todd's stuttering difficulties were noted. At first, they were quite severe and he began to have difficulty in school as a result but, nevertheless, his school performance remained at an acceptable level. While he continued to do fairly well in school, he began to withdraw from other children. The following year, it was reported that Todd did not get along well with other boys and that he was picked on and often beaten.

About that time, there was a gasoline explosion in Todd's house and his father was badly burned. Todd saw his father's flaming clothes and helped to remove them. During the father's convalescence Todd was very helpful and anxious to please him. At this time, when he was 10 years old, Todd's overeating began. Also, the symptoms and chief complaints for which he was later institutionalized began to appear and to become extremely troublesome.

Todd's psychotherapy began at a mental health center near his home. However, his parents felt that this outpatient weekly psychotherapy was not particularly helpful. Then Todd steered his bicycle into a tree, lost consciousness with a broken jaw, and was hospitalized for five days, but with no known sequelae. Later, when he was 11 years of age, he was sent to a boarding school, but within a month he was discharged because of his unacceptable and uncontrollable behavior. After he returned home, he threatened to harm his younger brother with a knife, and his mother called the police and had him placed in a detention home overnight. Another extremely aggressive acting-out episode at home frightened his parents so much that they called the authorities and had him placed temporarily in a state mental hospital. At this point, Todd was accepted for private psychiatric residential treatment.

PHYSICAL AND NEUROLOGICAL EXAMINATIONS

A comprehensive physical examination conducted at the time of Todd's admission to the residential treatment center revealed no significant findings other than marked obesity. He weighed 155 pounds but, according to medical charts for normal physical development, he should have weighed about 90 pounds. A neurological consultant examined Todd and found him to be "an intelligent and cooperative patient whose attention span was limited." He also reported that "the generalized obesity is dietary in type, without any evidence of thyroid or pituitary dysfunction." No gross neurological abnormalities were noted, and his motor power, sensations, and reflexes were intact. This neurologist felt that if there were any organic difficulties they were very slight. However, an electroencephalogram (EEG) obtained soon after his admission was classified as "abnormal." According to this examination, "the record is consistent with a diffuse organic factor with particular localization in the right temporal area, and perhaps in the diencephalon." Thus, according to these medical examinations Todd did not appear to have any gross physical abnormalities other than being seriously overweight. Although there was a suggestion of some form of minimal brain dysfunction, this did not have pronounced effects that were easily detectable by neurological examination.

PSYCHOLOGICAL ASSESSMENT

On the Wechsler Intelligence Scale for Children (WISC), Todd obtained an IQ of 128, indicating a superior intellectual capacity. However, the examining clinical psychologist stated that Todd was functioning less efficiently, and considerably beneath his potential, as a result of his anxiety and self-condemning attitude. The test responses showed that Todd was very fearful and anxious, with tremendous guilt feelings that led to the need for constant punishment. The psychologist felt it unlikely that Todd's motivation and behavior would change unless the conflicts underlying his guilt were resolved and he could obtain some insight into his psychopathology. Although Todd showed certain psychoticlike features on some of the personality tests, he was not psychotic but merely attempting to escape from his guilt by withdrawing from reality.

It was felt, however, that if Todd did not become able to properly understand and cope with his guilt, these psychoticlike tendencies could become a more permanent part of his personality structure.

PSYCHIATRIC EVALUATION

The psychiatrist who evaluated Todd's mental status at the treatment center reported that Todd's thoughts were very much centered around food and eating. He informed the psychiatrist that he had three things against the institution. First there should be two separate groups in the dining room—the quiet group and the noisy group. Todd considered himself in the quiet group. Second, there should not be such a waste of food—children should be allowed to take only as much food as they could eat. Todd complained that after each meal a great deal of food was thrown out, saying, "No one thinks that there might be some children who are still hungry." Third, Todd felt that he should be allowed to work in the kitchen. He stated, "I could skip a whole meal every day if I were allowed to help there. Let me try it at least. Then, if you think I am not suitable, I'll quit."

Todd readily admitted his difficulties in adjusting to the institution and described the hardships he endured in living with the other boys. He stated that he was teased and "pushed around." There were very few boys or adult staff members whom he liked, and he got along much better with girls.

The psychiatrist discussed Todd's need or desire to "elope" from the institution, and Todd indicated that being away from the institution lessened his anxiety and tension. He said, "I have heard that this is one of the best places in the world, but it makes me jumpy." When the psychiatrist asked him to compare his difficulties at home with those in the institution, he said, "Being here, I think this place is worse, but at home I think that place is worse." Todd's statements often revealed extremely ambivalent feelings toward his parents. However, on direct questioning, he always declared that he loved his parents.

The examining psychiatrist observed that Todd was extremely self-deprecatory and thought of himself as a very bad person. It was felt that Todd's anxiety and deviant behavior were connected with a tremendous amount of guilt. However, the psychiatrist readily admitted that he did not fully understand the basis for this guilt. In probing the traumatic events in Todd's life, the psychiatrist persuaded him to talk about the experience of pushing his cousin through a glass door, of crashing his bicycle and breaking his jaw, and of seeing his father on fire and being severely burned. Although these and other negative experiences reported by Todd probably played an important role, an obvious "cause" could not be found to account for his feeling of worthlessness.

In response to the psychiatrist's questioning, Todd revealed a very pessimistic outlook for his future. He semed to have a sense of impending doom and disaster in his life, and believed that he would be unable to avoid jails and would eventually end up in a state reformatory. He talked about these things in a rather nonchalant manner, as if they were being determined by fate and, although he understood them intellectually, there was nothing he could do about the unhappy times ahead.

Occasionally, Todd also expressed the fear of insanity, relating certain experiences that could be viewed as episodes of estrangement and depersonalization. Also there were episodes of loss of reality about himself. On several occasions, he reported feeling abnormally huge and, at other times, he felt as if he had lost all weight, or as if his legs did not touch the ground and he was floating in the air. He said that he frequently experienced feelings of unreality and that things in his immediate environment appeared strange, unfamiliar, and indistinct. He had been having these disquieting experiences for the past couple of years, and they engendered considerable anxiety.

After completing the diagnostic interviews, the examining psychiatrist was still baffled by Todd's psychodynamics and defenses. He found this case exceptionally difficult to diagnose, and felt that predictions for Todd's future adjustment and long-range outcome were bleak.

RESIDENTIAL TREATMENT

At the time of admission, Todd showed severely aggressive acting-out behavior toward other children, but soon this was replaced by a professed helplessness and an inability to protect himself. He was unable to enjoy group participation and formed no friendships with other children.

Throughout his entire stay he had a great deal of difficulty around meal times, always demanding more food, complaining about being starved, and behaving very badly in the dining room. Since he was severely overweight when he was admitted, the staff would have liked somehow to have controlled his weight, but Todd managed to gain weight steadily throughout his institutionalization. He evidenced a voracious appetite and appeared driven to consume huge quantities of food. There were, however, certain foods that he liked more than others, and these were the fattening foods. In fact, Todd occasionally traded some of his less preferred meals for other children's helpings when the meal consisted of things that he especially liked (for example, spaghetti and other starches). With this arrangement, when some of his favorite foods were being served, he would have control of almost all the food at his table.

An incident that occurred within the treatment center is particularly interesting. It not only reveals Todd's severe psychopathology but also his cleverness and ingenuity. He took a large tootsie roll and chewed it into a rather lumpy-looking brown substance that resembled feces. He then flushed a toilet to ensure that the bowl contained clean water and placed the substance in the toilet water. Gathering a group of other child patients to witness the act, Todd got several of them to promise him food from their future servings in the dining rom if he would eat the "shit" that was in the toilet. After securing these promises and making arrangements to collect the bets, Todd took the candy out of the toilet bowl and ate it. Thus he earned a considerable amount of food, which would be paid to him later.

Todd also showed a preoccupation with all sorts of sexual activities. He often exhibited his penis to boys and girls, lifted the skirts of female staff members, and physically molested female patients and child-care workers. On occasion he practiced fellatio on a number of boys. Whenever he was reprimanded for any of his unacceptable behavior, his immediate response was to run away or threaten to do so. If unable to run away, he would verbally and physically attack staff members and, at times, purposely urinate on the floor or destroy property. Even when he was not particularly upset, he frequently used obscenities and often sang obscene songs that he composed.

In the school at the institution, Todd was continually a disruptive influence in the classroom, making noises, singing, and creating a disturbance that made it difficult for other children to do their work. Moreover, he was very negativistic about doing his own schoolwork. In spite of this attitude, rather surprisingly, Todd was able to master academic material at his expected grade level with relatively little effort. Most likely, the fact that he possessed superior intellectual ability permitted him to function up to grade level even though he suffered from severe psychopathology.

Todd's stuttering continued throughout his period of institutionalization. In addition, he frequently hid pins and used them to pick at his hands and feet, tearing bits of flesh from his body. Obviously, he possessed a strong masochistic need to hurt himself. In keeping with this, in his interactions with child-care workers, he constantly provoked them to punish him. His self-concept was that of a very bad person, and much of what he did to himself or provoked others to do to him seemed to reinforce the negative feelings he had about himself.

The most troublesome behavior, however, was Todd's tendency to run away from the institution. These "elopements" occurred several times a week, and there seemed to be no way to stop them within the open setting in which he was being treated. That is, he was not residing in a closed institution with locked wards, but was in a setting designed for disturbed children who could be controlled without physical constraints. It was necessary to keep Todd constantly under close supervision, which required personalized attention from individual child-care workers, and this detracted from their ability to work with other group members. But in spite of this special attention, Todd managed to elope frequently.

Todd's usual pattern during these elopements was to go into a large city located a few miles from the institution and steal from collection boxes—boxes containing donations for the heart fund or cancer fund—or steal from ladies' pocketbooks in bowling alleys or the railroad station. Sometimes the money was spent on the movies but, mainly, it was used to buy food and candy. Todd would go into a diner or restaurant and eat hamburgers and frankfurters without stopping, until it became obvious to the proprietor that the boy's eating behavior was pathological. After Todd was picked up by the police and returned to the treatment center, he admitted that he stole the money to buy food because he was being starved in the institution. According to him, an escapade without something extra to eat would not be enjoyable.

During the cold winter months, Todd, often improperly clothed, ran away when the temperature was around zero. During these escapades, he frequently got into dangerous situations, such as hitchhiking along a darkened road and walking around freight trains in the railroad yard. Here is an example of his ingenuity: one winter evening, clad only in pajamas and a jacket, Todd left the grounds of the institution during a snowstorm and hitchhiked to a neighboring city. There, he stole money to buy a train ticket and got to New York City where he went on an eating binge before he was caught by the police and returned almost 200 miles to the treatment center.

DRUG THERAPY AND PSYCHOTHERAPY

Throughout Todd's institutionalization, he received daily medication such as Thorazine, Reserpine, and Dexedrine. These drug therapies were administered to help cope with his consistently uncontrollable behavior.

Psychotherapy was also initiated shortly after Todd's institutionalization and it continued for three months. Although he was able to discuss significant material in the therapeutic interviews, the therapist felt this period of therapy had been too brief to show appreciable gains. In the beginning, the therapist attempted to reduce Todd's troublesome behavior of running away from the institution by taking him on outside trips during the therapy sessions. This was not successful, however, and these trips with the therapist stopped. Consequently, Todd became negative toward the therapist and eventually refused to participate in psychotherapy.

Throughout this period, the therapist encouraged Todd to express his hostile feelings. Much of the material brought up by Todd related to his parents, especially the father. On several occasions, he expressed a great disappointment in his father. However, during psychotherapy, he never revealed an improvement in the ability to cope with his strong guilt feeling. Moreover, a great deal of sexual material was presented by Todd in psychotherapy and its bizarre content suggested an underlying schizophrenic component.

TREATMENT OUTCOME AND SUBSEQUENT ADJUSTMENT

Obviously, this was not the type of institution that could contain a boy with Todd's pathological behavior. After six months of residential treatment, it was decided at a formal staff conference that Todd made no gains and should be discharged. It was recommended that he be placed in a closed institution where he would be protected from his uncontrollable impulses and would receive intensive psychotherapy.

Todd's official psychiatric diagnosis was a combination of "anxiety reaction" and "chronic brain syndrome of unknown cause," and his condition at the time of discharge was rated as "unimproved." Although his parents were still legal guardians, Todd was discharged into the custody of the Child Welfare Department in the state in which his family lived. The prognosis at discharge was "guarded," with possibilities that Todd might show psychotic features and continue to hurt himself and others if his serious psychological difficulties were not alleviated.

Following his discharge from the institution, Todd was seen in other child-treatment facilities and nothing was heard about him for several years until he was 18. Then a letter was received from a large state mental hospital where Todd was incarcerated, requesting information about his earlier psychiatric treatment. It stated that he was in serious trouble with the law and was suspected of starting a fire that injured innocent people and destroyed valuable property. Thus, the predictions about his future were unhappily confirmed.

2. THE CASE OF DEBBIE:
Eating Phobia in a 15-Month-Old-Girl

On a bleak day in January, a mother brought her 15-month-old daughter to the Child Study Center located in the psychology department of a New England university. Although other mothers brought their normal children here to participate in research studies, it was unusual for a child to be brought for consultation concerning severe psychological or physical abnormalities. The girl suffered from a serious psychosomatic disturbance: she would not eat food in the normal fashion and therefore had to be fed through a tube that was inserted into her stomach. By psychosomatic, we mean that psychological factors—learning problems—were leading to physical distress. This case was referred to the psychologists by the child's pediatrician.

DEBBIE'S EARLY HISTORY

Debbie was born from a troubled pregnancy during which her mother felt uncomfortable and experienced extreme fatigue and nausea. She was a full-term baby, and delivery was rapid and by low forceps. Her mother received oxygen during delivery because of a rapid heartbeat. At birth Debbie weighed seven pounds and four ounces.

Soon after birth, tachypnea (rapid breathing) in the range of 100, was noted and the child appeared plethoric (excessive flushing). The conjunctivae (lining of the eyes) were inflamed and Debbie appeared to be starry-eyed with some eye-rolling. Hypoglycemia (low blood sugar) was suspected and subsequently diagnosed, and Debbie was transferred to the intensive care unit where she was treated with intravenous 50-percent glucose. Seizures occurred at this time. Because of these abnormalities, she remained hospitalized for 16 days and was discharged with these complications: transient hypoglycemia of the newborn, poly-

19

cythemia (increased red cells), thrombocytopenia (decreased plate-lets), and central nervous system impairment.

When Debbie was three months old, after various formulas had been tried because of her poor feeding she was hospitalized and studied by several specialists. She had visual problems and her EEG revealed a marked abnormality. She was placed on a low-protein, high-carbohydrate diet, taking a sugar supplement 20 to 30 minutes after each feeding. The discharge diagnosis was leucine (that is, amino acid formed from protein) sensitive hypoglycemia.

During the next few months, Debbie continued to have difficulty in eating. She had little interest in food and would often refuse to eat even when her mother tried to get her to do so. The mother reported that, at one point, she improvised a procedure to get Debbie to open her mouth and take in food. Her mother slapped her buttocks gently, and when Debbie opened her mouth to cry or utter an exclamation, her mother put food into the back of her mouth. For a while, this worked and Debbie obtained nourish-ment in this way; then she started to gag and fuss, and the tech-nique was abandoned.

When Debbie was seven months old, the feeding problem became so severe (she weighed 9 pounds, 13 ounces) that tube feeding was required. She was brought to the hospital again and a tube was put into her stomach (gastrostomy) where it remained until it was surgically removed. The stress involved giving the special diet to Debbie, who now actively resisted all oral intake, was relieved by having tube feeding available as a last resort. However, for seven months she got all her daily food through the tube. Usually, this took three feedings a day—with her mother filling the bottle and waiting for the contents to drain into her stomach.

When Debbie was 15 months old, her pediatrician requested that the psychologists use their skills and techniques in an attempt to modify her abnormal and disabling behavior. She no longer needed the special diet and was off medication.

Before the psychologists saw Debbie, she was reevaluated by a pediatric-neurologist to ensure that her feeding disability did not have a physical basis; that is, they wanted to be certain that there was no physical reason why Debbie did not take food through her mouth. The medical report definitely indicated that there was no organic basis for her inability to eat normally. This consultant was enthusiastic about the intended plan to apply operant conditioning techniques in attempting to get Debbie off the gastrostomy. He was convinced that she possessed the functional capabilities of sucking, chewing, and swallowing.

INITIAL LABORATORY SESSION

When Debbie's mother brought her into the Child Study Center, the psychologists were pleasantly surprised to see a happy, pretty, little blonde girl with big brown eyes. She had a healthy, well-nourished appearance. Debbie was placed in a highchair and the initial procedure was to give her the opportunity to use various food-related objects. She voluntarily grasped and played with a baby's bottle with a nipple on it, occasionally putting the bottom into her mouth and then putting it down. She also played with a plastic cup but did not raise it to her mouth. Little tidbits (for instance, Cheerios) were placed on the tray in front of her, and Debbie played with them but did not put them into her mouth. She also held onto a spoon and played with it, but when baby food was put on the spoon, she did not put it into her mouth. In other words, she played freely with most of the food-related objects when permitted to do so, but whenever they contained food, she avoided them.

The next step was to encourage Debbie to put certain things into her mouth. Milk was put into the cup, which was placed in her hands and pushed toward her mouth, but she pushed it away and spilled the contents. The spoon containing baby food was brought to her mouth, but again she spilled it and turned away. Now, her eyes started rolling back into their sockets. Her mother tried to put a nipple on a baby bottle filled with milk into her mouth and, as her mother became more forceful, Debbie became agitated—crying and resisting attempts to put the nipple into her mouth. Soon, she reached the stage of extreme agitation—she cried loudly, became flushed, and showed signs of severe emotional upset. Obviously, these attempts to force her to take food orally were not successful.

The next step was Debbie's tube-feeding. A glass vial filled with a five-ounce mixture of blended food was connected to the tube that was implanted in her stomach. At first, her mother held her in one arm, and with the other arm held the glass vial in the air so that the food flowed down the tube into Debbie's stomach. Debbie immediately showed signs of discomfort and was unhappy with the procedure. After a while, her mother laid her on the table and held the glass container and tube over her head, letting the contents drain into the stomach. Debbie thrashed around, turned vividly red, and showed severe signs of emotional distress, almost like a temper tantrum.

Her mother said that when Debbie had taken the entire contents of this glass vial she would probably throw up. Following almost every feeding, Debbie vomited a great deal of what she had taken in. Emptying the total contents into her stomach took time, and she cried vigorously throughout. When the vial was empty and the tube disconnected, as predicted, Debbie spit up and vomited most of the food. However, quite surprisingly, within minutes after this seemingly traumatic feeding experience, she again became relaxed and was enjoying herself. She sought her mother's attention, clung to her, and gradually became her normal self. When placed on the floor in front of a large mirror that covered one wall of the laboratory room, she was pleased to be able to look at herself and to play in front of the mirror. When the empty baby bottle was made available, without forcing it on her, she handled it and put it to her mouth. Most of the time, however, she had the bottom of the bottle, rather than the nipple, in her mouth. The cup was again handed to her while she sat on the floor, and she was perfectly willing to pick it up, play with it, and put parts of it into her mouth.

Because of these observations, a program of behavior modification was implemented with Debbie.

BEHAVIOR MODIFICATION SESSIONS

It was decided that the best site for operant conditioning was the learning laboratory at a nearby children's hospital, which is equipped with a polygraph, assorted transducers, and equipment that could be used in feeding Debbie. Specifically, this laboratory contained a feeding device consisting of a transducer connected to a polygraph enabling recordings of mouth contact and sucking behavior, along with the required instruments that made liquid food reinforcement contingent upon the child's mouthing and sucking activity.

The original plan was to follow a well-controlled "scientific" procedure with Debbie, trying to obtain objective recordings of her behavior throughout the conditioning sessions. A highchair was obtained with a tray containing a hole through which a tube connected to the polygraph could be inserted. At the end of this tube there was a commercial nipple through which dextrose could be administered. The tube and nipple rested in the tray in such a way that she could reach for it, pull it to her mouth, and engage in whatever play activity she wished. The intention was to capitalize on the fact that although she had a strong aversion to other people placing things in her mouth, she had a tendency to willingly place her own fingers and other objects into her mouth. It was hoped that she would do this with the nipple and that, after recording her baseline level of activity, we could administer taste reinforcements, thereby increasing her willingness to engage in sucking behavior that led to food entering her mouth. It was hoped to "trick" Debbie into liking to put the nipple into her mouth by giving her considerable social and taste reinforcement.

The device for this experimental work with Debbie was not very attractive to her. She did not show the natural attraction for the nipple that a child her age ordinarily has, and she was not interested in exploring the nipple or putting it into her mouth. It was decided, therefore, to change the procedure quite drastically.

The next step was to have Debbie's mother sit in a chair holding Debbie in her arms, put a blank nipple into Debbie's hands, and wait for her to touch her own mouth with it. When Debbie touched her mouth with the nipple, both her mother and the laboratory assistant immediately followed this behavior with social reinforcement by smiling at her and saying, "Good girl, Debbie." It was discovered that Debbie liked to see herself in the mirror. Thus whenever she put the nipple near her mouth, the assistant closed the glass door to the observation chamber, enabling her to look at herself while simultaneously being praised, cuddled, and rocked. The technique worked very well, and throughout these daily sessions in the laboratory, she spent more time with the nipple in her mouth. Gradually, this was replaced by distinctively colored cups, and she again was reinforced (rewarded) for bringing the cup to her mouth. Her mother would sing to her and cuddle her, and the experimenter said nice things while he permitted her to look at herself in the mirror.

Gradually, it was possible to put small amounts of a milk formula into the cup, which Debbie eventually put into her mouth and swallowed. Each time that a successful behavior occurred, the usual reinforcement came from her mother and the assistant. Her mother hugged her affectionately and sang pleasant songs to her. Then a musical device was constructed and added to the procedure. The mother could control this music box with her foot while Debbie held a cup of food. Whenever she brought the cup to her mouth, her mother pressed the pedal and played the music that Debbie liked. In response, Debbie began to drink milk from the cup. Then she was given a spoon to place in her mouth, at first with no food on it. When she put the spoon to her mouth, she again received the social reinforcement and was also given some milk to drink because, by this time, she enjoyed this part of the feeding procedure. Next, they put baby food on the spoon and Debbie began to eat from the spoon, while obviously enjoying the various reinforcements obtained.

During a two-week training period in the laboratory, Debbie gradually increased her oral food volume until she was taking about 14 ounces a day. Then her mother reduced the amount of food given to her by stomach loading, while tube-feeding her only once a day instead of the three daily tube-feedings she received previously.

CONTINUATION OF THE
CONDITIONING PROGRAM AT HOME

The sessions at the hospital were discontinued for a while, and Debbie's mother was instructed to use these techniques with Debbie at home. Shortly thereafter, she brought her back to the hospital laboratory and demonstrated the successful feeding behavior that Debbie maintained. Now, her mother was somewhat reluctant to have the tube removed from Debbie's stomach. Although she was using it infrequently, she thought that at times it might be necessary to give Debbie supplemental food in this manner. However, the tube came out of Debbie's stomach accidentally and the

reinsertion was difficult. Since she now took her her daily requirements of food orally, the tube was kept in her stomach only one
week longer. Then it was removed by a pediatric surgeon. By this
time, Debbie was eating and drinking normally.

FOLLOW-UP EVALUATIONS

Three months later, Debbie and her mother returned to the laboratory for a follow-up evaluation. Her mother reported that
Debbie's feeding was proceeding very well and that everything was
fine. While the mother still occasionally used the music box at
home, she said that Debbie could be fed regular foods without undue concern for feeding difficulties or the need for special handling.

A typical breakfast consisted of juice (usually apple-cherry) and
cereal with a little fruit and cold milk. A typical lunch included
meat (turkey, chicken, veal or beef), vegetables such as carrots,
green beans, peas, or beets, and fruit such as applesauce, peaches,
pears, and again cold milk. At dinner, Debbie had almost the same
menu as at lunchtime and, later in the evening, she was given milk
and some food that was left over from the day's prescribed
amount. Sometimes in the evening she had things like cookies or
ice cream. With the present approach, she had been getting 24
ounces of whole milk from a cup each day.

Another follow-up session was held with Debbie and her mother
approximately nine months after the initial contact. The mother
reported that Debbie continued to eat three meals a day, with
additional milk at bedtime. Now the meals included sandwiches,
crackers, and cookies. Her mother said that at the time of the
initial contact in January Debbie weighed 21 pounds and, now,
she weighed only 17 pounds. Her mother was still worried about
the fact that Debbie remained at the borderline of acceptable
weight for her age (approximately two years), but she tried not to
become overly concerned.

In the laboratory feeding session, Debbie sat in the highchair
and very easily and contentedly ate a bowl of food (a mixture of
meat, beans, and applesauce). She used a spoon and ate very well.
Then her mother gave her a cracker, which she also ate. When
Debbie was satisfied with the amount of food she had taken from
the bowl, she handed it back to her mother. Also, when she had

almost finished the cracker and decided that she did not want any more, she handed it back to her mother.

Her mother also proudly stated that Debbie was happy, active, playful and very well liked by other children. Debbie was being seen in the Home Development Guidance Program conducted by a local special school for young children with varied types of neurological impairment, and it was reported that she had been showing continued improvement in all areas of functioning. Although she remained somewhat underweight, in spite of normal feeding patterns, this may be attributable to metabolic imbalances associated with hypoglycemia and the central nervous system difficulties she experienced. Nevertheless, when last evaluated, Debbie was making good progress, and it is hoped that this truly lovely little girl will be able to lead an essentially normal life.

3. THE CASE OF DONNY:
Emotional Conflicts, Asthma, and Eczema

From the time of Donny's arrival at the children's psychiatric hospital, he was a very easy boy to live with. An average sized seven-year-old boy, he was usually agreeable, cheerful, and happy. The staff found him to be quite affectionate and cooperative. At first rather shy and reserved, he was nevertheless generally liked by the other children and was accepted with no noticeable resentment. He worked well into the routines, conforming very satisfactorily and understanding almost immediately what was acceptable behavior. When difficulties arose, it was almost always possible to reason with him.

Donny eagerly participated in most group activities, showed skill with playground equipment, and a great interest in sports. In spite of his shyness, he generally preferred to play with a small group of children rather than alone, although some of his play was perhaps typical of a slightly younger child. For example, Donny showed a great fascination with sand and water play, although his similar interest in forts and castles was more typical of his age level. He liked to finger-paint and seemed quite artistic, taking an interest in crayon and water-color activities. In some ways he was an ideal audience for the adults, listening with interest and attention when they told stories to the children. Similarly, he showed considerable interest in music and even developed a beginning ability with the guitar because of his good sense of rhythm. He seemed anxious to learn new activities and seldom complained, even when asked to try something that he could not do.

Generally, Donny did extremely well, adjusting almost immediately to the limits and rules of the hospital. He liked the adults and went out of his way to please them, maintaining acceptable behavior in the dining room and being very cooperative both in getting up in the morning and going to bed at night. Even when he was unable to go to sleep immediately at bedtime, he was usually quiet, although occasionally he told stories on his own to

27

those children who were interested and still awake. He was very capable of self-care, being able to dress, undress, and bathe himself quite competently. Occasionally, he was a little slow in these areas but, at a word of reminder from an adult, he would quickly complete his task. One of his most noticeable characteristics was his great consideration for the less capable children in his group. He was kind to them, made special efforts to be friendly, and often went out of his way to protect them against the aggression and taunts of the other children. This won him many friends and even the respect of the children who did the teasing. He seemed to like almost every child, with only one or two exceptions, and even toward the exceptions he seldom expressed his dislike.

Only rarely was Donny aggressive, provocative, or negativistic. He occasionally could be somewhat impatient and, a few times when frustrated or upset, became a bit obstinate and stubborn. On these occasions, he might direct verbal abuse or aggression toward the staff, but his reasonableness and good nature soon took over and he would often spontaneously apologize for something he had said. After a few months at the hospital, he might tease the adults a bit, sometimes playfully hiding or challenging the adults to "make me," when something displeased him. However, in the end and usually with a minimum of difficulty, he did what was requested of him. Only infrequently did he begin a fight or show aggression toward other children, unless provoked. But he was capable of defending himself and protecting himself in any situation, even with the older, larger children. Although there were changes later, this picture basically characterized Donny throughout his stay of several years at the hospital, and he was always known as an agreeable, pleasant, likeable, and affectionate boy.

REFERRAL AND EVALUATION

In contrast, the agency in Donny's home town had a somewhat different picture of him. They had referred him for residential psychiatric treatment after he had been found unsuitable by several foster homes and after difficulties in his own home with his mother had become seemingly insurmountable. He was viewed as a boy who was overactive, aggressive toward younger children, extremely demanding, moody, and attention-seeking. He was reported to be very difficult to control when frustrated, and was both enuretic and encopretic, wetting and soiling himself, particularly at moments of stress, anger, or anxiety. The agency considered him to be an extremely disturbed child, incapable of living in a family or foster home situation and desperately in need of emotional support and intensive psychiatric treatment.

All of these difficulties were found in a boy who had some rather severe medical problems that were very likely related to his emotional conflicts. These included severe bronchial asthma and a dermatitis of long standing that had appeared when Donny was three, consisting of severe eczema, both of which seemed related as well to his allergic reactions to a number of foods and other substances. Donny had been hospitalized several time for the eczema and the asthma. In spite of the obvious allergic reactions, medical studies suggested that the skin condition particularly was largely psychogenic, since it seemed to worsen during periods of emotional stress, and the agency psychiatrist made this interpretation of Donny's symptoms: "Theoretically, it has been suggested that a mother who cannot handle her child physically in a warm accepting way and has a good deal of hostility and resistance to the child, may have a child with skin difficulties. It has also been suggested that asthmatic reactions may develop in individuals who have a fear of losing the mother and a need to suppress their hostile feelings towards her because she might abandon them completely. Thus, asthma may appear as a kind of suppressed cry of rage."

Clinical evaluations at the psychiatric hospital reflected the agency's picture of a deeply disturbed boy more than they reflected the actual behavior seen in Donny's early days at the institution. Thus, the psychiatrist who initially interviewed him described Donny as a frightened, confused little boy, anxious and guilty about his hostile aggressive feelings, and in search of a sense of safety and stability in a world that he perceived as depriving, cold, and unloving. The psychiatrist described how Donny had been tense and restless in the interview, although making efforts to be friendly toward the doctor. Donny began by shooting at a target with a toy dart gun, and although not very successful in this he became quite stimulated, to the point of defecating in his trousers. The feces fell on the floor and Donny carefully picked it up and put

it in the wastepaper basket, saying nothing about it, apparently trying to pass off the episode with a great deal of denial, concealing
his activity and his anxiety as much as possible.

Following this he began to paint, asking the psychiatrist to spell
the word "poison" for him so that he could paint it. Having made
this request, he refused to answer any question about why he
wanted to paint the word poison. He then painted a picture of a
skeleton and remarked, "There is such a thing as a skeleton, but not
a live one. I am not afraid." Painting the skeleton to the waist, he
put a shirt on it and a belt around the waist. He mentioned having
some sisters but expressed no feelings about any member of his
family. He answered questions about them briefly, in a way that
fostered the impression that everything was all right at home. As
it turned out, his "sisters" were children who had shared the same
foster home with him.

Despite his denial and his attempts to portray himself as happy,
the psychiatrist suspected that there was a good deal of underlying
depression along with his anxiety and deep hostility. He described
Donny as a frightened child who was searching for a kind of stability in his world. "He perceives his environment as a depressing one,
cold and unloving, rocky and dangerous. He feels that he has been
deserted by his parents and that he is now hopelessly alone in a
dark, lonely world, confused about where he belongs and how he
should relate to the world and to the people in it. He wants to be
loved, cared for, and protected, but at the same time, would like to
strike back at the people he sees as depriving and rejecting.

"This conflict leads him into a vicious circle that seems to increase
his sense of isolation, frustration, and unhappiness. Donny appears
to be searching for love, but his defenses prevent contact with
people in the way that would satisfy him. He seems confused about
good and bad, healthy and sick, which parallels his confused perception of parental figures. Thus, he sees his mother in her relationship to him between seduction and rejection, the inconsistency
in the relationship probably giving rise to the suspiciousness and
distrust that characterizes him now. The frustrating aspects of the
mother seem to be the object of much of his hostility, and yet, she
is the mother who can be loving and compassionate with her child
when he is in pain. Some of Donny's problems stem from the fact
that love and attention were obtained only through physical illness; apparently, the only way he could convert his rejecting
mother into a comforting one was by being sick."

Psychological testing further showed that Donny presented a remarkable contrast of personality strengths and weaknesses. He appeared as a boy able to delay gratification, to organize experiences, and to question his own behavior. On the other hand, his suspiciousness, deep hostility, and many unfulfilled infantile needs left him in the grip of conflicts that required more treatment than simply being placed in an adequate family situation or in a good group home. There was a tremendous difference between fantasy seen in the psychological testing and Donny's behavior with his group in the hospital, since he was very active in his fantasy and yet relatively passive and controlled on the behavioral level. Aggressive, destructive, and hostile fantasies, with people tearing each other apart, killing each other, and mutilations, all gave what might have been assumed to be a picture of a very destructive child. However, his destructiveness appeared limited to his fantasy and was seldom, if ever, seen in overt behavior. The benign support of the hospital environment and the satisfactions gained from the adults who worked with Donny led him to suppress and to conceal these aspects of his behavior that might provoke another rejection; in this sense, the contrast between his behavior before referral and after he entered the hospital can be reconciled. At the same time, psychological testing, psychiatric interviews and his continuing severe psychosomatic symptoms indicated that he was still undergoing a great deal of stress and had many unresolved and severe conflicts.

HISTORY AND DEVELOPMENT

Donny's parents separated before he was born, although his father visited and maintained sporadic contacts with Donny and his mother. His father, a cruel man with an explosive temper, had beaten his mother, sometimes severely, and once to the point where she had to be hospitalized for two weeks. After his father left, his mother obtained a divorce and remarried, but this resulted in a second divorce. Donny had taken the stepfather's name and, in spite of the separation and divorce, still remembered him with fondness. The stepfather seemed to have been a fairly positive figure for the boy. The early years of Donny's life were stormy ones because his mother, being a disturbed woman, was periodically hospitalized for her emotional difficulties. She sometimes became extremely depressed, on several occasions had attempted suicide, and once was found wandering in the streets, confused, disoriented, and incoherent.

When together, Donny and his mother had an extremely variable relationship. She often punished him excessively, beat him unmercifully, frequently threatened to leave him, and used extremely abusive language toward him. At other times, overcome with guilt and remorse at her treatment of Donny, she went to the other extreme. She indulged him completely, let him sleep with her, and became physically seductive with him. She often came to his defense when he had difficulties with other children, and yet would frequently leave him alone in their apartment, sometimes overnight, while she went out with a man. On one occasion, she deliberately immersed him in an extremely hot, almost boiling bath in order to punish him, saying that she did not care if it killed him.

This vacillation between cruelty, extreme overindulgence, and protectiveness, was apparently very confusing to Donny, and he became cautious and careful in his dealings with others. During these years, he was often left in the care of his maternal grandmother who died when he was three; after this time, he more and more was left alone. His mother's behavior caused a neighbor to file a complaint for neglect and child abuse, and Donny was placed briefly in a foster home. His adjustment there was poor, however, and the mother succeeded in having him returned to her. At that time, she stated to a social worker who had interviewed her that she "hated herself" for doing the things she had done. On Donny's return home, she tried to compensate for her behavior by bribery, not refusing or denying him anything, particularly on an oral level.

Finally when Donny was about five years old, his mother became so disturbed that she was hospitalized for a prolonged period. Since the maternal grandmother was no longer available to care for him, he was placed again in a foster home, after having stayed at a neighbor's home for a brief period. He remained in this foster home for about two months, after which his asthma and skin difficulties became so severe that it was necessary to hospitalize him. Following this hospitalization, Donny was put in a second foster home. Here, the foster mother became very possessive of him and when Donny's own mother visited she became resentful and insisted that her son be removed. To satisfy Donny's mother, the placement was terminated and he was kept for a few days at a children's receiving center. This was interrupted by a second hospitalization because of his asthma and what appeared to be the early stages of bronchial pneumonia.

After his discharge from the hospital, he was placed in a foster home of another religious faith, on an emergency basis, since there were no foster homes available in his own denomination. This was a temporary placement, meant to be so, although Donny's adjustment during this time was probably better than in any other of the temporary placements. The foster mother here was patient and was able to show him a good deal of love. He responded favorably to this, as well as to the structure, the patience, and kindness of the entire family. His behavior and his physical symptoms improved greatly. However, when a home of his own religious faith became available he was transferred to it.

Donny became enuretic on the day of placement and shortly after this encopretic, and although the foster parents made great efforts to relate to him, the situation became worse. Once, after a frustrating incident, he screamed at his foster parents, "I hate you." The foster mother described him as being an active child, difficult to control, who pouted easily and became very moody when told to do something. He had moved his bowels on several occasions at home in the living room, in the bathtub, and even once at church. He began school while in this placement, and although there were no serious behavior problems, the teacher said he was lazy and he was often kept after school to finish his work. This foster mother found him to be very demanding, wanting constant attention. She tried to reason with him, and he seemed to understand but continued with the same behavior. Donny seemed unable to accept their love but, instead, despite his demands for their attention, kept them emotionally at arm's length. He maintained a reserved, detached manner toward them, which was more characteristic of an older child or even an adult. He often tested them to see how far he could go, in a rather indirect way, pushed them and provoked them, and only stopped when they finally became angry and expressed their feelings toward him. After this, he ended the provocative behavior but withdrew quietly into himself.

Eventually, Donny's own mother was discharged from hospitalization and was allowed, occasionally, to visit him in his new foster home. She made many promises to him, among them a promise that she would have a home for him by the following Christmas and that he could then be with her again. Donny became very upset after this, and his foster parents found it increasingly difficult to cope with him. His continual testing of their love and patience as well as his apparent lack of general emotional response to their overtures made them extremely "nervous" and frustrated, and they finally asked for his removal from their home. His agency had him evaluated again, this time psychiatrically at the hospital where he had been treated for his medical problems. The result was a recommendation for residential treatment. His foster parents agreed to keep him until such a placement could be made.

WORK WITH MOTHER

After Donny was finally institutionalized at the residential treatment center, his mother again went through a period of severe disturbance. She began, then quickly terminated, a common-law relationship with another man. After this, she became severely depressed and had obsessive thoughts and dreams of her son's being dead. She was finally admitted to a mental hospital in her community in a state of severe agitation and depression. She was seen first by a psychiatrist and then by a psychiatric social worker for treatment. The social worker saw her regularly twice a week, giving her a great deal of ego support and reassurance. Donny's mother, during this time, began to use her interviews as an opportunity to verbalize her anxieties and hostile feelings, rather than act them out as she had done previously. She showed better judgment and insight, and integrated her past experiences more constructively.

Following a period of hospitalization that lasted almost two years and began shortly after Donny's placement in the residential treatment center, she was moved into a halfway house, a sort of family care home, on a trial basis. She was treated on an out-patient basis during this time, with interviews continuing at the same rate of two a week. These interviews along with medication and the environment of the halfway house finally stabilized her so that she was able to begin vocational training and pursue it successfully. At about the time of the third year of Donny's hospitalization, she renewed her contact with him, first writing to him and then making a visit to the hospital. When she came to the hospital, the staff saw her as a woman who wanted to be a good mother without knowing how, but who obviously had made remarkable improvement; however, it was felt that her adjustment was still precarious. Placement with her in the future was viewed as being a possible, but not very probable, outcome after completion of Donny's treatment at the hospital.

PSYCHOTHERAPY

During Donny's initial interview with his therapist (a clinical psychologist), he was very clinging and affectionate, although this quality had an impersonality about it. He gave a first impression of being a very controlled and, in some ways, mature boy. He made no demands and accepted his therapist's explanations without a word. Thus, he showed no interest in the candy offered him and never asked for it, although he usually accepted it, never consuming the candy at the time but putting it in his pocket. There were no difficulties at all about limits during the therapeutic sessions; Donny accepted these almost too easily and, indeed, often anticipated them—a rather remarkable thing for a boy his age. Thus, when he and his therapist were shooting dart guns at a target, Donny remarked, 'We shouldn't shoot at the lights, should we?"

At first, beyond the very limited play with guns in which he showed a great deal of control, Donny gave no evidence whatsoever of any kind of hostility. He acted in many ways like a "model" boy. He related to his therapist more as an object of fantasy than as a real person, still maintaining his autonomy so that he remained self-sufficient and permitting only a limited, very controlled, and guarded interaction with the psychologist. He seemed to expect that his interviews would answer all his problems and needs, and he seemed to be making an effort to avoid the kind of behavior that might disturb this happy picture. At the same time, he did not enter into a genuine relationship with his therapist. Beyond the superficially affectionate overtures, he expressed almost no feelings at all, so that the first goals of the therapist centered around forming a more genuine relationship with him to break through the fantasy image that Donny had of him and, in this way, to penetrate his defenses, coming to more significant levels of basic feeling. This process extended over a long period of time and was made difficult by the fact that much of Donny's behavior was characterized by a defense against involvement, perhaps to prevent the kind of disappointment that he had experienced so many times in the past, not only with his mother but also in his several foster homes.

In the beginning, Donny avoided any direct expression of feelings, particularly hostile ones, toward his therapist. Then he slowly began to engage in aggressive play, starting with the toy dart guns and target practice and gradually incorporating toy soldiers, around which he was able to verbalize a good deal of aggressive fantasy. From this, he moved on to the point where he was able to show hostility toward his therapist, often in a half-joking, half-serious way. This expression of hostility, muted though it was, made him very anxious and required constant reassurance, permission, and support. Then the problem became one of either complete suppression or of complete loss of control and, on two occasions when he allowed himself an open indulgence in genuinely hostile fantasy and direct aggressive verbalization towards the therapist, Donny—as he had in his initial diagnostic interview—became encropetic. However, eventually, he learned how to handle these feelings in a more moderated manner, expressing realistic anger and frustration but without a complete loss of control.

Another of Donny's difficulties were his needs around dependency. Once, he seemed convinced of the dependability of gratifications and, both in the hospital and on a lesser but important symbolic level in the interviews, he began to express almost insatiable demands. He requested many material things that may have seemed to him less threatening and more easily obtained than genuine affection and acceptance. For example, Donny told the therapist what his mother would give him for Christmas but completely avoided the topic of whether she really cared for him. His denial in all of these areas was at first intense. Interpretations by his therapist often led to sullen negativism, with Donny turning his head the other way, beginning to drown out the psychologist's comments and interpretations by whistling. Again, his feelings emerged slowly but they did emerge and, as this happened, he became a more real, if somewhat more difficult, little boy to deal with.

It was observed in interactions with the other children and adults in the hospital that Donny became more aggressive, irritable, and demanding. Occasionally he began to provoke fights with some of the children who had been offensive toward him previously and began frequently to resist some of the demands made upon him. Indeed, at times he made a point of violating certain rules and routines of the hospital, as if to try his new independence and ability to express himself. Communication among the staff around his needs and the mechanisms at work in his treatment led not only to an acceptance of his behavior but to a great deal of reassurance and support as well, with, however, limits occasionally being placed gently but firmly when necessary.

One of his more intense periods of feeling was when he became very interested and concerned with the other children seen by his therapist. He felt an obvious rivalry with them and, although at first he simply withdrew in the presence of another patient of the psychologist, he eventually made matter-of-fact remarks about them and then reported some of their misdeeds. On one occasion, he used blocks to spell out the names of each of the other children and then knocked the blocks all over the room. Finally, he came to the point of demanding to know who was the best liked, who among all of the children the therapist would keep if he could only have one. From this developed a great deal of confused, wishful fantasy regarding his home, mother, relatives, and the multitude of relationships he had in foster homes. Basically, however, the change observed was almost more in the quality and amount of affect that he was able to express than in the content of what was said. Donny seemed to be responding with real feelings to real situations rather than with fantasy and wish fulfillment. Again, with the increase in the genuineness of his feelings, there was an increase in what might be called a regression into a more infantile level of adjustment. His superficial maturity gave way both in the group and with his therapist to a more direct expression of dependency and hostility.

During this time, concurrent work was also done on a purely physical level to help control Donny's allergies and to relieve his asthma and eczema. A great deal was accomplished from this point of view, although the physical symptoms continued to show connections with his emotional problems. Thus, at a particularly frustrating time for him, when a visit from his mother had not materialized and when she even failed to write him, and when his request to be transferred to a group of more competent older boys

had been turned down, his eczema and his asthma became considerably worse. This occurred when he still was unable to show
his frustration directly in behavior or in words. He reacted to both
difficulties, that is, the failure of communication from his mother
and his inability to win what he saw as a promotion, not with
obvious disappointment or frustration, but with intensification of
his allergic symptoms.

In spite of individual psychotherapy, Donny still retained a core
of depression, involved with the separation from his mother, his
confusion about his family and origin, and from guilt regarding
his hostile, aggressive feelings. There seemed to be a fear of loss
and an expectation of rejection and deprivation, although he appeared better able to live with these feelings and to be a far more
capable, strong, and genuinely mature boy. His course in the hospital proceeded, then, from an initial excellent adjustment to one
of more open aggression, negativism, and occasional loss of control
to a return to the very affectionate, cooperative condition that he
initially showed. The second time around, however, he was much
more real in his feelings. When first seen, Donny had been shy and
frightened but had kept his control and his safe distance from
others, although he had related in a superficially mature, affectionate way with adults and was generally protective and helpful with
the other children. He gradually became more aggressive and as-
sertive with the other children, although seldom openly. Unless he
chose to make an issue of a particular situation, he seldom had
trouble with the staff, but sometimes he created difficulties almost
as an experiment or as a trial balloon to see what effect his hostility
would have. By the end of his stay, Donny finally returned to a
point where he got along very well with everyone, peers and adults
alike, but where he had also begun to learn to express some of
his negative feelings in an appropriate and often constructive way.

FOLLOW-UP NOTE

Although the staff of the hospital recommended group placement
for Donny, feeling that because of the early history and extremely
disturbed relationship with his mother, placement with her would
be most inadvisable, the child welfare agency was unable to afford
further placement, even in a nonpsychiatrically oriented group-

living situation. On the other hand, Donny's mother actually had improved a great deal. Indeed, a social worker from the hospital who visited her in Donny's home town to prepare for Donny's arrival noticed that the gains were very impressive. She had obtained her own apartment and had made it a pleasant and attractive home. Using the skills obtained in her vocational training, she had begun a small business and was doing extremely well, not only supporting herself but gradually paying off the debts she had incurred when starting her business. She was even able to set aside a small amount of money to, as she said, "Pay for Donny's education." For these reasons, she presented the most attractive alternatives among the various placement possibilities and Donny was returned to her after his discharge from the hospital.

A year later, a note sent by the agency to the hospital reported that Donny was doing very well in his adjustment at home and was building on the gains he had made in his treatment at the hospital. Both Donny and his mother were still being seen in intensive supportive casework by the staff at the agency. They noted that although Donny and his mother sometimes found their new situation of living together strange and discouraging, they were nevertheless able to cope with these problems and to derive much satisfaction from their relationship. Donny's mother continued to do well in her business and he was attending school regularly and doing well, although it had been found necessary to place him at first in a special education program. His mother had obtained a big brother for him with whom he developed a good relationship. There had been an outbreak of Donny's ezcema on his return home, but this had improved a great deal with continuing treatment, both psychological and medical, from the agency.

3

BEHAVIOR DISORDERS

The diagnostic category "behavior disorders" includes children who engage in activities that would be judged delinquent or pre-delinquent. They "act out" their conflicts, expressing them in behaviors that are socially unacceptable, such as drinking alcohol, smoking pot or taking drugs, running away from home, stealing or damaging property, and physically hurting others. Some also engage in various sexual practices that can get them into serious social and legal difficulties.

Statistics indicate that many of these children come from lower-class socioeconomic backgrounds, often from broken homes and with parents who themselves are unable to cope with everyday living. The seemingly high incidence of delinquency among children from lower-class backgrounds has prompted social scientists to emphasize the need for preventative measures aimed at the ills and inequalities of society itself. They feel this would do more to prevent the development of disordered behavior than the individual therapy provided after the children have already gotten into trouble.

It should not be overlooked, however, that children from middle- and upper-class backgrounds also show behavior disorders and, in many instances, the parents are just as powerless in redirecting their children's energies as are parents from the lower classes. For various reasons, the statistics pertaining to delinquent behavior could be biased. "Crimes" by lower-class children are more likely to be reported to police and referred to the courts, while more affluent parents are apt to personally pay for damages incurred by their offspring and then have them seen by private psychotherapists or at child guidance clinics rather than sent to institutions for delinquents. The lower-class youngster who is apprehended for taking a stranger's car for a joyride is likely to be sent to the local training school and thus become a tally mark on the statistical chart showing the incidence of juvenile delinquency. The middle-class youngster who takes a neighbor's car without permission is more apt to be returned to his parents with a warning by the local police, and a recommendation that he be seen by a psychiatrist or psychologist, with no record made of this delinquent behavior. If this same sort of differential handling by police and other authorities holds true for all kinds of acting-out behavior, it would help to explain why behavior disorders are commonly believed to be the almost exclusive province of the underprivileged.

The cases presented here are from lower-class families suffering from severe social pathology. They were not selected to show these sociocultural characteristics but, instead, because they are unusually interesting cases. The fact that these children had been institutionalized for their behavioral difficulties, rather than being treated by private practitioners while living at home, makes it more likely that they would be from lower socioeconomic family backgrounds.

It is also noteworthy that these three cases are males. This is to be expected, however, since there is a much lower incidence of behavior disorders in girls in all child-treatment settings throughout the United States. Another consistency among these three children was not anticipated—the fact that they all were conceived out of wedlock. This was not a consideration in selecting the cases for study. After choosing them on the basis of other criteria, a detailed review of their case records uncovered this fact. In each case, the mother had a history of serious marital conflict and was not living with the father at the time of the child's placement in the residential treatment center.

Interestingly, however, in spite of the terrible beginnings that these children endured, they were in much better psychological shape than some of the other children whose cases are described here. Although they were seriously disturbed, they were not psychotic, and two of them actually managed to attain a very adequate level of emotional and behavioral adjustment by the time they reached adolescence.

These three cases vividly reveal the important influence of "role models" on the behavior of children. Without a strong, stable, and responsible father with whom he could identify, each of these boys was in great need of a competent male adult to serve as a model for a healthy psychosocial development. While the therapeutic contributions of qualified members of the helping professions (psychiatry, psychology, and social work) are amply demonstrated by these cases, they also highlight the crucial role that can be played by paraprofessionals (aides, attendants, child care workers, and volunteer visitors) who influence the social learning of children in residential treatment.

This section begins with the case of Mike, a boy who suffered about as much social and sexual pathology as one could expect any child to endure without becoming psychologically damaged beyond repair. Witnessing his mother engaged in drunken sex orgies with strange men, in bed with her while she delivered a child, and subjected to homosexual practices in early childhood, this unsocialized and severely depressed youngster somehow managed to show remarkable recovery in the course of two years of residential psychiatric treatment.

The usual approach in most case studies is to start at the begining and proceed to the end but, in the case of Roger, we begin with his tragic ending and then go back to his early history and therapeutic treatment some years previously. Living through a childhood filled with turmoil, rejection, and failure, Roger repeatedly tried to escape from life's trauma by running away, but there was never a permanent place of refuge to be found. His final attempt to escape must be judged as a supreme failure, although it succeeded in freeing him from the caged existence that seemed to be his destiny from an early age.

The case of Tommy calls attention to several highly critical issues within the field of abnormal child psychology. Among these is the significance of racial differences between child and therapist. Tommy, a black child, found it difficult or impossible to establish a therapeutic relationship with some staff members but got along with others very well. More important than the adults' skin color seemed to be their understanding of this youngster's prior experiences and the extent to which they did not force themselves on his privacy. It proved more therapeutic to permit him to work on his personal and social difficulties in his own way and at his own pace. With a child who comes from a lower social class background similar to Tommy's, the emphasis must often be placed on nonverbal therapy. One should not expect such children to freely verbalize their problems to therapists who approach them with a middle-class, academic orientation that values verbal facility and intellectualization.

Tommy's case study also provides compelling evidence relevant to another major contemporary issue—the validity and ethics of IQ testing with lower-class children. Many organizations throughout the United States are speaking against this practice, which is felt to be especially detrimental to black children. The "labels" that get attached to children as a result of psychological testing (for example, retarded, defective, or dull are believed to have lasting damaging effects, preventing these youngsters from enjoying educational opportunities that should rightfully be theirs. In the case of Tommy we see a striking example of what could have been a grave injustice to a black child whose intelligence test performance was profoundly influenced by the psychological and social conditions under which he was tested. Fortunately, the treatment of this disturbed child was not adversely influenced by his test performance, and the therapeutic program eventually accomplished highly successful results.

RECOMMENDED READING

Bandura, A., & Walters, R. H. *Social learning and personality development.* New York: Holt, Rinehart, & Winston, 1963.

Glueck, S., & Glueck, E. *Physique and delinquency.* New York: Harper, 1956.

Kozol, J. *Death at an early age.* New York: Bantam Books, 1967.

Quay, H. C. (Ed.) *Juvenile delinquency: Research and theory.* Princeton, N.J.: Van Nostrand, 1965.

Redl, F., & Wineman, D. *Children who hate.* New York: Free Press, 1951.

4. THE CASE OF MIKE:
A Severely Traumatic Childhood

During the early stage of Mike's stay in the residential treatment center his only comfort was his own thumb. He stayed by himself, passive and forlorn, and his only visible emotion was a pervasive look of sorrow. His characteristic pose was with his left thumb grasped in his right fist and the thumb of the right hand inserted in his mouth. Whenever you saw Mike you could be certain that he would be sucking this thumb, from the moment he woke in the morning until long after he fell asleep at night. Even in the dining room, Mike managed to suck his thumb between mouthfuls of food.

This good-looking 10-year-old boy, with large brown eyes and dark hair, had been transferred from another institution for neglected children. In the previous setting, an older boy had killed a younger boy who resisted his homosexual advances, had dismembered the body, and had hidden it under some rocks. An inquiry revealed that Mike had been forced to engage in sex play with this older boy, and he was suspected of knowing about, but not reporting, the killing. Mike denied having been involved in the killing but also said that he did not feel sorry for the murdered boy. However, this incident led to the closing of the institution, and Mike, who was a ward of the state, was sent to the private psychiatric treatment center.

BACKGROUND HISTORY

Mike's mother was seven months pregnant when she married his father. This man had a court record since the age of 16 for various charges, including breaking and entering, rape, incest, and indecent assault. He continued to engage in criminal activities after Mike was born, mainly dealing in stolen goods, and the couple spent a stormy five years together. Actually, the father was away from home much of the time, traveling about the country, living with other women, and constantly in trouble with the law. When he was at home, he tended to be completely permissive with Mike, with no attempt at discipline or control. When Mike was five years old his parents were divorced and, soon thereafter, the father received a prison sentence for robbery and assault.

Since Mike's father did not support the family, his mother worked nights as a waitress in taverns. When Mike was one year old, a baby brother was born, followed by two sisters within the next two years. Within five years, Mike's mother gave birth to four children. A particularly deviant incident was reported in connection with the birth of the fourth child. A maternal aunt stated that when she entered the hotel room in which they were then living, she found the unattended mother in the midst of giving birth, with the umbilical cord still uncut, and Mike lying in the bed beside her.

Throughout this period, the mother drank very heavily and often brought male customers home when the tavern closed. Home consisted of one furnished room in a cheap rooming house or rundown hotel, and the mother and her children were constantly on the move. The children would be left alone or under the care of people living in the building, or they were placed with various relatives. Although some of the children spent parts of their earliest years with relatives, Mike stayed with his mother throughout all of the moving and the years of battle between his parents. He was also present for the drunken sex parties that took place very frequently. One of the taverns that his mother worked in was located near a naval base, and often at two or three o'clock in the morning she would bring sailors home for a drink and whatever else they might be seeking from this intoxicated, emotionally disturbed young woman. There is no doubt that Mike saw his mother engaged in activities that would make the "traumatic" childhood experiences described by Freud seem relatively innocuous.

At one point, Mike's mother established a more permanent relationship with a navy enlisted man, and lived with him as man and wife. This man was also drunk a good part of the time, and there is suspicion that on occasion he engaged in sexual activities with Mike. Since this man was married and not supporting his family, he and Mike's mother were subsequently arrested for committing adultery, and she was put on probation for neglecting her children.

The children were placed in various institutions or foster homes, and the mother's pathological behavior became even worse. It soon became so troublesome that she was institutionalized in a state mental hospital with the diagnosis of alcoholism and delirium tremens, with severe anemia and cirrhosis of the liver.

Thus, with a psychopathic, overindulgent father serving time in prison and an alcoholic mother committed to a mental hospital, Mike was placed in a state home for children where he became intimately familiar with homosexuality and murder. Is it any wonder that when this lonely, 10-year-old boy arrived at the residential treatment center he presented a pathetic picture of severe depression bordering on psychotic stupor?

PHYSICAL AND MENTAL STATUS UPON ADMISSION

Physical and neurological examinations conducted soon after Mike's admission revealed a physically normal boy with no sign of neurological impairment. Intelligence tests resulted in an IQ of 90, but it was felt that Mike was much brighter than the tests showed and that he was penalized by the inadequate and interrupted schooling that he had experienced during the past years. School achievement tests showed him to be functioning between a second- and third-grade level when, according to his chronological age, he should have been entering the fifth grade.

The mental status evaluation conducted by a psychiatrist revealed a frightened, introverted, extremely dependent child. There was practically no spontaneous talking on Mike's part, and he offered only very brief, monosyllabic replies to the psychiatrist's questions. According to this examiner, Mike had no clear ideas about his role in life and harbored conflicting and confusing ideas about birth, death, and sex. The psychiatrist stressed the fact that Mike had little opportunity to identify with an adequate male figure and that he had formed a rather strong identification with his psychopathic father. During the interview, Mike expressed the desire to return to living with his parents, and he denied the fact that they were separated. The psychiatrist's overall diagnostic impression was "neurotic character with considerable autistic phenomena and sweeping intellectual retardation resulting from depression."

RESIDENTIAL TREATMENT

Soon after Mike's arrival at the treatment center, he was assigned to a living unit consisting of a group of boys about his
age, placed in a special education class, and assigned to a psychotherapist. In each of these areas—daily living, school, and pycho-
therapy—Mike interacted with a strong adult male figure.

The child-care worker in charge of Mike's unit was a young but
experienced male who was a good athlete and was in the process
of completing his own education. He had been working for several
years after graduating from high school, and he recently had begun
taking college courses while working full time. He was generally
regarded as one of the most capable child-care workers ever to
work in this residential treatment center. Throughout many hours
of the day, Mike was in the company of this young man who filled
the role of "father-figure" for the group of boys—getting them up
in the morning, eating meals with them, participating in games
with them during recreational activities, watching TV in their
living area, and sometimes helping them get to bed at night.

The schoolteacher in Mike's class had served as a child-care
worker before joining the school department in the treatment center. He was a qualified special educator with special interest and
skills in the area of graphic expression, and he was exceptionally
good at employing unconventional procedures in motivating disturbed children with a history of school failure to become interested in conventional academic subject matter.

Mike's psychotherapist was a clinical psychologist who had recently joined the institutional staff. He and Mike arrived at about
the same time and had become acquainted during the first few
weeks. When therapy assignments were made for the coming year,
both the therapist and Mike seemed pleased with this arrangement.
Mike was seen in individual psychotherapy on a twice-weekly basis
throughout his two-year stay at the institution.

In the beginning, the therapist attempted to establish a "therapeutic relationship," mainly providing Mike with support, guidance, and encouragement. Although the therapist's orientation was
basically psychodynamic, with occasional interpretations of feelings and attempts to help Mike gain some insight into his emotional difficulties, the main emphasis was on changing Mike's
values and behavior in a more socially desirable direction. Upon

entering treatment, Mike's "ego-ideal" was that of a psychopathic male who pushes people around, takes things forcefully from others, and fights with the law. He did not value hard work, either in school or in athletics, and saw little virtue in excelling at scholastic or athletic endeavors. His basic orientation was essentially antisocial with a very poor self-concept, a tremendous amount of underlying anxiety, and feelings of helplessness in an unfriendly world. The goal of residential treatment, including psychotherapy, was to modify Mike's view of himself and the world and to help him achieve some degree of mastery that would enable him to better cope with life's obstacles after he left the treatment center.

GENERAL COURSE IN THE TREATMENT CENTER

Initially Mike was extremely depressed and withdrawn, interacting very little with other child patients. Gradually, however, he became more outgoing and then became the leader in this group. Mike seemed to be making excellent progress until, after about 10 months in the treatment center, he received word that his mother had died. Although he had been showing considerable improvement, he now became the leader of a group of acting-out children who engaged in a great deal of delinquent activity. He became extremely difficult to manage except by a few male staff members whom he seemed to like. During this stage in his treatment, in the beginning months of the second year, Mike got into so much trouble that it became doubtful whether he could remain in this particular institutional setting. However, with a great deal of therapeutic work devoted to this troubled boy, in talks with staff child-care workers and in individual psychotherapy, Mike gradually gained control over his delinquent behavior.

During the first year, he did not do very well in school. Then he started to show some improvement and, during the last several months of his stay in the institution, he showed tremendous advances in school performance and became highly motivated to learn. In fact, while his academic progress had previously been slow, he now advanced a whole school grade within a two-month period. Mike's teacher was greatly pleased with his behavior and performance in school and thought that the prognosis in regard to future school work was very favorable.

Mike also became more contented in his everyday activities and continued to be a leader in his group, although now he was a positive influence on the other boys. He no longer engaged in delinquent activities, but spent most of his time in athletics where he was an outstanding performer. During his final summer in the institution, shortly before his discharge, he was 12 years old and the best athlete in the treatment center, excelling in swimming and baseball. Just as he learned a great deal in school, he learned and benefited considerably from the athletic training. Mike was not only well liked by his peers but also established excellent social relations with the adult staff members. By the time he left the institution, he presented no management problems and his personal and social adjustment were greatly improved.

This rather remarkable improvement resulted from the great amount of time and attention that were devoted to Mike by staff members in all phases of his treatment. His unit leaders (child-care workers) liked him very much, and he benefited from the good relations he had with them. His schoolteacher worked extremely hard and successfully with him. Moreover, he had the same psychotherapist for individual therapy during his two-year period of residential treatment. In all spheres of activity, Mike had made great strides. And most important, Mike's identification had changed from psychopathic males to socially healthy and acceptable males.

This change in "ego-ideal," noted clinically, was also evidenced in Mike's figure drawings. As part of a psychological assessment battery administered to Mike at the time of his admission, at the end of his first year, and at the time of discharge, Mike was requested to draw a person. It is believed that this projective technique provides an indication of the individual's perceptions of himself. In Mike's case, on the first occasion he drew a gangster, complete with a mask and gun, in the process of committing a holdup. A year later he drew a picture of a soldier, again armed with a gun, but this time engaged in combat in defense of his country. Finally, at the time of testing prior to discharge, Mike drew a detailed picture of a baseball player in the process of hitting a home run. Thus, the projective tests and the behavioral observations indicated that Mike's self-concept and his view of other human beings had improved markedly in the course of residential treatment. At this point, it was felt that the prognosis (prediction of future outcome) was good, although Mike needed additional therapeutic help to reinforce the gains he had made and to help him cope further with his deeply rooted emotional disturbance. However, after his successful stay in residential treatment, he was much better off psychologically and socially, and seemed well prepared to meet the challenge of a new environment.

PSYCHOTHERAPY

As mentioned earlier, Mike was seen by the same therapist throughout his two-year stay in the treatment center. Although the detailed notes of individual therapy sessions contain much interesting content, they are too voluminous to present here. However, to give the flavor of what transpired in the therapeutic interviews between Mike and the clinical psychologist, we include excerpts from a therapy summary presented at a staff conference devoted to Mike's case after he had been in the treatment center for 18 months.

The therapist had seen Mike for approximately 120 therapeutic interviews during this period and reported the following information. In the beginning, Mike was extremely depressed, withdrawn, and not very communicative. He spent considerable time fighting with a large stuffed dummy in the play therapy room. He also devoted much time to war games by using toy soldiers, describing much aggression, mutilation, and destruction. Soon, he began mentioning some of his past experiences. He talked about his mother and her illness, his plans for joining her and reuniting their family in the future. After several months in therapy, Mike mentioned the murder of a boy in the previous institution where he was placed. Mike avowed that he did not like the boy who did the killing but he also did not like the victim.

Mike was progressing very well in therapy when, unexpectedly, he received word that his mother had died. Following this, his play and fantasy activity revealed a preoccupation with death, funerals, and unhappiness. He showed great longing for some sort of family relations and wondered about his brother and sisters. Around Christmas time, several months after his mother's death, he received a letter from his father and new stepmother, which included pictures of themselves and expressed a great love for Mike with plans for having him join them after he left the institution.

Mike now talked about his real mother at great length and always in very idealized terms—how beautiful she was, what a good swimmer she was, and how all men wanted to marry her. According to Mike, she did not really drink very much, and she became physically sick because of having to work while also taking care of her children. The therapist said nothing to contradict this positive maternal image.

The news from his father elated Mike considerably, and he appeared much more alert and happy in his therapy sessions. While not wanting to sadden him, the therapist pointed out the reality factors that might make it difficult for Mike to be reunited with his father and stepmother in the very near future.

At this point in psychotherapy, Mike spent several sessions working at the blackboard in the play room, drawing pictures and working on school-related activities. He spent time writing the alphabet, spelling, working with numbers, and showed great concern for mastering these academic skills. The therapist reported that recently Mike had engaged in very little aggressive play and generally seemed quite calm. The characters in his drawings and the heroes in his games were now strong figures, such as athletes, hunters, and sheriffs, and he showed much less concern for "bad guys" in his fantasy life.

At the close of this therapy summary, it was mentioned that in recent weeks the therapist devoted much discussion and attention to the problem of Mike's getting into difficulty in everyday activities at the treatment center. Mike explained that he had learned bad habits from the kids he had met in the various homes and institutions, and stated that he was trying to keep out of trouble but that it was not easy. The therapist concluded, "It is quite evident that Mike basically likes it here and is honestly trying to control his impulsive acting-out behavior. However, because of his psychopathology, he finds it difficult not to maintain his status and position as the powerful leader of the other children who engage in delinquent activities." Mike advanced well beyond his troublesome stage during the final months of treatment and appeared to benefit greatly from his therapeutic interviews.

TREATMENT OUTCOME AND SUBSEQUENT ADJUSTMENT

Since Mike had now reached his 12th birthday, which was the upper age limit in this residential center, it was necessary to discharge him. Although his condition was rated as improved and the prognosis was favorable, the consensus of professional opinion was that Mike needed further residential treatment. He was a ward of the state in which he had lived originally, and the Child Welfare Department was prepared to pay for his continued psychiatric treatment in another private setting if one could be found. The closest suitable placement was located about 400 miles away, and this institution required that Mike be seen in person for a diagnostic evaluation before accepting him for treatment.

It was decided that Mike's psychotherapist should accompany him on this journey and help prepare him to accept this transfer if he were found suitable by the new institution. The plan was to fly to the large city located near this institution, spend the night in a hotel, visit the institution the following day, and return that evening. This was an evaluation visit to see if Mike was acceptable for treatment, but with plans to return to the original treatment center to await word of his acceptance or rejection.

It was an extremely hot summer day when Mike and his therapist made their journey. Since Mike had never been on a plane, it was an exciting venture, and his spirits were quite good although, naturally, he was anxious about this new place that he might be sent to. On checking into the newly opened, attractive, air-conditioned hotel, the therapist, without Mike's knowing it, informed the desk clerk that the boy tended to be nocturnally enuretic (that is, a bed wetter) and that a rubber sheet should be put over the mattress of his bed. The clerk and therapist agreed that when no one was in the room, a protective sheet would be placed on the twin bed nearest the window, which would be Mike's bed for the evening.

Mike and the therapist spent the day and evening enjoying themselves—going to two movies, eating in an Italian restaurant, and having late snacks at night. The following day they took a short train ride to the institution, and Mike spent several hours being interviewed and taking psychological tests. In the evening they had dinner at the airport and boarded their flight back to their "home" institution. Looking at Mike as their plane approached the landing, the therapist suddenly became aware that throughout their entire trip Mike had not sucked his thumb. Although this habit had greatly diminished during the two-year stay, Mike continued to suck his thumb occasionally, when he was particularly anxious or upset. However, in the face of what was obviously a very exciting and in some ways very threatening experience, Mike had not shown the regressive behavior that characterized him in the past.

Although Mike and his therapist did not discuss the matter, on Mike's return he proudly informed his child-care worker that he had not wet the bed in the hotel. Interestingly, Mike no longer wet the bed during the brief remainder of his stay in this institution. Therefore, even though the therapist had never directly focused his attention on Mike's infantile symptoms of thumb sucking and bed wetting, now, at the end of the period of residential treatment, Mike was finally mastering this socially undesirable behavior. In other words, while these unacceptable behaviors had never been discussed directly in psychotherapy, they now showed great improvement.

The therapeutic approach employed was in keeping with the psychodynamic model, which advocates working with underlying dynamics and causes rather than focusing on symptomatic behaviors. Although in this case there certainly had not been an exclusive reliance on orthodox psychoanalytic principles, there had been a basic psychodynamic orientation coupled with a considerable emphasis on social learning (modeling). The strict behaviorist would immediately attack the symptoms and attempt to modify them. In Mike's case, the therapeutic approach was to attempt to improve his psychological state and then change his motivation in the direction of an increased emotional maturity. As a result, his undesirable symptoms eventually diminished. Thus, if this case is judged as a success, which it certainly seems to be, it must be credited to a combination of psychodynamic therapy, milieu therapy, and a heavy application of the principles of social learning theory.

As a result of the evaluation visit, Mike was accepted eagerly by the new institution and soon made the transfer. At Christmas his therapist visited him in the new setting, where he had been doing very well, and brought him a bicycle bought with money donated by several staff members who fondly remembered Mike and wanted to do something to show how proud they were of him. During the following Easter vacation period, Mike took a train, all by himself, and spent several days visiting his old treatment center. He was now almost 13 years of age and certainly in much better shape, emotionally and intellectually, than when he entered residential treatment three years before. He was functioning almost up to his expected grade level and had made an excellent social adjustment to the new institution. His future now looked much more hopeful, but the road ahead would be filled with obstacles for a boy with Mike's early history and with no true family to rely on.

5. THE CASE OF ROGER:
Acting-Out Character Disorder

PROLOGUE

Shortly after the nine p.m. cell check in this particular state maximum security penal institution, the two cell mates pulled off a ventilator grill in their cell. Since both of them were of slender build, they managed to squeeze through the ventilator shaft into an attic. They crawled out a window and made their way along a catwalk to the roof of the building. Climbing down a drainspout to the prison yard, they hurried across an open area, climbed a hurricane fence, and made their way swiftly and quietly to the outer wall. With a 30-foot makeshift rope, fashioned out of bandage cloth, with a hook formed from a piece of pipe and insulated with rubber tape, they secured a grasp on the top of the wall. The first man up, holding fast to the wall, used a pair of insulated wire cutters to cut the bottom strand of the electrified barbed wire. He slid through the opening and escaped. The second man up, in the darkness, accidentally brushed the barbed wire and was jolted off the wall by the force of 4500 volts. He landed on his head and died instantly.

This news item might have been merely of passing interest: a 23-year-old man was accidentally killed in an escape attempt, without mention of his background. In this case, however, there was more than a passing interest because, just 10 years previously, Roger had left the care of a residential treatment institution which, at the time, had great concern about his future.

HISTORY FROM BIRTH TO
TIME OF ADMISSION AT AGE 11

Roger arrived at the residential treatment center accompanied by his agency social worker. He was a slightly built, rather small, 11-year-old boy, who was wearing toy six guns in holsters on his hips and carrying a toy rifle. He was obviously prepared to defend himself against the worst and, in view of his background, had every reason to expect the worst.

Officially, the chief complaints that led to Roger's referral for residential treatment were:

1. Difficulty in adjusting to foster homes since age two.
2. Unmanageable at school since age five.
3. Fire-setting.
4. Running away from home.
5. Difficult to manage, hyperactive, and extremely "self-oriented."

Roger was born out of wedlock. His putative father initially offered financial support to his mother, although he did not continue to live with her, and eventually broke off all contact insofar as is known. Therefore, Roger's earliest period of life was influenced primarily by his mother, whose background is not well known. She had at least eight siblings herself and, supposedly, did not get along well with the rest of the family. She was described, when Roger was referred, as "an unstable person, soft-spoken and passive, who would like to be a good mother but who didn't know how." It was difficult to enlist his mother's cooperation even in offering a developmental history for Roger. Although she lived only one hour's drive from the residential treatment institution, the travel was excessively burdensome. She made one trip, but seemed quite disturbed, terribly threatened, and highly anxious. Because she felt so overwhelmed, the interviewer had to provide frequent rest pauses, aspirins, and emotional support. The mother claimed that she had no money for food, that she had borrowed the bus fare, and that she had never been this far from home before. She said that her physical condition did not permit her to hold a job for more than two weeks at a time but, otherwise, nothing was known about this alleged physical condition. The interviewer felt that Roger's mother was unreliable in her reporting. She claimed that Roger was "too active," that from the beginning he was always into everything. During the first six months of his life, his mother lived with her sister's family and various family members cared for Roger. Although the circumstances were not known, he was boarded on a farm between his sixth and his eighth month, and then was returned to his mother.

His mother reported a great deal of difficulty in toilet training him. He refused to perform on the toilet, urinated, and then defecated after he had been removed. There also is a suspicion of an eating problem, in terms of his refusal of certain foods, but details are lacking. As Roger approached the age of two, his mother obtained adoptive parents for him, but Roger displayed his temper tantrums with the adoptive parents and, after two weeks, he was sent back to his mother. By this early age, Roger had been separated from his mother for two definitely known periods, and also had a number of mother figures. His attempted adoption at age two, which resulted in a clear rejection of him, was merely the beginning.

Between the ages of two and four, Roger was placed in a number of foster homes. The child welfare agency that was responsible for him received conflicting reports concerning his adjustment. On the one hand, it had been reported that he was well adjusted in various homes and, on the other hand, it was reported that he was quite unsuccessful in being able to adjust. More likely, the latter was true. Otherwise, he would not have been in six different homes, During this time he had intermittent contact with his mother, but the details are not known.

When Roger was four years old, his mother remarried. This was the occasion for Roger to be returned to his natural home. Unfortunately, the stepfather was physically abusive to both Roger and his mother, especially during his frequent intoxication. Roger reacted with considerable fear of this stepfather; he also became physically abusive to his mother and destructive of household items. He began to steal, to light fires, and to be cruel to animals. Physical punishment of him in the form of whippings seemed to have no beneficial effect. Roger did, however, begin running away from home. Ultimately, his mother felt she could not control him at all. When he was seven years old, she complained to the Society for the Prevention of Cruelty to Children, about the stepfather's abusive treatment of Roger. At the age of seven, Roger was temporarily placed in a shelter and, from there, he was put in a foster home. He lasted in the home for one month. Then he was placed in another foster home for four months. He was considered to be a severe discipline problem and was removed. His next foster home lasted about one month because he started a fire. Then he was placed in a group institution for foster care for children. On the second day, he was sent to a hospital for treatment of scabies and, during the hospitalization, he was considered unmanageable. He had to be strapped to the bed. He bit a nurse and was considered to be the "worst" child that they ever dealt with. He stayed in the hospital for a month, then was returned to the group home. He spent a total of two months in this home, but eventually the home was closed because of criticism about its child-care methods. It was accused of being extremely rigid and excessively punitive.

Roger was next placed in a diagnostic home for wayward children. Here he was treated much more kindly, even therapeutically. An EEG revealed "cerebral dysrhythmia," although the relationship of this to his behavior was unclear. Psychological tests showed that he had average intelligence but that he was extremely emotionally disturbed. At the time, when he was approximately seven and one-half years old, Roger was recommended for referral to the residential treatment center to which he was ultimately admitted. However, this admission did not occur at the time of the initial referral. It was reported that Roger had some likable qualities, so that he was not considered hopeless in a treatment sense, but it was noted that he regressed considerably at times.

From this diagnostic setting, Roger was placed in another private home. Reports indicate that this was the first foster mother who was capable of handling him, although the type of handling and the nature of the relationship were unknown. The period of about a year was the longest time that Roger stayed in one foster placement. During this time, the residential treatment center evaluated Roger and put him on the waiting list for the earliest opening.

Although it would appear that circumstances had changed for the better for Roger in this last foster home, events took a turn for the worse when he was placed in a parochial orphanage at the age of eight and one-half. Here he was quite destructive, troubled the nuns by masturbating during chapel, and generally was considered a management problem. However, he supposedly enjoyed a pleasant visit during the Christmas holiday with his mother and stepfather. Because of this, at the age of nine and one-half, he was sent home to live.

Within three months he was returned to the orphanage because his mother felt she could not handle him. On his return, the nuns described him as being much worse than he had been before he had gone home. He frequently screamed and was even more destructive than before. He physically attacked his peers, threw knives, continued his masturbatory behavior, and stole whenever the opportunity afforded it. He appeared to be a follower rather than a leader and occasionally ran away with older boys. He seldom showed genuine affection and never showed generosity or sharing. He would lie readily, and he had developed the ability to cry real tears when the occasion suited him. His stealing reached monumental proportions. His locker was found to contain medals, keys, and anything and everything that he could grab. As the nuns said, "He would steal an eye out of your head if you're not watching." Punishment varied with the sister in charge, so that Roger could never be sure how severely he would be reprimanded or disciplined for a particular act. He did spend that Thanksgiving and Christmas at home, but this was a very unsatisfactory arrangement. By now, his parents thoroughly rejected him and returned him early from the Christmas visit. On his return to the orphanage, his parents "practically pushed him inside the door with soiled pants."

During the previous summer, Roger was living at home. Prior to this, he had been accepted for residential treatment and was on the waiting list for admission which, it was anticipated, would occur in the fall. However, an official of the agency in charge, upon reviewing the case and seeing that Roger was in fact at home, concluded that the referral for residential treatment should not be pursued because, as was stated in the official letter, "he no longer needed inpatient treatment."

For the next year and one-half, Roger's life was much the same. Ultimately, the sisters requested that he be removed from the orphanage. They felt that he needed "severe treatment" and "discipline by males." He was placed in another orphanage, which was run along somewhat less rigid lines, but here he had the problem of being so far behind academically that he could not attend public school. Since this was a requirement of this orphanage, he subsequently had to be removed. Also, he showed a great deal of regression, frequently smearing mustard when it was served and, on one occasion, smearing feces. He continued to steal. He was placed for five months in a group home with adolescent boys who were retarded with some problem behavior. His adjustment was not known, although it was stated that he seemed to be happier in this setting.

Finally Roger was admitted to residential treatment just one month short of his 11th birthday, with his toy guns on his hips, with his rifle, and accompanied by an agency worker assigned for the trip.

DIAGNOSTIC STUDIES AND TREATMENT PROGRESS

During Roger's three years in residential treatment, he received individual psychotherapy, special education through the residential school facilities, engaged in small group activities in a therapeutic milieu, and received several diagnostic evaluations.

The first of the evaluations occurred one month after admission. His electroencephalogram at the time was considered "borderline abnormal," raising the question of whether there was a delay in maturation or a specific localized abnormality. Actually, two subsequent EEGs at yearly intervals showed practically the same tracings, without any definite conclusions being drawn. Again, the relationship between the EEG abnormality and overt behavior was basically unknown.

The psychological evaluation at the time showed a verbal IQ of 82 which was at the low end of the dull-normal range, a performance IQ of 108 which was average, and a full-scale IQ of 94 which was at the low end of the average range. Roger was described as an impulse-ridden child with unusually strong hostile-aggressive drives. He was considered as a child who had been severely emotionally traumatized and whose expectation was for adults to be punitive. At the time, the psychologist stated, "I feel this is a very difficult case—to intervene in a process that has been going on for 11 years. I don't think there is any doubt, however, in anyone's mind, that this boy should not return to his home, but should be thought of as material for a group placement when he leaves our program." The diagnosis was "passive-aggressive personality."

During the course of Roger's treatment, there was an improvement in the frequency and degree of his more violent temper tantrums, and he became better able to accept frustration. He was somewhat puzzling because, at times, he had periods of excellent behavior and good relationships whereas, at other times, he was highly manipulative and showed an apparent lack of guilt or anxiety about stealing and other delinquent acts. Interestingly, because of his stealing, he was placed in rather low esteem by his peers. Although he could act in a friendly manner, he really developed no close relationships with the staff or his peers. He did show signs of being suspicious and jealous that perhaps an adult might be giving more to another child than to him, and he competed furiously for what he considered his just rewards.

Roger's lack of emotional involvement with others was observed also in individual psychotherapy. Despite being seen twice a week for an hour for approximately two and one-half years by the same male therapist, who was experienced in the treatment of children, Roger did not let any close feeling develop between himself and his therapist. Progress was seen in terms of the development of an ability to delay immediate gratification, but his therapist reported that Roger was apt to resort to acting-out behavior if his demands were not quickly met. He was quite demanding, even infantile in this respect, continually seeking gratification and, as had earlier been reported, was very much out for himself. In playing games with his therapist, Roger showed that he could not afford to lose. He would become aggressive and attempt to destroy the toys in the playroom. He could not accept any interpretation of his behavior; he denied and reacted against any acknowledgement of feelings. He manipulated his therapist, always seeking something to get or some situation in which to use the therapist against the child-care staff. He obviously could not trust, and he seemed to see people as figures to exploit in terms of his needs at the moment.

During the course of Roger's second year in residential treatment, he passed his 12th birthday, which was generally considered to be the age commensurate with the developmental level at which the program at this institution ceased to be effective. Some progress was noted in terms of development of controls, but it was felt that the controls were external to him and certainly not integrated within him. In view of his increased ability for self-control, the fact that he was making some gains in this area, and was able to adapt to the treatment setting, it was recommended that Roger be kept one additional year.

During his third year in treatment, Roger was again evaluated. On the WISC he had a verbal IQ of 81, a performance IQ of 106, and a full-scale IQ of 92. It may be noted how generally comparable his intelligence test scores remained. He was described as a boy whose primary means of coping with intense anxiety was by impulsive acting-out. This was felt to reflect Roger's characterological immaturity. He appeared to present enough ego resources to recover control of himself, and he appeared capable of instilling more stable patterns of adaptation as long as ongoing external support and limits were provided. He showed that he could be critical and resentful of women and, therefore, he maintained a distance from them since they provoked a great deal of anxiety in him. He was viewed as a severely disturbed boy who needed continuous therapeutic support in an environment that was protective and well structured but not overwhelming.

As his third year of treatment ended and the time for his leaving of the institution approached, there was much concern regarding Roger's future. He continuously needed controls from without because he had not, in the opinion of the staff, truly integrated and internalized these controls nor the standards and identifications that were their basis. Now, a child psychoanalyst commented that Roger was "emotionally defective." "His conscience is defective and the intense deprivation he has had early in life leaves him with no nucleus for identification. The danger is that he will become delinquent. He has not changed fundamentally."

At this point, major efforts went into future planning. The problem of determining a suitable placement for Roger, now in his 13th year, with his history of acting out, with his need for external controls, and with his anxiety still present and leading to impulsive behavior, posed much difficulty. As one staff member said, "His prognosis is extremely guarded even if a good placement is found." Certainly, Roger was adapting to his environment. However, basic gains in terms of personality change were very small. A discharge date was set and then postponed, in the hope that in the intervening months more progress would be made in terms of finding a proper placement for Roger. However, at discharge, actual placement plans were indefinite both to the residential treatment center and to the child welfare agency. Referrals had been pursued with regard to three residential placements of a group sort, all of these being unsuccessful. The social worker at the residential treatment center reported that "the agency was contemplating Roger's return to his mother. This was definitely recommended against." On the day prior to discharge, a temporary foster home placement was secured, where there were five other foster children, and Roger was sent to this home upon his discharge from residential treatment.

EPILOGUE

It is difficult to obtain adequate follow-up data on children who have been in residential treatment facilities. This is a nationwide problem. In Roger's case, the scanty information that was obtained indicates that he did not last more than a few weeks at the initial foster home placement. Since he was at a fourth-grade level academically when, according to his age, he should have been entering the seventh grade, and because of his short attention span and difficulty in concentration, he needed special education. He thus ran into difficulty with the public school being unable to provide for his academic needs, and subsequently was placed in a detention facility for youths. Then, as had been feared, he was sent to live with his mother. By now, the stepfather was no longer in the picture but, after drifting in and out of the home for over a year and getting involved in minor delinquent activities, Roger finally recognized that there was little gratification or positive feeling of his mother toward him. For a time it is believed that he lived with some young adults who were slightly on the shady side of the law. He was involved in joyriding in automobiles and ultimately was placed on probation for theft. He was then placed in a foster home setting, but nothing is known regarding the nature of this. Later, he was involved in a breaking-and-entering felony for which he was actually sentenced to prison.

He served about three and one-half years and then was paroled. During this time, Roger was inconsistent in his occupational endeavors, since he had no actual job skills. He did not develop any strong or particularly meaningful ties insofar as could be determined. He was always felt to be a "nervous" type of person, high strung, always on the go, but not going anywhere in particular. It is believed that he continued to steal, although his actual record does not indicate many convictions. He did violate his parole and incurred a new sentence for breaking into a liquor store with two companions. It turned out that one of them drank as much of the loot as possible, and this interfered with his driving to such an extent that the police became suspicious. When they found several cases of liquor in the car, questioning led to the incrimination of his companions, one of whom was Roger. The amount of money obtained was less than $50.

While in a city jail awaiting final sentence, Roger attempted and was successful in escaping. Again, he was with other companions, all of whom were older, although by now he was in his early twenties. He was subsequently apprehended, since he had no definite plan as to what he would do on escape. Consequently, he was given an additional sentence for escape and was sent to the maximum security facility of the state. While serving this sentence, Roger attempted once more to leave the situation. All of his life he had found every residence in some way unacceptable and was either rejected outright or attempted to run away. The exception was the residential treatment center but, unfortunately, that institution eventually had to discharge him because of age and program limitations. His subsequent delinquent activities made it very clear that his home eventually would have to be in a penal institution. His last attempt at escape from this fate cost him his life.

COMMENTARY

Roger's background is filled with instances of abuse, punishment, inconsistency, and rejection. This sort of pathological early development is an aspect of motivation for so-called criminal behavior in many instances. In Roger's case, it is abundantly clear.

It is also significant that Roger was nearly 11 years old when he was placed in a situation where he could achieve the stability and interpersonal help that he obviously had needed for many years. When he was seen by the staff of the residential treatment center, it was mentioned that there was some doubt about the extent to which successful therapeutic intervention could be made, in view of his age and background. Also it is unfortunate that his original admission had to be delayed because of an administrative decision on the part of the child welfare agency. In terms of child development, one may consider the extent to which Roger's basic character was formed early, and how persistent his maladaptive behavior was throughout his life. When we consider his relative lack of affective involvement with others, his tendency to manipulate, his supposed lack of guilt and anxiety over misbehavior, and the frequent descriptions of him as self-centered and egocentric, the old label "psychopath" comes to mind. In terms of the theoretical understanding of psychopathic character development, Roger seems to have several of the components.

We cannot be sure whether there are underlying organic elements in Roger's case. This is frequently a question mark in terms of severe acting-out behavior. Although the EEG results are suggestive, they are certainly not conclusive. Moreover, even with abnormal brain wave recordings, the correlation between this and overt behavior is often difficult to establish.

Finally, it was obvious from the time of Roger's admission to residential treatment that plans would have to be made for his ongoing care in a special setting once he left residential treatment. Despite these forecasts, the fact remains that these plans were inadequately accomplished. It was not at all surprising that he finally was sent back to his mother, in view of the frequency with which this happens because of well-meaning individuals who feel that children should be with their natural parents. The failure to obtain a suitable placement, such as a group home with a therapeutic environment, is not surprising either. These homes at the time were rare, and they continue to be far less available than the need for them. Even with such a placement, it is questionable whether Roger would be able to build on those aspects of his personality that seemingly were arrested in his earliest years. Perhaps if the investment could have been made in his treatment three or four years earlier, it might have been possible to salvage him.

6. THE CASE OF TOMMY:
Dramatic Effects of Personality on IQ

Tommy's mother was several months pregnant before she married his father. This pregnancy terminated in the normal delivery of a healthy, full-term baby, who was breastfed for 5 weeks, walked at 15 months, and was toilet trained at 2 years of age. When he was less than 1 year old, his mother gave birth to a daughter. By the time Tommy was 4 years old, his mother divorced his father, remarried, and had another child, but this marriage also ended in divorce.

Following a stormy early childhood, when Tommy was 9 years old he became a candidate for residential psychiatric treatment. His father had now been away from the family for several years, and the available information about him was scanty. However, he had completed 2 years of college prior to army service and later attended a university for several months. Social agencies found him very difficult to work with and described him as being extremely hostile. He was a good athlete in his younger days and had participated in college sports. According to his mother, his father tried to "make a man out of Tommy" by the age of 3, teaching him to box and encouraging him to develop athletic skills.

Tommy's mother attended school until the 11th grade when she became pregnant and had to leave. She had two illegitimate children prior to meeting Tommy's father, and both children had been turned over to the Child Welfare Division for adoption. At the time of Tommy's institutionalization, his mother was contemplating a third marriage. She said that this man was very fond of Tommy and that they would be happy to have him return home after completing his residential treatment.

Two years prior to Tommy's institutionalization, his mother sought assistance from a child welfare agency and requested placements for her three children. At the time, she and her children were living in one room in her sister's crowded apartment. Her main concern was Tommy, whom she was completely unable to control. He was only seven years old, but he would steal money from her pocketbook and then deny it. He returned home late from school and often stayed outdoors playing until the late evening. His mother's efforts to discipline him were either ignored or he responded by swearing at her, telling her to "shut up" or striking her back if she tried physically to reprimand him. There were behavior difficulties before, but they became more and more unbearable after the mother's separation from her second husband. She insisted that living with Tommy was an impossibility, and the agency sought a foster home for him because they considered him to be "an emotionally rejected child."

After several months delay, Tommy was placed with foster parents who were warm and relaxed with him, and allowed him to move at his own pace. Nevertheless, he became negativistic and difficult to manage. His unacceptable behavior eventually became even more pronounced and included such activities as ripping the bedclothes, breaking the springs in his bed, and becoming enuretic (bedwetting) every night. He played mostly alone and sometimes talked to himself. Also, he picked the sores on his skin and his nose until they bled, and he was occasionally encopretic (defecating in his pants). He was very destructive with his clothes and purposely tore his winter coat.

Although the foster parents said that they liked Tommy, they explained that he was very irritating to live with. He began getting into more serious difficulties with other children in the neighborhood and, when the foster parents had to rescue a young boy whom Tommy was trying to hang with a rope on their front porch, they requested that the agency remove him from their home. Following a seven-month period with the foster family, Tommy was placed in a children's receiving home. During this time, his mother was very sick with tuberculosis and was receiving medical treatment for her illness.

Tommy was seen for a psychological diagnostic study at the children's receiving home, and the findings were summarized as follows: "Tommy is a very disturbed child whose self-concept is badly damaged and who has a great amount of objective anxiety. He expects and wishes for physical attack. While his adjustment is fairly good in the receiving home, this diagnostic study indicates that he would probably act out hostility in a more emotionally threatening, and less protective, environment. In his interpersonal relationships, he demonstrates difficulty tolerating any form of frustration and easily becomes very hostile. Tommy has experienced a traumatic and confusing life and has witnessed much violence between parental figures. He has a strong tie to his mother, but it seems based primarily on guilt and on fear of what he had done to cause the turmoil in his own life and his mother's physical illness."

The diagnostic evaluation stated that Tommy could not benefit from a foster home placement at that time because he needed professional help on a daily basis. Therefore, it was recommended, that he be institutionalized for long-term psychiatric treatment in an attempt to rehabilitate him and his family before he could be returned home. On the basis of this recommendation, he was admitted to the residential treatment center where he stayed for almost three years.

COURSE OF TREATMENT

When Tommy arrived at the treatment center, he was described as a well-built, good looking, black, 9½-year-old boy. He initially appeared frightened and noticeably depressed, but was extremely sullen and distrustful of all aspects of his new surroundings. As a ward of the state, Tommy was accompanied by a social worker who left him at the treatment center, a long way from his home and family.

Soon after Tommy's arrival, he was given a battery of psychological tests. On the Wechsler Intelligence Scale for Children (WISC), he obtained a verbal IQ of 69, a performance IQ of 87, and a full-scale IQ of 75. The full-scale IQ placed his intellectual functioning in the "borderline defective" category. However, the examining psychologist felt that Tommy's potential was considerably above the borderline range of intellect.

Tommy's performance on the projective tests revealed a very frightened boy with a particular fear of males, whom he tried to avoid as much as possible. His fantasies and perceptions were constricted, and he avoided emotional involvement with people. He perceived others as being highly aggressive and attacking. Moreover, he showed confusion in regard to sex and aggression, with a very poor identification with males as a result of his anxiety and fearfulness. When he could not avoid the demands that were frightening to him, he tended to act out in a negative way and became extremely hostile. On the basis of this initial evaluation, the psychologist recommended long-term treatment with a male psychotherapist.

The young psychiatric resident who saw Tommy on a twice-weekly basis found that it was extremely difficult to establish a relationship with him. Tommy actively rebelled against psychotherapy and, on several occasions, he was verbally and physically abusive toward the therapist. One reason for this might have been that the psychiatrist stressed verbal interaction and attempted to interpret Tommy's psychodynamics, but Tommy found this particularly distasteful. In interactions with the other child patients and with his child-care workers, Tommy also was nonverbal and acted out his hostile impulses and feelings very freely.

After about six months of psychotherapy, the psychiatrist wrote: "Initially, Tommy was very suspicious and quiet. In some instances he was withdrawn and apparently very depressed. Gradually, however, he became more aggressive and in his play activity resorted mainly to shooting darts and throwing rubber balls at the wall. He acted out much of his hostility in play, and also, in some of the sessions, he was physically aggressive to me. On one occasion, he lifted up a chair and threatened to hit me with it and had to be restrained physically."

Tommy frequently used foul language and made insulting remarks about the therapist's religion, appearance, and personality. Many of the phrases were so vile that, in a "nontherapeutic" setting, they would provoke retaliation and physical attack from the person receiving them. Within a professional therapeutic relationship, however, the adult did not retaliate when Tommy made these verbal attacks. Whenever they participated in games, together, Tommy made the games into aggressive encounters, doing his best to provoke and upset the psychiatrist. Several times, when the psychiatrist was unable to cope with Tommy and could no longer accept his insulting comments or physical attacks, the sessions were terminated early.

Then Tommy went through a phase of refusing to attend his psychotherapy sessions, preferring to stay outdoors and play with the other children. It was summertime, and he wanted to remain at the outdoor swimming pool. When his child-care worker sent him to the play therapy room, he went there in his bathing trunks and refused to enter. After this, he flatly refused to see the psychiatrist for psychotherapy sessions. On a few occasions when he was more or less forced to see the psychiatrist, Tommy became so destructive with toys and equipment in the therapy room that the session had to be terminated. At the time, the psychiatrist diagnosed Tommy as suffering from "anxiety reaction" and stressed that he was extremely anxious, depressed, and constantly expected to be punished and attacked. Therefore, Tommy employed the defense mechanism of attacking others before they could attack him.

Toward the end of the summer, after about six months of therapy with the psychiatrist, Tommy's behavior and outlook started to change markedly. After having canceled 10 therapy sessions in a row, Tommy approached the psychiatrist and said he wanted to go to the playroom. From that point on, he became more relaxed and apparently enjoyed attending his therapy sessions. He started building plastic models, usually warships or rockets, and became meticulous about observing the proper length of the therapy sessions. He wanted to be certain that his sessions were as long as those attended by the other child patients.

The psychiatrist observed that Tommy's anxiety had diminished considerably, and he hypothesized that one reason for this was Tommy's improved status in the group. Tommy seemed to be enjoying many rewarding experiences in his daily life, and his self-esteem was increasing noticeably. His psychiatrist commented that "even his cleanliness and grooming have markedly improved." Tommy still did not want to talk about his personal problems with the psychiatrist or his child-care workers. Nevertheless, the psychiatrist, who was preparing to leave the institution, strongly recommended that Tommy be permitted to stay at least another year and, as soon as possible, be assigned another therapist.

Tommy was then assigned to a male clinical psychologist who saw him for individual psychotherapy during the remaining 18 months of his stay in the institution. The therapist moved slowly in probing and interpreting psychodynamics. He permitted the material to come from Tommy at his own pace and tried not to upset him by imposing on his privacy. The following verbatim material is taken from the psychologist's reports of therapy written for Tommy's case record.

"Tommy appeared very eager to start his therapy sessions once he heard I would be his 'interview man.' Whenever he saw me asked when we would start our interviews together. From the beginning I was impressed with the intelligence, maturity, and reality orientation revealed in his conversation. He immediately asked about my job, salary, education, and family situation, and was very interested in other children I had seen for therapy in the past or was seeing at present. I explained my function as a therapist and the purpose of our interviews—that I was here to help with problems, difficulties, or anything that bothered him. He seemed to understand, but for a long while he did not speak of any serious difficulties or personal problems.

"During one of our early therapy sessions, we discussed an incident in which Tommy had hidden from the child-care workers and they had been unable to find him for quite some time. When we discussed this, Tommy said that he had not been upset but was 'just messing around,' trying to fool his unit leaders. He emphasized that he hid under beds in the various living units and had not gone off boundaries. That is, he seemed very concerned that I realize although he had shown this troublesome behavior, he really had not broken any serious rules. I used this occasion to remind him that whenever anything bothered or upset him, he could always talk with me about these problems.

"Shortly thereafter, when a female child care worker was leaving the institution to get married, Tommy stated that the kids liked her and would miss her. When he saw various ladies being interviewed or touring the institutional grounds, he wondered if they would be the 'new miss' for his unit. When a new unit leader was hired, Tommy was not too pleased. In fact, he engaged in a rock throwing incident against her, which I talked with him about in psychotherapy. I explained that children become upset when somebody leaves whom they like and are used to, and often have trouble accepting a new person. I tried to get Tommy to realize that it is not right to physically attack other people merely because they frustrate or upset you. While not saying much, he seemed to be accepting of my explanations and suggestions.

"On another occasion he started the interview by saying his unit leader had told him to discuss with me the fact he had fought with another child. Whenever anything like this came up, Tommy acted as though he meant no harm, was only fooling, and did not mean it. These occasions were used to reiterate that I was glad he could talk to me about such things, and that the purpose of our interviews was to help him understand himself and the difficulties he encountered."

During this period, approximately 18 months after the first psychological examination, Tommy was readministered the battery of psychological tests. He showed decided improvement in his behavior during the testing session and an unusual improvement in his test performance. In contrast to the mentally retarded qualities evidenced in his first performance on the WISC, his current scores reflected an exceptional intellectual endowment. His previous verbal IQ of 69 showed an astounding increase to an IQ level of 111. Although the scars of his early years of abuse and rejection were still limiting the adequacy of his perceptual processes as well as his use of fantasy and emotional responsiveness, he now appeared to be more relaxed, less fearful, and more competent. His conflict-ridden feelings about aggression continued to dominate his test productions, but he was more amenable to psychotherapeutic assistance than he had been in the past.

Tommy was now completing his second school year in the treatment center and his schoolwork had shown considerable improvement. On the scholastic achievement tests administered at that time, he performed at the 6.8 grade level whereas, according to his chronological age, he should have been entering the sixth grade. His teacher described him as a diligent student who showed a keen interest in his work. During the second year, he had been more relaxed with his teacher and had verbalized more freely in the classroom. He showed great improvement in personal neatness and in all written work. Moreover, the teacher reported that his behavior in school had been excellent throughout the year. Tommy knew that he had done well and was very proud. His therapist praised him for his fine performance, and they spent much time on the topic of his going to public school the following year. He was ambivalent about this, but seemed to favor the idea.

By now, Tommy occasionally talked spontaneously about his

family members. He mentioned going to the store for his mother, and he happily recalled that she would give him a nickel to buy a chocolate cupcake, which he loved. He also became an avid reader of the sports pages in the newspaper and spent time in therapy discussing the topics that he read about. A world heavyweight championship boxing match was in the news, and this motivated him to talk about his father and athletics. He idolized the black heavyweight champion, and several other black superstars in various sports were his heroes. Tommy was a highly competent athlete, and he derived pleasure from athletic participation, but he continued to be a poor sport. He expected perfection from himself, from his teammates, and from the adults. His frustration tolerance continued to be very low, and whenever anyone made a mistake, he became extremely upset. Now, however, Tommy seemed to look forward to his sessions, and therapy was progressing slowly but satisfactorily.

In the fall, Tommy began attending public school, and much therapy time was spent in discussing his school work. He had trouble learning the meaning of words and worked hard to master this one area that had caused him trouble. Early in the term, he remarked that the work was easy, but he said that he knew it would get harder later on, and he hoped that he would continue to do well. He often spoke about his teacher, who was a strong male figure (he was 6 feet, 3 inches tall and weighed about 230 pounds). He was a former outstanding football player and Tommy had a great deal of admiration for him. When Tommy obtained his first report card in the fall, he received several grades of "excellent" and placed in the highest quarter of his class. He was very proud of his accomplishment, and his therapist congratulated him wholeheartedly. They talked about his graduating from high school and eventually going to college.

Tommy continued to show in intense interest in all college and professional sports. He was especially interested in football, but he also liked basketball and spoke frequently about becoming a professional athlete when he grew up. Actually, one of his primary motives for going to college was to participate in athletics. His therapist told him about scholarship opportunities, explaining that a boy who was both a good student and an outstanding athlete could go to to a college of his choice without cost to his family.

Tommy liked the idea of getting a free education, since he was well aware that his family did not have money for college.

Once, Tommy's therapist took him to see an Ivy League college football game in which the captain of the visiting team was a black athlete who turned out to be the star of the game by scoring three touchdowns. Although Tommy definitely rooted for the black football player and was highly impressed by his performance, he also cheered for the local team to win the game and was noticeably disappointed when it lost. The allegiance to the local university may have been related to the fact that the therapist and some of the other personnel at the treatment center were also affiliated with this university. With the advent of the basketball season, Tommy began following closely the attainments of another local college team that was having a very successful season. He mentioned that he would like to have one of the black basketball players as a volunteer visitor at the institution and looked forward to this possibility, but it never materialized.

Tommy rarely went to his therapy session with any perceived serious problems that he wanted to discuss. However, he voiced complaints about a male child-care worker whom he did not like. Tommy was still not eager to talk about personal experiences, and he resented that this particular child-care worker often pressured him to talk about things that he found upsetting. Whenever his difficulties with adult staff members were discussed, the therapist used the occasion to provide some interpretations about feelings of aggression and taking the feelings out on others. Tommy did not say much in response to these attempts at clarification and interpretation, but the therapist had the feeling he was listening and gaining personal understanding.

Tommy spoke more frequently about home and family members, spontaneously brought up events that happened back home and expressed his hope for a future with his family. He became very interested in food and on several occasions, mentioned the kind of food his mother used to prepare for him and compared it with the food at the institution. He had been corresponding with his mother and grandmother and received a letter from his mother, saying that she planned to visit him soon. He seemed thrilled about this and was looking forward to her visit. In talking about his mother traveling to the institution, he mentioned his father, and the therapist asked for clarification as to whether he was referring to his original father or his stepfather. This served as a stimulus to motivate Tommy to talk about some personal matters he had never discussed previously.

Tommy spent considerable time telling his therapist about early experiences with various fathers. He said that his real father used to drink a great deal and was very mean to the children and their mother. Once when he was four years old, his father pulled a knife on the three-year-old sister and acted as if he were going to kill her. Tommy had a vivid recollection of this traumatic event. However, in spite of the unpleasant memories, he said that he liked his father. He also pointed out that he did not blame his mother for getting a divorce, since she had to work while his father wasted money and mistreated her. Tommy said that his mother then had married another man and that he, too, was a heavy drinker. Moreover, he gambled away his earnings and did not even provide the family with enough food. Thus, the mother also divorced this man, and Tommy felt that this was completely justified.

Tommy then talked about his present stepfather, whom he liked best, and recalled several happy experiences with this "nice man." He mentioned the names of his original father, second father, and third father, and indicated which of the children belonged to each. There were three different family names among the four children from this one mother. Tommy's therapist pointed out to him that although we sometimes recognize upsetting and bad things about parents, we always remember the good things about them, and this is why Tommy liked something about each of these men, even if they were not good to his mother. Also, the therapist told him that it is natural for a boy to be fond of his mother and want to take care of her. He was hoping to make Tommy understand that although there might be unpleasant aspects to parental figures, it is natural to love them and want to be with them.

Tommy, now 12 years old, was looking forward to the end of the school year and returning home to his family. He also felt ambivalent about leaving and commented that recently time had been passing very rapidly, and he did not mind staying a few months until the beginning of summer. As the time of discharge approached, he mentioned that sometimes, instead of going directly home, the children returned to the receiving home where they stayed for a few months to see whether they were ready to live at home. There, he said, they would test your conduct, see if you would run away, and watch how you got along with people. When asked how he felt about this, he replied that he would not mind this too much as long as he was sent home after a short stay in the receiving home. His therapist assured him that in view of his excellent work in public school and the way he had been getting along with the other children in the treatment center, he should have no trouble making a good impression in the receiving home before being sent home. Tommy agreed, and seemed optimistic that all would turn out well.

Shortly before leaving, at the end of the academic year, Tommy made first honors in public school. His teacher reported that Tommy had been rather quiet in class, but he had shown considerable improvement in relating to others. He got along exceptionally well when the children engaged in their school athletic program. Moreover, he was very popular with his classmates and was elected class treasurer. His teacher also said that Tommy showed a good sense of humor but that he had an undercurrent of sensitivity; his personal confidence had to be won before he could work up to capacity.

On the final psychological testing, administered just prior to his discharge, Tommy maintained the gains that he had shown previously. His full-scale WISC IQ, at this time was 115, falling within the "bright normal" category. Thus, during almost three years of residential treatment, Tommy showed a truly remarkable gain of 40 IQ points! Many signs of superior intellectual potential were present in his final test performance. Tommy continued to show a certain aloofness and distance from people, but he now appeared far less threatened by interpersonal relations and much better able to express his feelings.

The psychologist, in his therapy summary prepared soon after Tommy's discharge from the treatment center, said:

"I felt that Tommy and I had established a warm, meaningful, and trusting relationship, and that we truly liked and respected each other. Therefore, I felt sad to see this therapeutic relationship come to an end. But I also knew that for Tommy to continue growing, it was necessary for him to leave the security of the treatment center and face the further challenges that awaited him back in his natural environment."

ADJUSTMENT AT DISCHARGE AND RECOMMENDATIONS FOR THE FUTURE

Tommy obviously had made great strides and showed a tremendous amount of intellectual, personal and social improvement as a result of his residential treatment. He still had many basic conflicts, continued to be somewhat suspicious, and was not too open in interpersonal relationships. Yet, he was more trusting, verbalized more freely, and seemed more stable emotionally in all aspects of life at the time he was ready to leave the treatment center.

It was recommended that Tommy, now 12½ years old, should be returned to his mother, while continuing outpatient treatment at a child guidance clinic. It was felt that he was ready and able to function adequately in a public junior high school. He certainly possessed the intellectual endowment to do well academically and, moreover, he had demonstrated his competency in public school the previous year. His inner conflicts had been sufficiently resolved, and his emotional maturity was at a level that should permit him to live effectively in the community. Thus, he had made considerable improvement, and the prognosis was good. It was realized, however, that Tommy's future success and functioning would depend greatly on the adequacy of the home situation to which he returned.

SUBSEQUENT ADJUSTMENT AND LONGER RANGE OUTCOME

Tommy went to live with his mother and stepfather. He attended junior high school and, according to the last report, he was doing very well. However, the question of whether he would make it sucessfully through high school and college was not known. At the time of the follow-up report, it was felt that with proper guidance and encouragement Tommy could continue to make good progress. But he was still susceptible to frustration and emotional upset, and a few failures along the way could have highly negative effects on his eventual attainments. Although he definitely possesed the potential and the motivation to achieve in this society, he would only do so in surroundings that nourished the seed and appreciated the growth. It is very doubtful that his internal strength and drive for attainment were sufficienly strong to keep him working toward socially sanctioned goals in an environmental context that ignored, or continued to neglect, his abilities and his hopes.

4

LEARNING DISORDERS

Some children with learning disabilities also have behavior problems and other forms of emotional disorders, but this diagnostic category is reserved for children whose primary difficulty is an inability to learn in the ordinary school situation. Learning disorders take many forms and can result from a variety of causes; often there is a question of psychological versus organic causation. In some instances, there is a known physical impairment, with children suffering from sensory defects (abnormal vision or hearing) or obvious neurological damage (cerebral palsy, grossly impaired motor coordination). And in many cases there is mental retardation of varying degrees. Children suffering from these physical defects and mental deficiency constitute a large portion of this broad classification called learning disorders. However, the physically handicapped and mentally retarded are *not* the focus in this casebook.

There are many children who are intellectually bright, but who fail in school. These children are often called "underachievers" and, in many cases, the causes of the learning disabilities and school failure are entirely psychological. A rather prevalent subvariety has been termed "passive-aggressive underachiever," which means that the child uses school failure as a way of passively expressing aggression against his parents and other authority figures. Often this expression of emotional conflict through school failure is done unconsciously, with the youngster being totally at a loss to account for his inability to obtain good grades in school, in spite of perfectly adequate intelligence as measured by conventional IQ tests.

There is another subvariety of children with learning disorders who are believed to suffer from "minimal brain damage" or "minimal cerebral dysfunction." It is called by various names, all implicating some form of "minimal" neurological impairment, yet in most of these cases it is impossible to produce neurological or medical evidence of this hypothesized organic damage. The children look perfectly normal, and medical examinations and brain recordings (EEG) show no signs of abnormality.

These children are often hyperactive, restless, impulsive, and explosive—a cluster of characteristics forming a syndrome known as the "hyperkinetic impulse disorder." Because hyperkinetic children find it extremely difficult to sit still, have trouble concentrating and attending to details, do not like to work for delayed gratification, and have a low frustration tolerance, they are very apt to experience school failure. However, with many hyperkinetic children, psychostimulant drugs (for example, amphetamines) produce a striking improvement in behavior and school performance. The effectiveness of these drugs in treating this type of childhood disorder was a chance discovery several years ago, and it remains paradoxical and difficult to explain. That is, a drug such as Dexedrine, which tends to speed up or excite a normal person, has exactly the opposite effect with hyperkinetic children, calming them down and making them better able to concentrate. To date, all attempts at accounting for this finding have been theoretical and speculative, but there is no doubt that in many cases the drugs do work. From this positive drug effect, it is reasoned that there must be some form of undetectable neurological defect that benefits from the drug action; thus, the concept of "minimal brain damage."

Although drug therapy is often recommended for hyperkinetic children, other therapeutic and educational procedures are used with the majority of children who show learning disabilities. The primary approach to treatment is "special education"—a specialized area within the educational field, devoted to the teaching of children with severe school problems. Special education is further subdivided into teachers who specialize in teaching the mentally retarded, the physically handicapped, or the emotionally disturbed. In most public school systems today, there are teachers and facilities devoted to helping children overcome their learning disorders, from whatever cause.

As mentioned earlier, children with learning disabilities frequently show other behavioral difficulties. When these maladjustments and school failure result from emotional conflicts, psychotherapy may prove beneficial. These various treatment approaches (drug therapy, special education, and psychotherapy) were all used to good advantage with the cases described in this section.

The three children in this group of learning disorders come from very different socioeconomic backgrounds than the children who were studied in the section on behavior disorders. The present cases were treated in private practice and outpatient child guidance centers, *not* in institutional settings where they had been sent by child welfare agencies. These child patients were from intact families, with parents who were paying the private practitioners (pediatricians, psychiatrists, psychologists) or the child guidance centers for their diagnostic and therapeutic services. Although there is ample psychopathology in these cases, it is expressed in a form that is less offensive to society, which accepts learning disorders more than antisocial behavior.

According to psychodynamic theory, learning involves an aggressive component; thus, children who have difficulty coping with their aggressive impulses are often unable to learn in the normal school setting. To the extent that a child cannot express aggression in his social surroundings, he is likely to encounter difficulty learning to read and to master other academic skills. The psychodynamic orientation suggests that if a child with a learning disability is helped to express his aggression in a therapeutic setting, he will be better able to use his aggressive drive in coping with school work.

The case of Ricky provides findings that fit very well with this psychodynamic interpretation. Raised in a family in which all members had great difficulty expressing their aggressive feelings, Ricky experienced school failure at a very early age. Although bright enough, he was unable to read and had repeated the first grade. However, through a program of psychotherapy with a clinical psychologist, Ricky gradually became better able to express hostility and aggression in his play activities and then showed marked improvement in his school performance. Thus, the clinical evidence from this case study confirms the psychodynamic hypothesis of an association between aggression and learning.

In the case of Carol, we see pervasive negative effects on personality and social adjustment resulting from the experience of school failure. The detrimental influence of anxiety and a poor self-concept were particularly evident in her IQ test performance. Projective tests were used to uncover Carol's unconscious motivation and conflicts, and her responses to the Rorschach inkblots and the Thematic Apperception Test (TAT) revealed a considerable store of underlying hostility and resentment toward family members. Carol's ambivalence toward her father (with strong attraction toward him coupled with feelings of rejection and resentment) provides a vivid example of the Electra complex described by Freud—the female child wants to replace the mother in a love relationship with the father, but she fears hostility from the mother and thus feels resentment toward both parents. In Carol's case, amphetamines and psychotherapy were used in combination for the treatment of the hyperkinetic impulse disorder, with highly successful results.

Carol is a little older than most cases of hyperkinesis, since this disorder is usually outgrown by late adolescence. The case of Robby provides a more typical example of hyperkinesis and its related learning disabilities. His short attention span, overactivity, and irritability were observed at a very early age. And, like many hyperkinetic children, in spite of his exceptionally high IQ, he was unable to cope with schoolwork at the third grade level. Fortunately, however, a daily dosage of amphetamine was remarkably effective in treating this hyperkinetic youngster.

The various forms of therapy that are employed with cases of learning disorder are currently being seriously questioned by some members of the helping professions and by many educated laymen. Drug therapy for treatment of children with school problems has been compared to placing active children into pharmaceutical straitjackets and making them into helpless zombies. Psychotherapy has not been clearly demonstrated to be worth the time and expense involved in most cases. And special education has been said to stigmatize children by placing them in special groups with "labels," which remove them from the regular educational and social programs. Here, we will not attempt to resolve these controversies; instead, we note that some of the procedures that were found highly effective in the present cases do not always work so well. Thus there are several important issues, both practical and ethical, to be considered before recommending widespread application of these treatments for children with learning disabilities.

RECOMMENDED READING

Frierson, E. C., & Barbe, W. B. (Eds.) *Educating children with learning disabilities.* New York: Appleton-Century-Crofts, 1967.

Hellmuth, J. (Ed.) *Learning disorders.* Vol. 3. Seattle: Special Child Publications, 1968.

Johnson, D. J., & Myklebust, H. P. *Learning disabilities.* New York: Grune & Stratton, 1967.

Trapp, E. P., & Himelstein, P. (Eds.) *Readings on the exceptional child,* 2nd edition. New York: Appleton-Century-Crofts, 1972.

Wender, P. H. *Minimal brain dysfunction in children.* New York: Wiley-Interscience, 1971.

7. THE CASE OF RICKY
Psychogenic Learning Disability

As Ricky's mother phrased it, he was born "neat and polite." He had been a model child in every way but one: when he was eight years old, he had repeated the first grade and "slipped through" into the second, but he could not read. He had absolutely no grasp or understanding of reading, although he did well in other subjects including arithmetic. He began nursery school at the age of four, had a good time, and was popular with the teacher and the other children. However, his mother was quite upset because he did not learn to write his name. She felt that this was perhaps because "boys' hands mature slower than girls' hands."

When Ricky was five, his parents moved to a different state and he began kindergarten. He made a great effort to learn to write his name and, eventually accomplished this, to his mother's relief. He had a good year in kindergarten, again showing every sign of enjoying the experience and of being liked by the others in the school. When he began first grade, however, he had great difficulty with reading. His mother described the first grade teacher as a very good one; she not only had an excellent program for the first grade children but was able to give Ricky some extra remedial help. In spite of this, he did not learn to read and, by the end of the year, his mother and the teacher agreed that it would be best for him to repeat the grade, which he did the following year.

This time, when Ricky repeated the grade with another teacher, very little issue was made of his difficulty. The teacher liked him, but paid less attention to him and, at this point, in his mother's words, "he slipped through" into the second grade, still without having learned the skills appropriate for this promotion. The following year when Ricky was in the second grade, his parents were called to the school and told that he was not achieving anywhere near his potential and that he probably needed help; a referral was made to the child guidance clinic.

Ricky was tall for his age and was a leader in play because of his size and skills. He was good in throwing and catching. However, in the classroom he seemed unmotivated. His teacher said "he can't read and doesn't desire to read." Daydreaming and shyness characterized him in this situation. He seemed happy in a passive way and was very likeable, but the teachers sometimes felt that they did not really know him and had not really established a relationship with him. He could do oral arithmetic quite well but seldom, if ever, volunteered. He gave the impression of being a boy who knew a great deal more than he was willing to show. With this degree of passivity in school, he had accepted (without making any objections or even appearing to mind) the fact that he had to repeat the first grade.

Ricky's parents also found him to be slow in learning. As they put it, "he has to do well or he won't try at all" and, with some insight, his mother remarked that sometimes his lack of interest covered up his fear of taking the risk of failure. Generally, he was described as a very responsible boy around the home who could play well by himself, but who did equally well with other children. His parents had seldom seen him angry, although he could become quite stubborn if he was aroused.

When Ricky was examined by the school psychologist shortly before his referral to the clinic, he was found to have above-average ability, although his scores on the standard intelligence test had fallen in the two-year period since he initially was examined in the first grade. The psychologist who had first seen Ricky found him to be unresponsive, giving little clue to his feelings and verbalizing no more than necessary. He volunteered nothing but, on the other hand, he was cooperative in attempting to respond to all of the test items given to him. The second time Ricky was seen, he appeared to be restless, although he tried to control this, was able to cooperate well, and was willing to work hard on everything assigned to him. The contrast between his restlessness and his effort to cooperate was striking; it was as if Ricky had to control himself to keep from running away from the situation.

In the second examination, he was found to have an intelligence probably at the superior level, to do particularly well with verbal abstraction, to have a good knowledge of vocabulary and information, and to be quite adept at perceiving nonverbal visual relationships. However, he showed a great deal of difficulty in relating events and people to each other and in explaining interpersonal and social relationships verbally, a trait also seen on the projective testing. Thus, on the Thematic Apperception Test (TAT), he described the pictures rather than tell coherent stories about them, and he remained as superficial as possible. He avoided imputing motives or feelings to the characters in his stories and, from his stories, he appeared to be a lonely, depressed youngster who was unable to form close personal relationships with other people in spite of his ability to relate readily on a more superficial level. Both psychologists found that Ricky showed a great deal of perfectionism. "He tries to make up for his feelings of inadequacy by being an especially good boy and by denying his own feelings. By doing so he does not come to grips with his feelings and is unable to resolve his inner conflicts." He was a rather withdrawn, static person who was unable to move forward and who seemed particularly concerned about the investment of energy and aggression that is necessary to learn. As in the classroom, he appeared as a passive boy who tried to please others, but he seemed afraid to compete actively in the challenge of learning.

After Ricky's referral to the clinic, on the basis of a third psychological evaluation, the psychologist was impressed by Ricky's strong defenses. Perfectionistic, repressing his feelings, and denying any difficulties, he showed an avoidance of any kind of involvement with others, either openly or in his daydreaming and fantasy. In regard to the daydreaming and fantasy, his responses to the Rorschach cards were revealing. He looked at the cards silently for a long time and protested his inability to see anything: "I can't make anything out of this." Then he picked out small details of the ink-blot and gave to one a vague response and to the other a popular response, completely ignoring the compelling human shapes and the possibilities that they provided for an expression of imagination. Thus, Ricky had worked out some relatively effective ways of superficially relating to other people and of interacting to meet conventional demands, but he did this without getting himself deeply, meaningfully, or emotionally involved to any extent.

The psychologist felt that Ricky must retain his impersonal detachment from actual people. For this reason, problem-solving activity of any kind was threatening for Ricky because, by potentially leading to self-reflection and inner life, it could open up the possibility of an awareness of his true feelings about others. It was felt that his way of handling his feelings could be involved in his learning difficulties. Some of the force of his feelings was evident in his repeated TAT theme of a mother "making" a child do something that the child did not want to do. He repeated this a number of times, and the feelings of anger it produced were obvious but quickly suppressed.

Ricky's inability to tolerate his feelings of rebellion and anger caused his inability to tolerate any awareness of his deeper feelings. His need to remain detached from others and to be as passive as possible was viewed as a means of avoiding situations where his angry feelings might erupt beyond control. The reason why aggression was so threatening to this boy was unclear, although his relationship with both parents showed a good deal of insecurity, with Ricky perceiving his parents as communicating much anxiety about the children: "They are worried that the children might be hurt or lost." From Ricky's TAT productions, the family picture generally was one of an overanxious, inhibited, and perfectionistic group of people, none of whom were really able to cope with negative feelings—their own or those of others.

DEVELOPMENT

Ricky was the second of three children, with a sister one year older and a brother two years younger. He was from an attractive, upwardly mobile, upper middle-class family, which was supported comfortably by the father's position as assistant to the president of a manufacturing firm. The parents were both hardworking, sober, and industrious people of Protestant, New England background. They described themselves as a quiet couple with a modest social life, which centered around church activities. They occupied a large home in a well-to-do suburb and had a number of people besides members of the immediate family living with them.

The paternal grandmother, an elderly and rather grouchy woman, lived in their home and the parents took pains to please her. In addition, his mother had from time to time acted as a temporary foster mother to a number of children whose parents were unable to care for them. Thus, when Ricky was about a year old and his sister was two, his mother had taken in a baby girl, the child of an unmarried teenager who had attended their church.

She had done this at the request of the minister and took care of the child for about one year. This pattern was repeated a number of times, with his mother feeling that it was both a religious and social obligation to help out in this manner.

At the time of the referral to the clinic, an older man and his young son were living in Ricky's home, and the boy was about Ricky's age. The man's wife had died a short time before and this was to be a temporary move until he could again establish a home of his own, with a housekeeper. The main theme running through these efforts was Christian sacrifice and charity, with his mother feeling strongly that she should help others in this way.

Ricky was born about two years after his parents married, when his father was still in the service. There was nothing unusual about his birth or early development. His mother recalled no problems whatsoever; labor was induced and no anesthesia was needed or used until the very end. During Ricky's first week of life, he was colicky but, within a few days, on the advice of the doctor, the proper feeding formula was found and he very quickly became a "good baby" and a good eater. He was always happy, easygoing, and had a big smile. He was somewhat slower than the other children, walking and talking at about 13 months, but he was toilet-trained between one and one and one-half years of age without much difficulty. Weaning took place at age one, again with no problems. Indeed, until the time he began school, there had never been any problems with him. He got along well with both of his siblings, although occasionally there was mild resentment because of his sister's mothering him and bossing him. His mother felt, however, that this occurred less than in most families and that Ricky was sometimes as concerned and protective of his sister as she was of him. He was equally close and affectionate with his younger brother and seldom, if ever, showed any of the resentment or sibling rivalry that one might expect between a middle child and his very close older sister and younger brother.

Ricky was always popular with other children, both with his siblings and outside the family as well. There were only a few unusual events in his development. The first occurred at about age three, when he was beaten up by a neighbor's child and was quite upset by this. At the age of four, he had a spell of tipping over neighbors' birdbaths and turning on their water faucets. Also, he would occasionally get a neighbor's hose, turn it on, and play with it, unaware that this could lead to difficulty. These, however, were the extent of his behavior problems until shortly before coming to the clinic for treatment, when he was somewhat upset and had occasional outbursts of temper. On the other hand, he had continued to take piano lessons, was good at athletics, and was popular. He had begun to develop an increased interest in television, particularly cowboy and war films and especially those involving fighting and shooting but, behaviorally, remained passive and good natured for the most part.

FAMILY BACKGROUND

Ricky's mother was a woman of average size, well groomed, trim, very attractive, pleasant, and cooperative. When seen initially by the social worker, she spoke with concern and bewilderment about the problem she had with Ricky and the inconsistency in his being friendly, outgoing, and popular while still having a learning difficulty. After giving the history that has been summarized above, she talked a little of her own past life, but this was in response to direct questioning by the social worker. Her previous experiences were at times quite vivid but, at other times, they were rather foggy and vague, and some events were clouded with questions and mystery.

She was the older of two girls, having a sister four years younger than herself with whom she had remained very close. She described the divorce of her parents when she was about six years old, her father's subsequent remarriage and, at this point, things became foggy and confusing. Ricky's mother said that her parents, in spite of their divorce, always seemed to get along very well. She did not understand, and no one had ever told her, the reason for their separation. Her father, she said, was a demanding, perfectionistic person, " a tough man to work for," whose employees often talked about his strictness but, at the same time, he was very likable. Ricky's mother stayed with her own mother whom she also found very likable. Nevertheless, she saw her father frequently and grew up very close to him. "He taught me how to drive, to fish, and to hunt." She grew up as something of a tomboy, having a close relationship with her father, generally "hanging around" with a group of boys in the neighborhood and doing many of the things they did. She explained that this was a result of there being no girls available.

Again, in spite of the divorce, Ricky's mother remembered that there was very little shown in terms of negative feelings or behavior in her family. Her father, mother, and stepmother got along well, often had dinner together, and spent Holidays together. On the surface the relationship was good, and none of the three (father, mother, and stepmother) ever really got angry, even about such a disruptive thing as the divorce. Her father and stepmother eventually had another child who, his mother said, was practically a half sister and half daughter to her. It seems that she really did not feel the full force of the divorce or its meaning until she became a teen-ager. At this point, she found it embarassing that her parents were divorced and often pretended to others that they were really living together.

She described her relationship with her mother as being "fun," but in a manner that suggested that she and her mother were more like sisters, discussing all the decisions that had to be taken and participating like partners in raising her own younger sister. Once, somewhat inappropriately in this discussion, his mother remarked, "It wasn't that I wasn't treated as a child when I was younger." As an adolescent, she described herself as being very shy and sensitive, and attributed some of this to her newfound embarrassment regarding the facts of her parents' divorce and to the other children's teasing, particularly the boys. However, she did well in school and later went to college where she became a dental technician. She gave the impression of being an extremely capable, intelligent, and very personable woman who had a great deal of difficulty expressing feelings, both about herself in her own childhood and about her children at the present time.

Ricky's father was an equally attractive person, tall, well dressed, and intelligent, with a rather serious, "sourpuss" expression. He rarely smiled or laughed but, when he did, his whole demeanor changed. He described his own childhood as being unhappy in a home marked by frequent separations and difficulties between his mother and father. He was an only child. His father was a brilliant man who set up several businesses, but they repeatedly failed. He described how he had several times attempted to help his own father in business and tried to pick up the pieces when one of the many ventures fell apart. His father's problem was alcohol! At times he had a great deal of money, but he died practically penniless. He thought of his father as being a good man, strict, but fair, self-made, and a "gentleman all the way." He said he had never witnessed an open argument between his parents, but he knew that they occurred because this was explained to him by both parents at the time of their divorce.

His mother had never been well and had remained an invalid until the present time when she was living with him and his family. He had stayed with his mother at the time of the divorce, and he described a childhood in which he "had to grow old too fast." Even as a boy of 10 or 12, he was helping to maintain his mother, and in spite of the separation kept contact with his father, helping his father out of difficulty from this time through his college years. He blamed his parents for his never finishing college and, at the same time, admitted that it probably was his own fault. He nevertheless had done extremely well in business, being assistant to the president of his firm in a position where he acted as a trouble-shooter, often traveling to his company's other offices and factories where there were problems. Ricky's father also impressed one as being an intelligent man who, in his own words, had never really had a chance to be a child or to be loose, easy, and free. He seemed to have covered his feelings with a great deal of effort, and he had done so fairly effectively, resorting to intellectualization and perfectionism. On the surface, the whole family were attractive, happy people who functioned smoothly as a group and handled themselves "properly." Also, they gave a strong impression of being unable to express themselves, to feel free and, particularly, they needed to inhibit any kind of negative, hostile, or aggressive feelings.

TREATMENT

Because much of the problem in Ricky's inability to learn seemed dependent on his inability to express his feelings (particularly his negative ones), and since this appeared to be a problem with the entire family, the treatment involved not only Ricky but also his parents. In some respects, the more significant parts of the treatment may have occurred with his parents. Ricky himself was seen in therapy by a psychologist, individually, for about one year. At the end of the summer, just before entering the third grade, he appeared as a very polite, well-defended boy. He was quite reserved verbally but, gradually over the year, he began to invest himself more actively in play with his therapist. Much of this centered around the use of toy soldiers and toy guns, with miniature battles being arranged in which the soldiers were lined up in formations and then mowed down with enthusiasm by Ricky. However, he was careful in these games to include the therapist and, indeed, usually insisted that the therapist take the first shot and make the first move. He did this in his typical polite manner, never presenting any difficulty behaviorally.

Ricky arrived on time and left on time, was punctual, and was always helpful in cleaning up the therapy room at the end of the session. It was with some difficulty that the therapist was able to get Ricky to the point where he could make any kind of mess without discontinuing his activities at once, in order to clean it up. He seldom tested (let alone questioned) a limit and it was almost unnecessary to bring up the subject of limits in the sessions. Ricky's unusual instinct of knowing what was proper and accepted was exceptional for a boy his age.

Because of the problem that had been seen through testing and, in terms of the whole family diagnosis that centered around aggression, the therapist's major goal was to enable Ricky to open up, to show some of his feelings, and hopefully to express negative, hostile, and rebellious impulses in a direct way. On the verbal level, this proved to be an almost impossible goal to achieve. However, in his play, Ricky did move considerably so that toward the end, at least in terms of his behavior within the structured situation, he had developed a capacity to show a good deal of aggression. He seemed to need the therapist's permission to do this, and seemed much reassured when the therapist joined in himself although, of the two, Ricky was usually the more reserved, cautious, careful, and inhibited.

During this period, Ricky began to show more aggression outside of the treatment situation. Thus, he asked for, and received, an air rifle for his birthday, and he spent many hours shooting, first at targets, then at the river that ran in back of his home, and then at small animals in the neighborhood. Eventually, he transferred this activity to street lights and included in his "rampage" an episode of upsetting tombstones in a nearby cemetery. Ricky said nothing about this to his therapist until one session when he arrived early and went directly to the therapy room. Not knowing this, the psychologist waited for Ricky in the reception room until a loud crash down the hall attracted his attention. It had come from the therapy room. When the therapist entered, he found Ricky covered with paint, disentangling himself from a set of steel shelves that had toppled over on him. Going to the rescue, he helped Ricky clear himself of the debris, when both stood back, looked at the jumble, and began to laugh. Ricky commented, "I bet you won't laugh when you hear what else I got into," and related the story of his escapades at home. For once, he was able to verbalize his feelings and accepted the connection made by his therapist between his behavior, his play in therapy, and his feelings; he admitted that, "I guess I do get mad sometimes." He was surprised that his therapist could accept this fact and could even explain that everyone sometimes had these feelings—and they acted on them.

Finally, during the last few months of treatment, when Ricky had been attending summer school, he was able to discuss his problems in learning and, instead of the passive denial that was so evident before, he was able to admit that he was not doing as well as he should in school and to express a good deal of motivation to do better. He had begun to make progress, was proud of it, and hoped to continue doing well in the fall. Therapy with Ricky was terminated at the end of the summer. For the most part, he remained a well-controlled, polite boy, but with a degree of relaxation and an ability to be more flexible and expressive in his behavior, particularly around aggression.

Ricky's mother, in her treatment by a psychiatric social worker, had similar difficulties expressing her feelings. At first, she asked for direct advice and help in solving some of her minor problems with her children. The caseworker had the impression that some of the inhibited, rather "stuffy" behavior that was seen in Ricky was almost a projection of the way his mother felt: one had to protect oneself from feelings. As her own treatment progressed, she described how Ricky had begun to show aggression around the home. He even had fights with his friend next door. She admitted never having actually seen any of these fights but stated that Ricky would come in from outside, saying that he was not going to play with the boy any more, so she assumed that there had been some sort of difficulty.

Ricky's mother remarked that his attitude toward her had begun to change, and she gave the following example.

One night recently, she had said to the children that she was tired, was going to bed early, and that the children could put themselves to bed at eight oclock. She said that she would not actually do this, but that she was just teasing them a little. Ricky replied that he did not have to go to bed every night at eight o'clock, to which she responded, "Of course, you do, Ricky." Ricky answered, "Oh, no I don't. On Friday I can stay up later, because I don't have to go to school the next day." His mother considered this as evidence of Ricky's newfound aggression, giving perhaps an indication of the intensity of the inhibition in the family.

Ricky's mother stated that he was the last one of the children she would have expected to have emotional difficulties. "Ricky was such a good baby, so happy and calm, you could always depend on him. He would never be on the edge of a cliff or up a tree." She didn't have to worry that he was going to get hurt, "He always had such good common sense, he wouldn't attempt anything he knew wasn't safe." Ricky's younger brother was more adventuresome, although the older sister was a responsible, apparently very mature young lady who, even at her age, could be left with the care of the other two. His mother stated emphatically, "There is no rivalry among them. I treat them all alike. There is no competition among my own children for any reason nor has there ever been."

She followed this by explaining that she and her husband never allowed the children to see them disagree on anything. They always talked things over privately, particularly if it was an issue concerning the children or a decision that had to be made. Always, when a decision was made, each would back the other up to the fullest extent. She described the contrast between her own children and the boy who was currently staying with them, describing the other boy's "sloppy table manners," and the difference between this boys' behavior with her and her family and with his father. With them, the other boy was quiet, shy, extremely clean and careful, sometimes obsessed with germs, and always washed his hands and refused to eat anything if anyone else had touched it. She felt that this was because his mother had recently died of an infectious disease and that the boy was concerned about germs. She described the difference in his behavior when he was with his own father. "What that man has to put up with. I can hear them. He whines and cries and has tantrums and acts like a three year old. I don't let on that I hear, but he doesn't act like that with us. He has just sensed that we don't allow our children to behave like that, and he has never tried it with us."

His mother soon adopted a routine in her interviews, each time describing Ricky's behavior throughout the past week, offering something similar about other members of the family that seemed interesting or significant to her, and then sitting back and waiting quietly for her social worker's comments. Seldom did she seem able, willing, or interested in really involving her own feelings or in expressing them, over a period of months. Finally, however, she came in one day, went through her usual routine, and then having finished it, she described very quickly that it had been an extremely difficult week, that her father had become ill and died, and that she had buried him only the day before.

Until then, Ricky's mother had been completely calm, controlled, and self-possessed, but following these statements she burst into tears, describing how difficult it was to lose him, how she had been his favorite, how he had taught her to hunt and fish, and how cold he appeared in the coffin. She shuddered and clasped herself as though suddenly chilled, unable to speak. She recovered, saying, "I am all right," and went on to say that her younger sister had taken it well. Her half sister, however, had gone to pieces. She seemed troubled by the questions people asked about her mother and step-mother. She described the "one big happy family relationship with the two widows mourning their lost love side by side." But then she referred to the whole situation as a strange family, "her weird family," in which her mother and father were separated, but they always spoke kindly and protectingly about one another. Emotions were never allowed to interfere. She repeated that she did not know why they had divorced, although she knew that there had been a bitter fight for custody in which her mother had won. She again stated that she had always been happy with her mother who was very likable, but had been closer to her father.

After this outburst, Ricky's mother began to talk more and more about herself and less of her children and family in her interviews. She began gradually to admit and to show some of the feelings that she had held in check for so long. With this, she became more accepting of Ricky's own tentative efforts toward showing a mild degree of hostility. This never became intense, although it took his mother many sessions before she could accept even the small amount of resistance that Ricky began to show toward her and her husband. She stated that he was becoming more self-assertive, but that she was uncertain about this and not sure if she really liked it. For example, he had begun to refuse to eat certain foods. He had never done this before.

On looking back, Ricky's mother realized that she had been aware that there were things Ricky did not like, but that he had never openly said so. She remarked that the neighbors had also noticed a change in Ricky. The mother of his best friend saw that he was no longer so passive in his relationship with her son. The other boy's mother saw this as a very positive thing, but Ricky's mother implied that she still was not quite sure of how she felt about it. She contrasted his present behavior with the old Ricky, who had been such a good child, so sensible and obedient. It was not that he was a "goodie-goodie," she said, "he had his moments when he was all boy," although she was vague in describing what she meant by this. Gradually, however, his mother recognized her own need to protect herself from feelings, and she was able to relate this to the very complicated and mixed emotions she had had about her own parents and her childhood. She began to accept the fact that her children also could have feelings and began to feel more comfortable in allowing them to express themselves. She at least, was, intellectually able to accept the fact that Ricky would need to change in order to solve his difficulty; she was able to see that his inability to express aggression or anger and his tremendous inhibition had a great deal to do with his inability to learn to read.

During this time, Ricky's father was seen when possible in group therapy. These contacts were on again, off again because of his frequent need to travel on business, but he faithfully came to the sessions when he could. His father began as a stiff, rigid man whose remarks were mainly focused toward enhancing his own status and importance in the group. The rest of the members were rather hostile and cold toward him and, in fact, he was almost excluded by them in their discussions. However, he and another member of the group, because of some verbalized disagreements, eventually found themselves engaged in an openly aggressive relationship in which a good deal of temper and anger was expressed on both sides. This seemed to open up his father so that he could see his own rigidity and his fear of expressing aggression, except in the controlled, rational argumentative manner with which he attempted to maneuver in the group. With his adversary, his father found himself at the opposite end of the continuum. The adversary was unable to control his aggression and Ricky's father was unable to show it, except in a very refined gentlemanly and intellectualized way. However, they were attracted toward each other, and it reached a point where each was able to make rather perceptive comments about the other's difficulty with aggression.

Ricky's father, at one point, expressed concern about Ricky's behavior, which had become more aggressive, and was afraid that this might get out of hand. The matter had come up in a discussion of air rifles and whether boys should be allowed to have them. Ricky's father said, "Give a child a weapon like this and he could kill someone if he got angry." His adversary quickly pointed out that all boys felt angry at times, but that this did not mean they were going to kill someone—a point of view that was supported by the rest of the group. Gradually, Ricky's father described more involvement with his son and, through interaction with the other group members he was able to loosen up more and more, particularly through listening to their experiences and the difficulties they found in their own families. He even announced one day that he had given Ricky an air rifle.

FINAL NOTE

During the summer, while being seen in therapy and attending summer school, Ricky learned to read and made very exceptional progress. His reading approached the level of fourth grade, which he was due to begin in the fall. The school noted that he had "worked diligently during the summer, had learned to work independently very well, and had been an active interested competitor in the group. We can say congratulations for a job well done."

Concurrently, at home and in the neighborhood, although by no means an aggressive or acting-out child, Ricky began to express his preferences, wishes, and needs much more definitely, occasionally showing annoyance, irritation, or anger at his siblings or at the demands of his parents. His parents, while still extremely proper people, were able to accept some of these changes in Ricky, and they seemed much more relaxed themselves.

8. THE CASE OF CAROL:
People, Pills, and Performance

At the time of Carol's initial visit to the psychiatrist's office, she was described as a thin, potentially quite pretty, 14-year-old girl. She expressed great concern over her inability to achieve adequately in school—especially since she hoped, eventually, to attend college. She had experienced difficulty in coping with school work for many years and especially had trouble with mathematics.

Along with her academic difficulties, Carol had very few interests and no close friends. She described her lonely situation, staying home, bored, and restless with little to do. She felt rejected by other youngsters in her school setting and complained about being left out of most activities.

Carol admired her mother whom she felt was "very smart," but she also said that her mother was "quite pushy." She found many similarities between her younger sister (who also was very bright and quite aggressive intellectually) and her mother. She reported that her sister had a lot of friends and found it extremely easy to obtain excellent grades in school.

During the initial interview, Carol frequently described her main problem as not being able to keep her mind or attention on anything for very long. She often felt restless and fidgety, and found it extremely difficult to concentrate for more than brief periods of time. Very often, she would walk around aimlessly, move her hands or legs, and engage in various kinds of random motor activity instead of sitting in a still position. The psychiatrist formed the impression, based on Carol's conversation and choice of words, that she was quite intelligent and that her school failure probably was caused by emotional and neurological disabilities instead of an inadequate intellect.

PSYCHIATRIC INTERVIEW WITH PARENTS

After talking with Carol, the psychiatrist had a session with her parents and obtained the following information. According to them, her chief problems were that she was unhappy, antisocial, and unsuccessful in school. She was the middle child of three, with an older brother and younger sister. Her mother said the pregnancy had been perfectly normal, with delivery by Caesarean section prior to the onset of labor. Her mother reported that there were no obvious problems concerning the birth.

No feeding problems were described, although Carol sucked her two middle fingers and was a hyperactive child. She was a crib rocker and continued to show these rocking movements throughout her childhood, right up to the time of the present evaluation. Her parents stated that she had always been accident prone and showed signs of poor coordination. That is, although there were no obvious growth difficulties noted, Carol had remained awkward, hyperactive, impulsive, and uncoordinated throughout her childhood years.

By the third grade, Carol's academic difficulties were becoming evident. She had a history of receiving poor grades even though she seemed to be trying. Her main area of difficulty had always been mathematics, in which her grades were extremely poor and usually close to failing. All this time, as Carol was having school difficulties, her younger sister was an aggressive and precocious achiever in the classroom.

Based on his interview with Carol and the discussion with her parents, the psychiatrist reported that "a lot of what has happened to this girl, and the kinds of things complained about, could represent a mixture of hyperkinetic impulse disorder and specific learning disability, plus both secondary and independent emotional components." He recommended that she be given psychological tests for a more complete intellectual and personality evaluation before deciding on a course of treatment for her difficulties.

PSYCHOLOGICAL EVALUATION

The psychologist described Carol as a pretty, petite, highly anxious girl who was willing to talk, but who talked initially with little spontaneity or eye contact. Gradually, however, she became more relaxed. She repeated some of the complaints that she had previously spoken of: no friends, poor performance in school, inability to concentrate, and very few interests. She felt that other people misunderstood her desire to be alone, and then described how she liked to "retreat into another world," making up stories about scenes from movies with fantasies of herself as a heroine and glamorous star. She asked the psychologist, "Why am I so different? Why do other girls have hobbies and friends, and I do not?" Upon completion of the testing, when Carol seemed more comfortable with the examiner, she freely expressed her deep feelings of personal inadequacy and despair. She asked, "If you don't do good in school, and you don't have friends or hobbies, and you mess up everything you do, what would you think of yourself?" Then she said, "I'm just a nothing, I don't fit in with anyone."

On the intelligence test, Carol obtained a verbal IQ of 115, a performance IQ of 90, and full-scale IQ of 105. The psychologist felt that her performance reflected the effects of a variety of problems. Extremely high anxiety pervaded the entire test, and it had a noticeable effect on several of the subtests that are particularly susceptible to the damaging effects of emotional disturbance. In fact, it was difficult to determine how much of her poor performance was caused by real inadequacy and how much by overwhelming anxiety due to fear of failure. If she could not answer an item immediately, she became flustered and intellectually barren. She was extremely inconsistent within the subtests, often missing easy items and going on to answer more difficult questions correctly. It was obvious that she had great difficulty in concentrating and that her attention span was extremely limited. However, a few words of reassurance and encouragement helped her to maintain focus on the tasks at hand. On several occasions, she at first provided the correct answer but then, because of indecisiveness and uncertainty of herself, she would impulsively change the answer and spoil it, thereby losing points.

The examiner commented, "While her score is no doubt greatly jaded by the profuse anxiety, I feel strongly that there is also a basic perceptual disorder operating. Her ability to organize visual stimuli into meaningful elements or to conceptualize materials based upon visual information are seriously impaired. Much of her anxiety may be a reaction to her vague introspections. The anxiety reduces her attention span, increases distractability and lowers efficiency, causing what probably are minimal deficits to become disproportionately interfering."

When asked to draw a person, Carol drew a faceless, featureless, and ghostlike figure. Although she drew the male first, there was hardly any sexual differentiation, since both the male and female drawings were merely outlines. These drawings suggest serious identity problems and the possibility of significant emotional pathology.

The sentence completion test also showed Carol's low self-esteem and concern over her own inadequacy. Her tendencies toward withdrawal and an excessive fantasy life were again apparent. On this test, she showed signs of great hopelessness and despair, and she expressed considerable hostility toward her mother, blaming her for the difficulties she was having.

The Rorschach test revealed even greater signs of psychopathology, and Carol's fantasy was a panorama filled with bodily mutilation, anger, and death. People were seen as chopped up, split in the middle, beheaded, and disintegrated. Whereas on the figure drawings she produced only body outlines, on the Rorschach test her perceptions were almost totally of the gory insides of bodies that had been subjected to torture and various other forms of abuse. Responses to some of the inkblots revealed extreme depression and despair while, in response to other cards, her percepts were pervaded by anger, hatred, and uncontrolled aggressive needs. Throughout her performance on the Rorschach test, there was little evidence of intellectual control. She appeared either depressed and withdrawn or completely impulse-dominated, lashing out with strong hatred and fury.

These signs of psychopathology continued to be revealed on the Thematic Apperception Test (TAT). Carol's stories were highly constricted and overcontrolled, or they involved wild, uncontrolled anger and death. Her fantasies vacillated between those of the lonely, depressed introvert and those of the impulsive, aggressive attacker of other people. For example, in response to one TAT card, Carol told this story: "Here's an old lady, a spinster, sitting alone in her house and a poor man comes up, all bloody, crawling to her for help. She fixes him up, cleans him, and feeds him. Then she stabs him."

The clinical psychologist offered his impression that Carol was attempting to hide powerful, aggressive feelings that were pushing for expression. She seemed to feel that her mother had been overly controlling and aggressive toward her, yet she was unable to express hostility openly toward her mother. Moreover, she appeared to have an unusually close attachment to her father but, again, this was mixed with suppressed hostility, providing strong evidence of an unresolved Electra complex. In one TAT story, a young girl sacrificed her own life to help save her father who had been unjustly accused of murdering his wife. Another story was about an illegitimate female child whose father had been killed by her mother.

The examiner concluded that Carol hated herself not only for her own inadequacies but also for her femaleness and feelings of inherent evil. She tended to withdraw and retreat from others because she feared competing and feared what she might do to others if she openly expressed the hostility that she harbored. As a result, Carol had turned her anger and destructive impulses inward and, in many ways, was eating away at herself. The test results, together with the behavioral symptoms, pointed to a severe personality disorder involving withdrawal from other people and retreat into fantasy in the effort to control violent feelings and hatred toward herself and others.

The examiner stated that Carol's intellectual functioning and academic achievement were being greatly interfered with by both her visual-perceptual difficulties and her emotional disturbance. He felt that there was some form of minimal brain dysfunction that caused her to be overactive and unable to concentrate, with signs of poor coordination. These organic handicaps had led to a continued failure and frustration in school, and had compounded into a rather severe emotional disturbance.

On the basis of the psychologist's report and his own interview findings, the psychiatrist recommended that Carol be treated with amphetamines and also that she should begin treatment in psychotherapy with a female therapist. Thus, he prescribed Dexedrine and referred her case to a clinical psychologist to be seen twice a week for individual psychotherapy.

FOLLOW-UP PSYCHIATRIC EVALUATION

Approximately eight months after initiating treatment, the psychiatrist saw Carol once again. Here is the summary of his report based on that interview. "What a difference! Carol appeared in the latest mod fashion and seemed very confident and self-assured, displaying the attractiveness which was seen as potential in the initial interview several months ago. From her accounts, all goes well with the amphetamines (15 mg. of Dexedrine in tablet form), with no side effects. Therefore, this course of drug therapy will be continued for another six months."

PSYCHOTHERAPY

Following eight months of working with Carol, the therapist presented a report of progress. She described Carol as a small, skinny girl who looked more like 12 years of age than 14. However, she also mentioned that Carol possessed a classically beautiful face with expressive dark eyes and long dark hair. But as the therapist stated, "Unfortunately for Carol, at this stage of her life, this kind of beauty is more apparent to adults than to peers." In therapy, Carol revealed that she was dissatisfied with her own appearance and envied other girls who were better developed physically and had more of the prettiness that boys their age found attractive.

When Carol began the psychotherapy, she was leading quite a restricted life, staying home and trying to study, but gaining very little from the time she spent with open books and her inability to concentrate. Within a few months, certain positive changes had become apparent. She started to achieve much better in school and began having occasional dates. She seemed to approach success in school (getting good grades) and success in social life (getting dates) with the same investment of energy and emphasis on tactics and strategy.

At the end of the school year, following several months of combined drug therapy and psychotherapy, Carol's report card showed two Bs, two Cs and one D in comparison with her first quarter report card of one C, three Ds and two Fs. Thus, she had shown marked improvement within a relatively short time with this type of treatment. But, having started at an extremely low level, she ended up with a record that was still far from outstanding. Along with improved grades, she also enjoyed some dates with high-status boys in school and began to feel that her own status within the peer group had been improving quite noticeably.

The therapist's summary stated: "Carol is growing up at an accelerated pace after a slow start. She is trying to catch up with her age peers, both academically and socially and she is thinking, feeling, and reacting every step of the way. It is a pleasure to work with Carol, as she is so bright and responsive and so invested in growing."

BRIEF PSYCHIATRIC FOLLOW-UP

After Carol had been in treatment for about one year, she again visited the psychiatrist, who reported: "Carol looks and sounds great." They agreed to reduce her medication for a trial period, with Carol reporting the effects to the psychiatrist via telephone.

SECOND PSYCHOTHERAPY REPORT

Following approximately 18 months of psychotherapy, the psychologist reported that she had been seeing Carol regularly throughout this period and recently, they had decided to reduce the frequency of her sessions to once every other week. The aim of this change was to counter Carol's dependency on the therapist and to encourage her growing feeling of personal adequacy. At this time, Carol was doing well in school and had just received the best report obtained to date, with all Bs and Cs. She just missed an A in English and felt that the next year she would be able to obtain good grades in college preparatory subjects.

Carol had "forgotten" to take her medication during her spring vacation from school and immediately became miserable and irritable. She recognized her dependency on this medication to help her function at socially acceptable levels, and she wondered with the therapist when she would outgrow this condition. The psychologist offered the explanation that Carol was physically immature for her age and that perhaps it would take slightly longer for her to outgrow the physical condition that was believed to underlie the hyperkinetic impulse disorder. At the end of her report, the psychologist stated: "All in all, things are going well. Carol is maturing, becoming more empathetic with others and functioning better academically and socially. She is fairly dependent on me, but I am not particularly concerned about this at her present stage in development."

FINAL PSYCHIATRIC FOLLOW-UP

Following almost two years of treatment, the psychiatrist again had an interview with Carol and wrote, "This session was one of pure joy." He was extremely pleased with the progress she had made in all facets of her life. However, within recent weeks Carol had found it difficult to sleep and had been "all pepped up" during the day. According to him, this suggested that she was probably outgrowing the hyperkinetic aspect of her difficulties. Thus, they agreed that she would start not taking the Dexedrine for several days, reporting to him for a decision about the continuation of this medication.

LONGER-RANGE OUTCOME

Carol was taken off the medication completely and, for the next two years, she continued to see the psychotherapist only occasionally, whenever she felt the need for counsel, guidance, or support. She continued to do well in school, getting mostly As and Bs, and she found life much happier. Her parents also reported that the family life had become much more pleasant. Thus, the treatment of these personality and educational problems through a combination of drug therapy and psychotherapy must be judged as highly successful.

Interesting supplementary information was obtained from a letter Carol published in the "Letters to the Editor" section of her hometown newspaper. This newspaper had published several feature articles pertaining to the pros and cons of administering drugs to treat hyperactivity and learning disabilities in school children. Carol wrote:

"In regard to all the controversy on drugs for children, I feel I must take a stand. I'm 18 years old and a senior in high school. As a patient of a child psychiatrist for three years, I took three Dexedrine pills every morning for approximately one-and-a-half years. I was a hyperkinetic child.

"In junior high school I couldn't concentrate on my school work. As a result I received extremely poor grades. In fact, I was flunking. I did not have a friend, because I couldn't get along with them. I had no interests and could never stand up for my side of the argument with my brother or sister or classmates.

"After I was weaned from the drug, I never took any of those or other pills on my own. Contrary to the opinion of the opposed side, I am now a livelier, happier person and did not become a zombie. However, these drugs are not for everyone and should not be prescribed as such. For me, they worked. I also can't say they were miracle workers by themselves. I went to a psychologist for therapy and I still go to her occasionally for help with my problems. Thus, my grades have improved considerably every year, and I've been accepted by two college. I now have friends and, also, occasionally I can engage in a good argument!"

From Carol's self-evaluation of her problems and their outcome, and from the psychiatrist's and the psychologist's clinical impressions, it must be concluded that the course of treatment recommended for Carol was a wise one. She no longer took any form of drug therapy and was not dependent on her psychotherapist. She was able to manage her life without these forms of therapy, but she did so in a manner that would have been impossible if she had not, at the proper time in her psychosocial development, received the necessary medical and psychological help.

9. THE CASE OF ROBBY:
Hyperkinetic Impulse Disorder

An eight-year-old boy midway through the third grade, Robby was referred to the school psychologist because of "learning and behavior problems." When the psychologist spoke to his teacher, she pointed to Robby, a fair-haired, wiry, and attractive boy, who was fidgeting restlessly at his desk. "He can't sit still," she said, "and his writing is the messiest I have ever seen; he just won't try." All of the other children in the room were looking at the visitor with a mixture of interest and apprehension. Robby, after a brief glance, turned his attention elsewhere, looked out the window, then around the room, and then at a collection of keys that he took from his pocket. He seemed quite unaware of the visiting psychologist and the conversation going on at the front of the room. The psychologist, who had come to question the teacher at greater length concerning the referral, mentioned that he planned to give Robby a number of tests. The teacher immediately replied, "He'll be glad to go, he doesn't want to do anything here," in a loud voice easily audible to Robby. Robby did pay attention to this and looked at the psychologist with some curiosity.

Accompanying the psychologist to his office, Robby was ready and even eager to go. He knew where the office was and ran well ahead of his prospective examiner, around the corner, upstairs, and out of sight. During the testing situation, Robby was cooperative and verbalized constantly, frequently going off into irrelevant details and tangents. Often he seemed to forget what had been asked almost before the question was finished. He was first given the job of copying geometric figures, and he was very awkward with his pencil and very self-critical of his own performance. A typical comment, "That's terrible," was said in a rather unhappy way. He did, however, try to do his best, erasing and attempting to correct his drawings. At the same time, he seemed to expect disapproval and looked up cautiously at the examiner.

When beginning the verbal part of the intelligence test, Robby became increasingly restless and distractable, getting up from his chair, wandering around the office, and asking about the various objects he saw. He often talked about his interest in science, usually quite irrelevantly in terms of the questions put to him. Robby asked the psychologist many times about what he was writing: "Do you put down everything I say, do you put it all down?" Once when the examiner turned to some other materials, Robby picked up his pen and hid it, saying with some irritation when the psychologist asked for it back, "You don't have to write everything."

Robby's behavior during the testing situation alternated between attempts at perfection, when he would try over and over to improve his response to an item, and impulsive, frustrated replies in which he gave up almost without trying. The stopwatch seemed to upset him and, whenever it was used, he became slightly disorganized, seemingly more concerned about the stopwatch and the timing of his response than about the nature of the task itself. Tension mounted steadily, and Robby became increasingly frustrated, upset, and distractable, to the point where it was necessary to terminate the session.

When seen a second time, a few days later, Robby was much less active and distractable. This time he was happy to come along, particularly since he was having a rather difficult, tense time with his teacher. In the one-to-one situation he again made a good effort, seemed a little more confident in himself, and related pleasantly to the psychologist, although at times he did hurry his response too much. Because of this, he sometimes overlooked a number of details, particularly on the visual tasks that, otherwise, might have improved his scores a good deal. In spite of the difficulties in testing, he was able to obtain superior scores on the intelligence test and showed himself to be a boy of good potential who one might have expected to do extremely well in school. More regarding the results of the psychological evaluation will be presented later; however, at this point, to better appreciate the total picture, we will review Robby's family background and early history.

EARLY DEVELOPMENT

Robby was the oldest of two children, having a younger sister. His father was a lawyer, a busy professional who was passive with the children, leaving Robby's mother to discipline and raise them as best she could. With his passivity and lack of involvement, however, he was less angry and rejecting of Robby than was Robby's mother. He had been a law student at the time of Robby's birth. This had been a time of stress for the family, since the father had a great deal of work to do in his studies and was unable to devote more than a minimum of attention to his wife and child. He had continued this pattern, graduated from law school, and joined an important law firm in the city, which demanded most of his time and effort. Robby's mother was similarly well educated, having been a schoolteacher and having done a great deal of graduate work toward an advanced degree, with the goal of doing college teaching in history and political science.

Robby's mother was an insecure person. She had been adopted and always had a poor relationship with her adopted mother. She seemed to have a need to prove herself and to demonstrate her own adequacy to her own mother. In addition, she had been very anxious, nervous, and upset during her pregnancy with Robby, who was her first child. She expressed fears that she would have difficulty with his birth, and at the same time was very unhappy because she became pregnant so soon after her marriage. She told her husband that she was not yet ready and did not want to have a child. Nevertheless, after Robby was born, she became very overprotective and indulgent, as if to prove that she was a good mother. At the same time, she quickly became upset and angry at Robby's overactivity. She had high expectations of him, and he seemed to do everything to frustrate her wishes.

Even before Robby was born, he was a problem to his mother. He seemed to move and kick a great deal, and once she had exclaimed, "He was aggressive before he was born." The pregnancy was one of increasing emotional stress, which was not aided by his father's withdrawal from her because of the pressure of his graduate work. Robby's mother was finally hospitalized with mild toxemia shortly before Robby's birth, and she stayed in the hospital until the time of his delivery. He was a large baby, weighing 10 pounds, 1 ounce, and a difficult 18-hour labor was finally terminated with a Caesarian section When Robby was born he was a difficult, active and colicky child with many feeding problems and almost constant diarrhea. Shortly after his birth, his father finished law school, and the family moved into a small, three-room apartment, making them physically close in a very confined space. This made Robby's behavior even more difficult to accept. His father often worked late and left the mother alone with Robby and, when his father returned home for the night, he usually brought work with him, demanding quiet while he prepared material for the next day.

Inconveniently, Robby slept very little, cried during most of the night, and seemed immune to his mother's attempts at quieting him. When left alone, he often rocked back and forth in his crib or banged his head on the side. When sleep finally came, it was brief; Robby usually awakened before his parents, and his crying and rocking made it impossible for them to stay in bed. However, he developed very quickly and began to talk early in his second year. In spite of this, his speech even at the age of eight was still slightly infantile, and he had a noticeable articulation difficulty. Similarly, he walked very early, but was clumsy and often stumbled and bumped into things. He was always on the move, literally into everything, and he was very curious, constantly taking things apart to "see how they work." Often, he was found poking around in his parents' drawers or closets, and he carried this behavior outside of his home. Thus, at the age of four, he wandered into a neighbor's house and turned on the water in their bathtub, leaving the faucet on to flood the room. At eight he still could not tie his shoes, or even after repeated attempts could he learn to rid a bicycle. When he was placed in a day camp the summer before he entered the third grade, he could not compete in sports, could not catch or throw a ball and, for this reason, he was often excluded from the other boys' teams during group sports. He began to see himself as being weak and inadequate, cried frequently, and wanted to come home.

Robby had always been aggressive socially and tried to make friends, but he was able to hold very few of them. When he was only three, he hit another child with a metal toy truck, resulting in a number of stitches for the child. He was aggressive with other children, whether individually or in a group, and he refused to share his things or to play cooperatively with them. He seemed to see himself as a victim: "They don't play fair" was his standard statement after each of his attempts to enter a group ended in a battle. Robby always had to be the one to make the rules, and for this reason he was unable to last in a group for more than a brief period, either in the neighborhood or at school. Only when Robby could dominate, usually with a younger child in a one-to-one situation, did he have any success at all. He was extremely competitive and became upset and angry when he lost a game but, in spite of his rejection of other children, he could not take "no" for an answer when they in turn attempted to reject him. He was always teasing and provoking toward his younger sister, often driving her into the arms of her mother.

Robby's mother saw him as "aggressive and destructive," but she found his sister just the opposite. She had a much more pleasant pregnancy with the sister and perceived her daughter as an "angel." Robby's sister, born when he was about 20 months old, added to the already stressful situation in the family, although this was relieved somewhat when the parents were able to move to a larger house in a new neighborhood. Robby's reputation soon followed him. Along with his difficulties with other children, he was extremely impulsive. He often ran in front of cars or onto the roof and, as his mother said, "He does not know danger." He seemed to have no fear or awareness of possibly injury, although he had several accidents and, by the time he was eight, he had broken an arm, a leg, and at several times had stitches in his forehead.

Difficulties in the neighborhood increased to a climax when three other mothers called Robby's house, saying "We just had to find out what Robby's mother was like." Robby could not even give his mother the satisfaction of achieving adequately for his age level, let alone meet her high expectations. His room was always a mess, his things were scattered and dropped anywhere, and he seemed to have no interest or concern in self-care or in helping around the house. There were even difficulties about bowel training, and his mother perceived this as further evidence of Robby's aggressiveness.

Robby's relationships with his parents, particularly his mother, were variable. He did not like physical contact or affection, resisted it, and never expressed any himself. Yet, often he would not let his mother out of his sight and, as she said, "He drove me up the wall." She would become angry, rejecting him with her indiffer-ence. At these times, Robby would persist until he gained his mother's attention, and then, with similar indifference, would turn away from her. At times he made many demands on her and, al-though he denied the feelings that were usually associated with a mother, he was apparently very dependent on her. At the same time, as his mother said, "We get on each other's nerves." Robby seemed unable to communicate his feelings and showed little reac-tion to punishment or discipline. He never cried, even when spanked or slapped. He did, however, become frustrated about school and sometimes cried at his difficulties there. Often he was disobedient, but not so much in a malicious way as in a manner suggesting that he was simply unaware of what was expected of him.

Upset when faced with failure, Robby often spoke of his parents' as expecting more maturity and achievement than he could pos-sibly show. It was a vicious circle, particularly with his mother; Robby's overactivity made her angry and led her to reject him, which produced more tension and overactivity in Robby, and this led to further angry outbursts by his mother. Robby was often explosively irritable and aggressive. He had to have things immedi-ately, and he was unable to tolerate the slightest delay when he made a request. He sometimes was very depressed, but his moods were variable and changed for no apparent reason. He sometimes described nightmares of "elephants stepping on his head," and later had nightmares about school. Robby often depreciated himself. "I can't," was his usual reply, as part of this negative self-image, when-ever he was asked to achieve. He seemed to feel that he was bad, and he had fantasies of the police coming to take him away because of his behavior and his many troubles.

Robby began school at age four, when his mother brought him to nursery school three mornings a week. He had no trouble leav-ing her but, both here and in kindergarten, he was extremely active, showing all the social difficulties and the problems produced by his overactivity and curiosity that have been described above. He was the only child in kindergarten who was unable to learn to print his name, which was surprising to the teachers since he seemed to be an extremely bright child. In the first grade, he continued to have much difficulty in writing, and this was a problem that per-sisted for many years. He was a distractable child, unable to work on his own or in a group, and he had a particular difficulty with reading, often reversing words when writing or printing letters. He began to resist going to school, behavior that became intense in the second grade; Robby expressed a great deal of fear, to the point of panic, and cried when he could not do his work.

Robby's report card was very poor, and the teacher filled it with comments such as, "Won't adjust to class rules," or "He has no sense of responsibility," or "His desk and his work are always a mess." He received the lowest marks for adjustment and effort, but was nevertheless promoted to the third grade. His mother suspected that this was done because his second grade teacher simply could not stand him any longer.

In the third grade, Robby began the year by falling off a fence in the playground, and he broke his arm. His other difficulties intensified, and his first report card stated that "He often daydreams and seems detached," although more positively, "He does add a lot of information to the class." Nevertheless, the teacher said that he "can't sit still, never finishes his work, and talks about anything except schoolwork." She began to put on more pressure, particularly regarding his handwriting which remained illegible. By midyear, the teacher had become completely frustrated with Robby and had more or less given up. For this reason, she had called in the psychologist, hoping, as she phrased it, "You will find something wrong with him, so he can be put into a special class."

EVALUATION AND TREATMENT

Robby did surprisingly well on intelligence tests. He was given the Wechsler Intelligence Scale for Children (WISC) obtained a verbal IQ of 139, a performance IQ of 117, and a full-scale IQ of 131. Both the verbal and full-scale IQs fell within the very superior range of intelligence and the performance score reached the bright normal level. The psychologist thought that Robby was an extremely imaginative and creative boy of high potential and of high abstract ability.

On the WISC, Robby was at times perfectionistic, and sometimes he made wild, impulsive guesses, becoming frustrated when he was unable to answer a question correctly, and was quite variable in his behavior. He appeared, however, to be intellectually precocious and was preoccupied with areas that were far beyond the level of his class and teaching. There were many indications that he was bored with the school curriculum, which stressed rote learning and the repetitious practice of basic skills. There was much drill in his classroom; this, and his problem with handwriting, produced a great deal of conflict between himself and his teacher. The perceptual-motor difficulty was seen in his psychological testing when he attempted to copy geometric designs; on this task, his performance fell significantly below what would be expected developmentally for children of his age level. Often he had problems integrating the parts of the designs and, frequently, he rotated and turned them around, much as he did in writing and reading. As the same time, he had a good fund of information for a boy his age and showed extremely capable verbal judgment and reasoning, concept formation, and abstraction. His vocabulary was good, but he had some difficulty with arithmetic problems. On the digit span test, where he was required to repeat numbers in the same sequence as they were given to him by the psychologist, he failed badly.

On the nonverbal parts of the test, he often had great difficulty, especially on a task requiring him to learn and copy visually presented abstract symbols. He did poorly in other tests where visual details and slight changes in the visually presented drawings were important. On the other hand, he showed a good ability in integrating and copying both abstract and more familiar concrete types of designs and objects, when these involved the manipulation of blocks or puzzles. This was a bit surprising in view of his difficulty copying designs with pencil and paper, but on both WISC subtests, the Block Design and Object Assembly tests, he was able first to verbally conceptualize the nature and requirements of the task, and then, using this as a guideline, he proceeded to perform very well.

Overall, Robby's pattern was one of a boy of high potential who had much difficulty with visual details, particularly with tasks requiring sustained attention and concentration. His cognitive performance was surprising to the psychologist because of his reported learning difficulties in school. Obviously Robby had learned a great deal, although most of it was not the type of material that was demanded in the day-to-day classroom situation. However, he did seem to have a much better ability to read than had been recognized, although the psychologist could only concur with his teacher's evaluation of his pencil and paper skills.

Projective testing was also included in the battery, since Robby's behavior suggested emotional difficulties. His feelings about himself and his lack of achievement were summed up neatly in his TAT story about a boy who was "Studying something. He can't understand it, he tries, and he can't get it." He further stated that, "He is going to be in a contest and he will lose." Otherwise, much conflict centered around difficulties with his mother. His stories were replete with situations in which children were constantly being told "Not to do it," or a mother was angry because "Somebody broke something, and she is going to see who did it." On the other hand, his father was pictured as remote, unavailable, and neutral. In spite of these feelings, however, there was little other evidence of basic difficulties in his primary relationships; much of the problem seemed to be reactive to Robby's perception of himself and his inadequacies, and his frustrated efforts to please his parents. Indeed, the Rorschach indicated that he had more emotional strength than might be suspected, and that behind his scattered, sometimes disorganized behavior there was a good deal of emotional maturity. Robby's difficulty was his feeling of having lost before he had even started; he also had a feeling that he could not please, no matter how hard he tried.

To complete the diagnostic assessment, Robby was later studied by a psychiatrist, and similar observations were made. The psychiatrist reported, "While one might have expected a good deal of basic emotional conflict in this boy, such does not appear to be the case; rather he seems to present a picture of a child struggling with, and reacting to, a severe hyperkinetic impulse disorder." An EEG (brainwave) done at the same time showed that Robby was mildly abnormal, with "poor organization and with the type of pattern so often associated with hyperkinetic impulse disorder." Finally, in support of the diagnosis, a neurological evaluation revealed a number of the so-called "soft signs," in "a boy who constantly twitches, fumbles, falls, is messy, and cannot organize himself or maintain or focus his attention."

Recommendations based on the diagnostic picture included decisions to place Robby on medication; to attempt to provide him with remedial help for his visual-perceptual problem; and to suggest to the school that a change of curriculum involving more independent work, in order to take advantage of his high abstract ability, might be useful. Also, the parents were seen for several sessions by the psychiatrist, who tried to explain to them the nature of Robby's difficulties and to help them express their own feelings, frustrations, and sense of inadequacy in dealing with him. Individual psychotherapy for him was postponed to evaluate the other recommendations and, as it turned out, this additional form of treatment was never necessary.

Robby began on daily medication consisting of one five milligram tablet of Dexedrine. An immediate change in behavior was seen and reported by Robby's mother. Calling the psychiatrist about four days after Robby had begun taking this medication, her report was so glowing that the physician wrote in his records: "What a change, it's wonderful." It was reported that within a day of his beginning the medication, a neighborhood child had told his mother "Robby isn't kooky anymore." Even his sister remarked how controlled and reasonable he had become, and everyone noticed that he had taken up walking instead of running, and he was actually affectionate. At this point in school, he was given standardized achievement tests along with the rest of his class. For the first time he was able to finish these tests, and it was reported that, "He entered into school work more effectively." The dosage of his medication was adjusted, and a half tablet twice daily was found to be more effective since, on the earlier dosage, the effects had begun to wear off later in the day. The medication was eventually changed to another type, and the new type was even more effective.

From this point to the end of the school year, as was noted by the physician, "Behaviorally and academically, Robby continues to surge forward." He tried visual-perception training in the summer and, even though in the beginning there was a question concerning its helpfulness, progress was definitely seen by his teacher after he began school in the fall. He still worked better in a one-to-one situation than in a group, even with his visual-perceptual remediation. However, all went well at the beginning of the fall term in school until the end of the first month, when he began to resist going. He cried, again complained about nightmares, and gave indications of having developed phobic-like symptoms about school. He began to avoid his peer group as well. Robby's mother insisted that he keep going to school, but at the same time made efforts to discover the reasons for the latest difficulty.

It turned out that Robby's physical education instructor had ridiculed him because of his awkwardness, and several children had taken this up, teasing him in other situations as well, including after school. In the meantime, the physician observed that Robby's mother, after his great initial improvement, again began to pressure him toward greater and greater achievement, demanding perfectionism in homework and telling him that he might be going to a more demanding private school. Robby then began to express fear that he could not handle any schoolwork at all, and it was only with difficulty that he was reassured that he actually was doing quite well. This seemed to resurrect his negative self-image, with the effect so often seen in children of this type. That is, negative attitudes toward the self and feelings of inadequacy and inferiority linger to prevent achievement after the cause for these feelings and the original difficulties no longer exists. After a discussion with Robby's physician, his mother agreed to relax her pressures. Communication with his physical education instructor proved similarly effective, so that gradually Robby began regaining his confidence and showing progress.

In school at this time, Robby's concentration and attention had improved greatly, and the visual-perceptual training was followed by considerable improvement in reading. However, his writing remained very poor. This problem remained with him for years and continued to be a source of difficulty with each succeeding teacher. In addition, Robby was still bored with the standard curriculum but, in this area, efforts to work with the teachers were more successful. They began to give him independent projects after he had completed his weekly assignments. This led to Robby's completing one week's work in a day or so, followed by much enthusiasm and involvement with his independent reports and reading.

Things continued this well until later in the spring when Robby's father, "for an experiment," asked to have Robby's medication discontinued. This was done, and almost immediately Robby became disruptive, his behavior fluctuating, in the words of his teacher, "from wild to lethargic; he is incomplete." These qualities were very noticeable to his family, and, when his medication was reinstated, Robby immediately began to recover his previous gains. By the end of the fourth grade, on achievement tests, Robby's performance fell between the sixth and seventh grade levels in reading and arithmetic. Spelling and handwriting were still far behind at a low third grade level. However, in science and social studies, he was doing much better and placed toward the midpoint of the seventh grade in achievement. Thus, Robby was now using his superior intellect to good advantage, although he seemed to be able to do so only with the help of a daily dosage of amphetamine, and with a more appropriate curriculum.

5

NEUROTIC DISORDERS

People with neurotic disorders have at least one characteristic in common with those who suffer from psychosomatic disorders—they tend to take their troubles out on themselves. That is, rather than acting out in antisocial ways, they struggle painfully with their inner turmoil. These psychoneurotic disorders (known as neuroses) often represent exaggerations of "normal" responses to the stresses and strains of social living. At the root of all neuroses there is emotional conflict and anxiety. White has referred to the "nuclear neurotic process," which consists of frustration and conflict that produce anxiety and lead to the formation of neurotic defenses which are used to keep the anxiety in check. Although the defenses may prove effective in controlling anxiety for a time, they also prevent new learning and consequently become maladaptive.

The essential role of anxiety in the etiology of neurotic maladjustment was also emphasized by Freud, who called it "the central problem of neurosis." Based on his psychoanalytic treatment of adult patients, Freud was convinced that all neuroses originate in unresolved childhood conflicts. The sources of stress can be either intense, traumatic experiences with sudden onset or more chronic and threatening childhood interpersonal relations. As a result of acute or chronic stress, the child develops a neurotic protective organization, which requires considerable psychic energy to maintain, and thus interferes with healthy psychosocial development.

According to White, neuroses involve "overdriven strivings" which are exaggerations of certain ways of behaving that are universal in human behavior. It is the intensity and rigidity of the behavioral tendency that makes it neurotic rather than a normal striving. Horney proposed classifying overdriven strivings into three categories: (1) moving toward people, (2) moving against

people, and (3) moving away from people. These neurotic trends
are characterized, respectively, by an overly compliant dependency
on others, hostile striving to surpass and defeat others, and by
detaching oneself from meaningful human relationships. The normal person uses these orientations in a flexible manner, behaving
appropriately to the given social situation. But the neurotic individual overworks one of these three orientations at the expense of
the other two. The fact that the strivings are neurotic in any given
case is evidenced by:

1. Indiscriminateness (for example, the child constantly seeks
   approval from everyone).
2. Insatiability (the child feels rejected no matter how much
   affection he receives).
3. Overreaction (the child becomes unduly anxious and upset
   when the particular striving gets frustrated).

The chronic neuroses of adults are believed to result from these
neurotic trends established in childhood.

The above formulations derive primarily from a psychodynamic
view of human development, but learning theory approaches also
regard conflict, anxiety, and defense as the core of neurotic behavior. According to the behavioristic position, during the course
of seeking gratification for basic needs, the child learns to associate certain stimuli and responses with pleasure or with punishment and discomfort. He acquires (learns) behaviors that avoid
anxiety-provoking situations and continues to show these behaviors
even when they are no longer necessary. For example, having tried
but failed and having been ridiculed for it, the child now avoids
competition and refuses to strive for future goals. Or, having
sought the father's affection but obtaining either indifference or
overt rejection, the child avoids all adult males in the future, and
develops a self-concept of worthlessness. Actually, there are many
similarities among the behavioristic and the psychodynamic formulations of personality development, with both approaches perceiving the socialization process as a continuing series of stressful
encounters between parent and child. Freud's stages of psychosexual development (which require parental training of the child's
eating behavior, toileting, sex-role adaptation, and handling of
aggression) provide the foci for the fundamental social learning
that will produce an emotionally healthy or a neurotic child.

The case of Gail, presented in this section, shows classic Freudian psychodynamics in bold relief. She epitomizes the development of childhood psychopathology according to Freud. Her case history provides striking examples of several basic psychoanalytic concepts—like "castration anxiety" and "penis envy"—that non-Freudians find very difficult to accept. Family dynamics also play an important role in this case, with her mother and father struggling with their own problems and an unresolved Electra complex existing between Gail and her father. She seemed preoccupied with sex, yet extremely anxious about sexualized relationships, and she was afraid that she would die because of her evil thoughts. Although Gail was treated with psychoanalytically oriented therapy for several years, she did not resolve her unconscious conflicts, and she continued to hover between a state of severe neurotic maladjustment and one of psychotic reaction. Gail's terrifying thoughts and impulsive behaviors were extremely troublesome to her and her caretakers, and her neurotic protective organization at times seemed to be losing the struggle against her disabling anxiety. It might well be expected that such a classic case of childhood neurosis would prove very difficult to cure.

The case of Laura and Donna focuses on the symptom of elective mutism in identical twin girls. Elective mutism is a condition in which the ability to speak is present, but the individual does not or cannot talk to certain persons. This muteness is complete in these relationships, but selective to them, and the individual can communicate normally with other people. Significant aspects of the symptom include the fact that the difficulty lies in the motivation to speak, not in a basic inability to talk. The muteness may express a fear of unknown people, and usually develops around the age of three, as part of the oppositional behavior characteristic of this stage of development or around age six, when school begins. At age six, it is often a reaction to the anxiety involved in separating from the mother.

Elective mutism appears to be a neurotic symptom that is attributable to inner anxiety and conflict, and it is frequently the only symptom present. Often there is a too close attachment to the mother, depressive tendencies in the patient, much concern with oral matters, and somewhat emotionally immature mothers and fathers who are passive. Also, it is frequently observed that the parents do not have effective communication with each other. Aggressive and destructive fantasies of an oral type are frequently found in such children; the symptom is interpreted as being a form of control over the hostility.

This symptom has only rarely been reported in twins, although the psychology of twins seems to make it a natural situation for the appearance of elective mutism. It has been reported that twinship may be conducive to intense rivalry and jealousy. There is a good deal of competition between twins for their parents' attention and affection, which may lead to reciprocal hostility and may be activated as an intense aggressive reaction when the twins are older. Because of the close resemblance between identical twins, there may also be a confusion in self-identity. This has often been viewed as a major cause of delay in personality and ego development. The establishment of a twinship system or a sub-society leads to much mutual support between the twins and also to their isolation as a unit. This social isolation may frequently be paralleled by a delay in language, complicated by the fact that twins sometimes develop a secret language of their own, with the emphasis on communication being between themselves and not with others.

The closeness of the twinship can easily conflict with the hostility and rivalry that is also present. It may be necessary to suppress the hostility, not only between each other, but in general, in order to maintain the bond between them. In the present case, it is possible that anxiety about the hostile wishes between the twins was controlled by the symptom of elective mutism. The two girls harbored mutual resentment about being twins, as will be seen. However, in spite of this resentment, the symptom seemed to represent a kind of magical symbolic tie between them, which also maintained the benefits of the twinship in terms of mutual support and which, in any case, neither twin was able to break independently. Although most identical twins differentiate themselves eventually, at least by the time of adolescence, in this case the process was made considerably more difficult by their symptom of elective mutism.

In Roy's case, we see a youngster who started life from an extremely disadvantaged position. Neglected and rejected, left to live or die on a cellar floor with no family and no name, this black infant survived the ordeal, but he suffered from feelings of worthlessness and lack of identity throughout his childhood. In the several foster homes in which he lived, he felt unwanted and developed a highly negative self-concept. By the time he was institutionalized for residential psychiatric treatment, he was a very anxious youngster who showed signs of psychopathology associated with all stages of psychosexual development. That is, emotional disturbance indicated unresolved conflicts stemming from traumatic experiences at the oral, anal, and phallic stages of personality formation.

In interactions with Roy's white female psychotherapist, he revealed a strong Oedipal attraction toward this mother figure. He alternated between assuming the role of a helpless infant in need of maternal nurturance and a male lover with sexual desires and curiosities to be satisfied by the mother figure. In much of this, Roy showed a preoccupation with his blackness, expressing, consciously and unconsciously, the desire to be white. In this regard, however, it should be noted that this case study occurred several years ago, prior to the more recent emphasis on "black is beautiful." It is doubtful that a black child today would be so distressed because of his dark skin color. In view of the social and cultural changes that have been occurring, a child like Roy might now be much prouder to be black.

These three case studies should reveal the diversity of early experiences that can lead to childhood neuroses and the varied forms in which they can be expressed. Moreover, the process and effectiveness of child psychotherapy are highlighted in these case studies of neurotic children.

RECOMMENDED READING

Dollard, J., & Miller, N. E. *Personality and psychotherapy.* New York: McGraw-Hill, 1950.

Freud, A. *Normality and pathology in childhood.* New York: International Universities Press, 1965.

Freud, S. *The problem of anxiety.* New York: Norton, 1936.

Horney, K. *Our inner conflicts: A constructive theory of neurosis.* New York: Norton, 1945.

White, R. W. *The abnormal personality* (3rd edition). New York: Ronald Press, 1964.

10. THE CASE OF GAIL:
Castration Anxiety and Fear of Death

Gail was an attractive, light-skinned black child just turning ten years of age at the time of her admission to the residential treatment center. The chief complaints mentioned at that time were:

1. Hyperactive and destructive since one year of age.
2. Poor sibling and peer relationships throughout her childhood.
3. Problem behavior in school.
4. Preoccupation with and fear of death.
5. Preoccupation with marriage, sex, and reproduction since age seven.

This information was provided by Gail's parents who were described as "a good looking, well-educated Negro couple who presented a smooth, reserved, and sophisticated appearance."

Family History

Gail's father was born in the South, the third of four male children. He described his father as a carpenter who eventually worked his way through college, became a minister, and then died of a heart attack at a relatively early age. Her father reported that his parents were separated when he was three years old, and he continued to live with his mother although he was actually raised by his grandmother. He never knew his own father, and his only memories of him are based on what his mother told him—essentially that he was a cruel and sadistic man. However, Gail's father stated that his early life with his mother and grandmother was a very happy one, and he described his mother as being very talented and having a great deal of warmth and understanding. In describing his early life, her father stressed that he had not become

128

a delinquent, despite the fact many black children with his type of background tend to engage in delinquent activities.

Following graduation from high school, Gail's father joined the U. S. Army and rose to the rank of First Sergeant in the Infantry. He took several academic courses while in the service and also attended a university while stationed in Europe. After his discharge from the service, he went to work for an electronics firm and became a production planner, a position he has held for the past several years. During these past years, he also had been attending the extension division of a large Eastern university and needed only a few more credits to receive his bachelor's degree.

At the time of Gail's admission to the residential treatment center, her father stated that his ambition was to become a race relations worker. He was very active in community life—a member of the Rotary Club and a Sunday school teacher in a predominantly white church. He described his marriage as an extremely happy one, and he felt that their sexual relationship was very adequate, referring to his wife as "almost ideal." He said that her most favorable characteristics were that she was kind, gentle, and understanding.

Gail's mother was also born in the South, as an only child. When she was eight years old her mother died and her father soon remarried. She did not stay with her father but went to live with an aunt in New York, where she stayed for several years. Throughout her childhood, she moved frequently between various aunts in the North and South, and she described this period of her life as a very unhappy time, feeling as though she was always on the "fringe." When she was 17 years old her father renewed contact and offered to help her through college. She accepted this offer and their relationship has been good since that time. She placed special emphasis on her relationship with her stepmother, describing it as being "wonderful."

Following graduation from high school, Gail's mother attended a predominantly black college in the South for two years and transferred to a major Eastern university where she received a bachelor's degree, with a major in English and Psychology. She worked for a few years as a social investigator for the Department of Public Welfare and then received her master's degree in library science. She was employed as a librarian in a large public library until she became pregnant with her first child.

Gail's mother described her marriage as a good one but said that there had been some crucial areas of disagreement, especially regarding her employment after marriage. Her husband felt very strongly that her primary role should be that of a mother caring for her home and children, but she preferred continuing her work. She reported that she was very depressed after her first pregnancy and doubted that she really wanted to be a mother. She also confessed that with each subsequent pregnancy she felt "very confused and uneasy." She thought that perhaps her husband's difficulty in accepting her role as a professional worker, rather than a mother at home, stemmed from his negative reaction to his own mother working and not spending sufficient time with him during his childhood. However, in describing her husband she mentioned many positive features and stressed their "togetherness." Her major criticism was that he too eagerly committed himself to community projects and devoted a great deal of time to these socially oriented ventures.

When this couple had been married about 18 months, their first child, a girl, was born. She was described by Gail's parents as being an ideal youngster. In fact, the father referred to her as "a dream child." She was a very bright student who enjoyed school tremendously. The parents described her as being compassionate and completely opposite from Gail. They also said that the firstborn child and Gail had a good relationship, although the older child was very embarrassed by Gail's behavior when they attended the same school.

Gail was the second of three children, born one year after her sister. Her parents were initially very upset over this pregnancy because it had not been planned. Gail was a premature child, born after only eight months of gestation. However, her mother had no difficulty throughout this pregnancy and the delivery was not difficult. Labor lasted six hours, and Gail weighed four pounds, four ounces at birth. She was placed immediately in incubation where she remained for two weeks prior to being discharged from the hospital.

One year after Gail's birth, the third child, a boy, was born. Her parents said he was an average student, but one who placed high expectations on himself. Her father described the boy as impatient, stubborn, determined, and aggressive, but nevertheless manageable. The school personnel felt that the boy had good potential but was not working up to it. According to Gail's parents, her relationship with her younger brother was very poor, with a great deal of antagonism between them, and much overt fighting.

Developmental Background

When Gail was about six weeks old, she developed a case of bronchitis, which necessitated a brief hospital treatment. After returning home, her parents said she was fretful, irritable, hyperactive, and difficult to manage. During her first year of life, she experienced considerable difficulty sleeping and frequently had to be held during the night. She was receptive to holding and cuddling, and this seemed to be the only way that she could be managed satisfactorily. At about four months of age, she was hospitalized for a two-week period for an operation on an umbilical hernia. Shortly after this, she had to be hospitalized once again for treatment of a severe asthmatic bronchitis.

Gail was described as being accident prone as well as hyperactive from an early age. She frequently climbed out of her crib and fell on the floor. Her parents eventually placed a gate over the crib to prevent her from doing this, but this action was ineffective. Thus, they were forced to tie her up in the crib to prevent her from climbing out of it. When Gail was 15 months old, she walked onto a porch and fell about 12 feet to the ground. She was taken to the accident room at a local hospital but, reportedly, there were no serious injuries.

Toilet training began at 15 months and was accomplished by about 18 months. However, Gail remained nocturnally enuretic until age seven. The exact details surrounding toilet training could not be recalled by her parents. But they stated that her father assumed responsibility for the toilet training as well as for handling other developmental tasks accomplished by Gail. She had been a finger sucker during her first year of life. Through parental pressure she gradually eliminated this behavior, although she did become a nail biter.

When Gail was four years old, her brother ran into her with a bicycle and she sustained a serious wound on her leg that required hospital treatment. Following this, she became even more unmanageable, to the point where her parents had to use binders to constrain her. In describing her behavior at this time, her parents reported that her peer and sibling relationships had been extremely poor ever since they could remember. She was continually competitive, jealous, and domineering. Whenever these maneuvers did not succeed, she would resort to the physical abuse of other children.

Since Gail was two, she experienced bad dreams and nightmares very frequently. Usually, these dreams involved witches and people dying and being killed. When she had awakened from these dreams, she insisted on going into her parents' bed. At the time of her admission to the residential treatment center, many years later, Gail's parents reported that she had been permitted to get into their bed until she was almost seven years old.

When Gail was five, she entered kindergarten and seemed to enjoy the recreational aspects of school, but she did not like doing academic work and refused to follow her teacher's instructions. She became so negativistic and difficult to manage that the kindergarten teacher recommended that her parents seek professional help for her emotional and behavior problems. Consequently, when Gail was five and one-half years of age, she was accepted for individual psychotherapy at the outpatient clinic of a large hospital in a nearby city. She continued this individual psychotherapy, with a female psychiatrist, on a once a week basis for three years.

When Gail was six years old, she was admitted to the first grade in a local public school. Although she successfully completed first grade, the teacher described her as rebellious, nonconforming, hyperactive, destructive, unable to follow directions, and abusive toward her peers. Gail also continued to experience great difficulty sleeping and she developed many compulsive rituals around bedtime. She insisted that certain objects had to be touched in a certain order or arranged very carefully and that she be permitted to follow a specific ritual in looking under the bed for threatening objects and people before retiring. This was carried over into other areas, and she became very compulsive about her dress, tying her shoes a certain way, arranging her toys in prescribed patterns, and so forth. Even in her destructive play, she followed compulsive rituals. For example, she went through systematic, well-organized, and routine procedures in abusing and destroying dolls and other play objects.

Gail completed the second and third grades in public school, but she continued having a great deal of difficulty, making loud noises, refusing to conform, failing to concentrate, and being overly competitive and aggressive with other children. Her parents felt that her academic achievement had been minimal during these grades and that the teachers promoted her only because they knew that she was being seen by a psychiatrist for psychotherapy. Throughout these early school years, Gail continued to have trouble at home where she was very defiant and rebellious. At one point, her parents tried punitive methods in attempting to cope with her but, when this failed, they tried to reason with her and to obtain her cooperation through showering her with love.

Because Gail got along so poorly with the other children, she resorted to solitary play, but even here she was exceptionally aggressive and destructive. She frequently disrobed and dismembered her dolls, collecting the pieces and wrapping them in the blanket that she insisted on taking to bed with her at night. From about age seven, Gail became extremely fearful of death. This type of preoccupation became evident after Gail attended a funeral of a close family friend. When she viewed his body at the wake, she expressed a desire to kiss his hand but was advised against this by her mother. Both of Gail's parents reported that after this experience she frequently asked, "Why do you have to die if God is good?" Her father tried to explain that death was another phase of life and that she would sometime have to accept the challenge. Her mother said that she was unable to provide Gail with a comforting answer and was completely baffled by Gail's preoccupation with death.

During this period, Gail attended Sunday School, where her father was her teacher, and very frequently she drew pictures of a child crying for God's help. At this time, when approximately seven years old, she became unusually preoccupied with marriage, sex and, reproduction. She questioned her parents very openly as to whether they had sexual intercourse, and she became very upset and unhappy when they would not answer her questions. Gail approached a neighbor and asked him to show her his penis. Also, on several occasions, she was reported to have approached women in various inappropriate situations and asked them, "Are you going to lay out another baby?" Her mother attempted to answer some of Gail's questions concerning sex and childbirth but said that she always found it very difficult to find the right answers.

When Gail was nine, she was assigned to the fourth grade even though her teachers reported that in several academic areas she was working below this grade level. Her school behavior continued to be erratic and troublesome, as a result of her extreme restlessness and impulsivity. She usually refused to follow directions and posed a constant management problem.

Throughout this three year period, as mentioned earlier, Gail was being seen in psychotherapy at the out-patient psychiatric clinic of a local hospital. Soon after initiating psychiatric treatment Gail's psychological tests revealed that she had an obsessive-compulsive character structure with primary conflicts centering around her wish to be a boy. Consequently, she experienced great difficulty in controlling the fears and aggressive impulses that resulted from her self-concept of being damaged and defective. During the first year of psychiatric treatment, the prominent themes were her intense fear of being dirty and a related anxiety that she would not be liked or accepted.

Psychological testing which was completed after Gail had been in treatment for two years, revealed that she had regressed and was functioning much more poorly on intelligence tests and that she showed many more psychoticlike symptoms than she had two years previously. Her IQ had decreased from 100 to 88. However, it was felt that Gail was actually much brighter than average, but her severe emotional disturbances were greatly detracting from her ability to function anywhere near her intellectual potential. At the time of this second testing, the examining psychologist stated that Gail was losing her ability to test the reality of her fantasies, which were openly sexual. On the basis of her behavior and responses revealed on the personality tests, it appeared that Gail had undergone repeated sexual trauma and had been overwhelmed by sexual stimulation at a very early age.

During the third year of psychiatric treatment, Gail became even more disorganized and, at time, her fantasies and verbal expression became practically unintelligible. She was then nine years old, doing very poorly in school, unable to get along with her peers, and deteriorating in her psychotherapeutic relationship. At this point, the only possible remedy for this difficult situation would be to remove Gail from the home and public school setting and place her in a residential treatment center. Her parents were not eager to comply with this, but they finally agreed, and shortly before her tenth birthday, Gail was institutionalized at a children's psychiatric hospital.

PSYCHIATRIST'S EVALUATION

After Gail's admission to the treatment center, she was interviewed by a female staff psychiatrist who conducted a "mental status" examination. Because of her restlessness and impulsivity, it was necessary to see Gail on three different occasions to complete this examination. The psychiatrist thought she was very demanding, provocative, manipulative, and at times seductive. Her behavior and moods were almost totally unpredictable, and she was preoccupied with sex, boys, and death. Aggressive and destructive wishes against others were expressed very often. Masochistic behavior, such as hitting herself and banging her head on the floor, was constantly acted out. Her attention span was extremely short, and she was unable to carry on a reality oriented conversation. Although most children would be able to spend one hour in the psychiatrist's office, Gail's interviews could last no longer than 25 minutes. Toward the end of the sessions, she became increasingly impulsive, would run out of the room, hide behind the door, and make very loud noises. She seemed to be continually trying to provoke rejection, to the point of threatening to physically attack her interviewer so that she could apologize, saying that she was a bad girl and that she was sorry for what she had done.

The psychiatrist presented the highlights of her findings from the three sessions. During the initial session, Gail at first seemed to be in a pleasant mood and talked about various people that she liked at the treatment center. She talked about a boy she had met and said that she loved him. When the psychiatrist asked her why, Gail answered, "He is nice to me, he hit me right on my scar but I liked it." Then, she showed the psychiatrist a laceration on her arm, which she had received from falling off a slide. Her continual picking at the laceration and other scrapes on her arm made them very raw. When the psychiatrist asked her why she picked at the sores, Gail said she liked to because it made them look nice. Then, with no provocation or apparent reason, Gail suddenly stood up and started shouting, "I hate myself, I'm dumb, I'm stupid because I did those things, I don't want to die, I don't want to go into the ground. Can you help me so I won't die? But you wouldn't because you don't like me. I don't like you. I hate everyone in the world, I'll go kill myself!"

At the start of the second session, as soon as Gail walked into the office, she grabbed a toy gun, pointed it first at herself and then at the psychiatrist, saying, "We are bad and we both should die." The psychiatrist tried to reassure her by saying that she didn't think they had done anything bad and that all people sometimes had bad thoughts, but this did not mean that they had to die because of it. However, Gail did not care to listen to this, and she screamed, "I'm bad, I know it, my father called me a devil and I didn't like that!"

The psychiatrist finally was able to calm Gail a little and asked her to sit in a chair. Then Gail started to talk about another black girl patient whom she disliked very much, saying, "She doesn't have a mother or father, I'm glad because I don't like her. She is dark, I want her to die and go right down under the ground. I'll kill her with a knife, I'm going to stick it right into her stomach." At that point, Gail got out of the chair and lay on the floor. She said, "Im doing something bad every day and every night." She then pulled her pants down and pointed to her stomach saying she was itchy there. Finally, the psychiatrist got Gail up to her feet after she had been kicking the desk violently, and Gail continued with her rampage saying, "I don't like my skin, I'm ugly, I'm itching all over because I am bad." She then rushed over to the shelf that contained toys and found a tube of glue, which she said she wanted to eat. When the psychiatrist told her that she could not eat the glue, Gail turned around and said that the psychiatrist did not like her and that she never got her own way, and then she left the room.

At the start of the third session, it seemed as though Gail had been looking forward to her interview and, at first, she was pleasant and calm. She then asked for a particular toy, and before the psychiatrist could answer, Gail said, "You won't give it to me because you don't like me. If you want me to like you, you'd better give me that." The psychiatrist explained that she could not give away toys from the playroom and then asked Gail about school. She replied, "I'm in the fourth grade but I have no manners." Gail put her feet up on the desk and said in a very loud voice, "See, I'm bad, God hates me, I'm going to die." Instead of calming down, Gail acted even more wild and attempted to stand on her head on a chair, saying "I'm going to crack my leg because I'm bad, I'll kill myself." At this point, the psychiatrist stated, "I don't hate you, you're the one who wants everyone to hate you. Why?" Gail only replied, "I'm sorry."

During the third psychiatric interview, Gail voluntarily played with the hand puppets. She used the female and male puppets, putting one on each hand while she played the role of a minister. Then, she created a wedding scene beginning with the wedding march. She asked the male puppet, "Will you accept this woman for your wife?" and then asked the female puppet the same thing. After they said, "I do," Gail shouted at the top of her voice, "I pronounce you man and wife." She made the puppets kiss each other and seemingly engage in sexual activity by rubbing them against each other. After she separated them, however, she had them fighting and biting each other while she screamed very excitedly. At this point, she seemed to be unaware of anything else in her surroundings and, after continuing this excited sexualized and aggressive interaction for about five minutes, she stopped, saying "I'm sorry" and started to walk out of the playroom. The psychiatrist followed her closely and, as they walked by the other staff doctors' offices, Gail started to pull down her pants, and she pulled up her blouse, wiggling her body in a very seductive manner for all to see.

As they returned to the children's quarters, and because the psychiatrist was about to leave Gail, she told Gail that she soon would have a regular "appointment lady" with whom she would have weekly interviews. Gail turned and said, "You don't like me, you don't want to see me any more because I'm colored." Then she ran off, leaving the psychiatrist standing alone.

On the basis of several sessions with Gail, the psychiatrist described her as being severely neurotic and, at times, functioning very close to the borderline psychotic level of adjustment. Gail was extremely troubled by sexual and aggressive impulses and showed considerable confusion in this regard. She seemed to be unable to control her thoughts and actions and to be constantly under tension between impulses from the id and harsh controls from the superego. The psychiatrist recommended that this very difficult and challenging case be seen by a female psychotherapist.

PSYCHOLOGIST'S REPORT

After Gail had been in the treatment center for approximately four months, she was given a comprehensive examination by a male clinical psychologist. He described her as a pretty, round-faced Negro girl, with a ready smile and sparkling eyes, who was nearing the age of puberty. She was very happy to spend time with the examiner, showed much concern as to when the testing sessions would be held, and asked that she be seen regularly on a daily basis. It took three sessions to complete the psychological testing.

Gail made vivid declarations of love to the examiner, highlighted by flattery of his physical appearance. However, when she felt that her advances were rejected or when she found that the tasks were frustrating, she mixed extremely hostile criticism with the flattery. Once after asking and receiving permission to go to the bathroom, Gail tried to seduce the examiner to go with her. He reported that there were indications that Gail was masturbating in the bathroom. Upon return to the testing room, she did not concentrate on the tasks and admitted that she was "playing with her dicky." Toward the end of the session, she gave a very sexy exhibition of a dance while exposing her abdominal scars. During the second session, she put her chair in a precarious position and wanted to be saved from falling backward. Soon after this, she noticed a fly, screamed, and hid under the table begging the examiner to destroy the fly saying, "The fly will kill me, it will eat me up, I'm scared to die."

Gail's unrealistic fear of failure and her perception that the examiner would reject her if she failed led to a great hesitancy to work on the assigned tasks. She was much more preoccupied in seeking physical contact with the examiner, and she frequently reacted with intense rage when he would not give her the direct help that she sought on the tasks. Nevertheless, with the examiner continually expressing confidence in her ability, Gail completed the tasks that were presented to her, although she took an unusually long time to do so.

Gail received a full-scale IQ of 90 on the WISC, but her functioning was very irregular and showed the effects of severe emotional disturbance. At times, she responded quickly and correctly, but, often, she seemed confused and asked frequently that questions be repeated. On several subtests, she made poor responses to easy items while making very good responses to more difficult items. The psychologist felt that her actual intellectual potential was better reflected in her drawing of a man, which received an IQ score of 112 when scored in terms of norms provided for this purpose. On the projective tests, Gail's responses revealed very inadequate defenses that did not sufficiently protect her from intense inner conflicts. It was evident that she had a recurrent fear of being destroyed in the face of what she felt was absolute helplessness. In many ways, her responses to these tests showed a desire to be treated as a baby, continually protected and safe from harm. She projected her oral destructive impulses onto others and perceived the environment as an extremely hostile place. Because of her feeling of affectional deprivation, there was great aggressive turmoil reaching the point of a rage reaction. She seemed to view her parents as being angry and constantly fighting, and the examiner wondered if her fear of being destroyed might, to some extent, be traced back to an earlier fear of being hurt in interactions with her parents.

Gail was very uncertain about her body integrity and her sex. When asked to draw a person, she drew a picture of the examiner, showing great concern about the relationship of his body parts, which she carefully labeled. At the top of the drawing, she wrote, "Handsome Dr. B——" and, after carefully adding a penis to the figure drawing, she labeled it "Dr. B's dick." The examiner felt that this sexual preoccupation resulted partly from a basic confusion about her sexual identity. She wondered if she was once a boy who had since lost his genitals. Her indiscriminate wish for sexual intimacy also involved an attempt to be saved from destruction. She believed that her thoughts and behavior were bad and, consequently, that she would be further rejected by her parents and soon be "punished by God and the devil and go to hell." Thus, Gail's evaluation of her self-worth was extremely low; she felt possessed by the devil and feared ultimate annihilation.

In summarizing, the psychologist stated that Gail perceived sexual activity as both her salvation and damnation. That is, this type of activity was a possible source of nurturance and a way to have somebody save her from being destroyed, yet she felt that thinking about sexual activity was bad and that she would ultimately be destroyed. Her early history is filled with experiences that may have been traumatic: frequent separations from her parents during her hospitalization in infancy, sleeping with her parents for several years during early childhood, and possibly seductive toilet training by her father. All of these experiences, plus others which we may not be aware of, could have contributed heavily to the develop-

ment of her interrelated conflicts. Also, it appeared that her mother
may have been very cold and rejecting toward her while her father
acted in a feminine, seductive manner, thus further confusing her
sex-role identity and the development of age-appropriate behavior.
The examiner felt that the intensity and continuity of these early
experiences had greatly retarded the development of her adaptive
behavior; thus, her general functioning was now of a borderline
quality. He pointed out, however, that there were some positive
prognostic signs. Gail's higher mental processes, including her perceptions of reality, were relatively intact, and she showed a strong
need and desire for people to help her. However, the psychologist
concluded that, "If a great deal of therapeutic work by all those
involved is not carried out, Gail faces the danger of a full blown
psychosis especially in light of approaching puberty.'"

PSYCHIATRIC CASEWORK WITH PARENTS

While Gail was being treated in the out-patient clinic for the
three years prior to institutionalization, her father was being seen
by psychiatrists and social workers in that setting. He was diagnosed as a severe obsessive-compulsive character disorder, with
paranoid tendencies. The focus in the work with him was his
handling of Gail. The report that was received from the guidance
clinic stated: "We have been unable to ascertain the extent of his
intimacy with Gail and it may well be that it constitutes only
excessive embracing and coddling. He talks more, however, about
the problems of the American Negro and it has been hard to assess
just how crucial this issue has been in the parents' ability to trust
their workers and to cooperate in treatment."

Gail's mother was also seen in treatment during those three
years by several therapists in that setting. She was described as
"a strong self-sufficient woman who relies heavily on intellectualization and reaction formation to handle conflicts." In therapy she
talked in generalities, maintaining that she knew what to do, and
she had difficulty accepting advice. She identified Gail with her
husband and felt that both of them were emotional and impulsive.
She revealed serious underlying conflicts in the marriage, although
she avoided facing these troubles and placed considerable emphasis on keeping up appearances and outer control.

Throughout Gail's stay in the residential treatment center both of her parents were seen by psychiatric social workers for individual casework. Her mother, who was then a part-time librarian, approached the early casework sessions with a good deal of ambivalence. In one sense she seemed to be reaching out asking for reassurance of herself as a good mother and seeking help in dealing with her children. In another sense, she was saying that the staff really did not understand her problems and did not care about them. Part of this was attributable to the racial differences between her and the worker. However, after a session during which she vented a good deal of hostility toward the worker, she was able to become much more involved in the casework process.

In the early sessions the mother presented many conflicts in family relations and interactions. She complained about her husband's high expectations for the children and his demanding perfection from them. In many ways she seemed to be pointing to the father as the imperfect parent and looking for the social worker to support her opinions of how to handle children. It was obvious that the parents experienced considerable contention and disagreement in regard to disciplining their children. The mother relied on talking and reasoning with the children while the father thought that overt kinds of punishment were more effective.

As casework progressed the mother focused more on problems in their marriage. She described her husband's disagreement over her working and how he constantly took advantage of any opportunity to criticize her performance as a mother and homemaker. There appeared to be a good deal of friction here, although the mother always countered her negative comments and complaints with some statement about the father's good qualities.

The social worker felt that the mother was a strong, controlling person who was quite inflexible and rigidly held to whatever stand she might take. Although her affect appeared well controlled, there were signs of strong, explosive feelings underneath the surface. To some degree she appeared to reject the feminine role and to obtain much more satisfaction outside of the home. It was obvious that she was more successful and obtained greater enjoyment from her work than she did from her responsibilities as a mother.

Whenever the mother discussed Gail there was little evidence of softness or maternal warmth but more an air of cold detachment. She had hardly anything positive to say about Gail and usually the only mention of her was to ask how she was getting along in the treatment center. At one point in the treatment process there was a four-week suspension of visiting, and the mother showed no regret about this. In fact, she appeared visibly surprised when the social worker told her that Gail had missed her very much. When the visits were resumed and Gail presented the mother with a stack of gifts she had collected for her, the mother managed to leave them in the social worker's office, later saying that she had forgotten all about them.

In contrast to this rather detached relationship with Gail, the mother revealed a very close identification with her first-born child, describing her as quiet, bright, and an exceptional reader. While she would verbalize an understanding and appreciation of the differing personalities among her three children, it was clear that the oldest daughter was the only one she fully understood and accepted. Over the past several years the youngest (the only son) had been evidencing behavior problems and becoming of concern to the mother. She was thinking very seriously about having the child evaluated for psychiatric treatment at the outpatient clinic in the city where they lived.

At various times during casework the mother mentioned dissatisfaction with her early experiences involving various relatives with whom she lived, but she always countered these negative statements with something positive about the people and the settings. It was as if expressing hostility and dissatisfaction with these early experiences were too threatening and unsettling for her to face. The social worker was convinced that the mother harbored numerous unresolved conflicts from the past and that these greatly influenced her relationship with her own daughter. However, these conflicts had not been uncovered and focused on in casework since the social worker had serious doubts about probing too deeply into these repressed memories. She accepted the fact that the mother had established a rather strong defensive system and seemed to have achieved a relatively comfortable equilibrium.

A male social worker presented a report of his casework with the father following 70 regularly scheduled interviews during Gail's institutionalization. He stated that the father's basic difficulty was his inability to relate to or trust other people. The father relied on psychological defenses of rationalization and intellectualization and revealed a strongly obsessive-compulsive personality structure. He often referred to his daughter as being "a most unusual case" and, on other occasions, he would say, "The white man can never understand the black man." He devoted a considerable portion of his psychiatric casework interviews to discussions of racial issues and the injustices that the black man had suffered at the hands of the white man. According to the social worker "through this medium he has cried out his rage, his despair, his sense of having been emasculated, his confusion in assuming the role of man, husband and father and, saddest of all, his own self-hatred of his blackness."

On occasion, however, the father moved somewhat closer to discussion of troublesome experiences from his family life. He intimated that Gail's life had indeed been threatened even before she was born. It took him several months to reach the point of telling the social worker that Gail had come at a very difficult time. Then he became even more direct, stating that Gail had not been planned or wanted. Finally he stated that they had actually sought out a doctor with a view toward aborting the pregnancy. Interwoven with these bits of personal information were hints that he viewed his wife as somewhat lacking as a mother. However, he was quick to defend her and immediately after discussing his wife's depression around the time of Gail's delivery he hastened to make it clear that Gail always received the best attention. He also indicated that most of Gail's early mothering had come mainly from him because of the wife's depression.

In the course of psychiatric casework he occasionally talked about sexual relationships with his wife and discussed his long periods of "celibacy" as being largely determined by his wife's frequent unwell states. Evidently there were many times when he became stimulated, even implying that his wife played an active role in this stimulation, but then she would cut him off saying she did not feel well. Instead of expressing anger directly, the father tried to understand his wife and would make allowances for her distress. A possible indirect expression of his own anger was his statement that he wondered if his wife's headaches might be a sign that she was suffering from some form of malignancy that had not yet been detected. He seemed to be unaware of the hostile implications of his thoughts in this regard. After many months of casework the social worker reported that the father continued to be a frustrating case and to have changed essentially very little. Thus, the movement in casework was very slow and actually minimal. Moreover, the social worker believed there was very little reason to anticipate much further change.

PSYCHOTHERAPY

Soon after admission to the treatment center Gail was assigned to a female psychologist for psychotherapy. On being informed that she would see the psychologist for therapeutic interviews, Gail appeared overjoyed, and immediately inquired how much candy she would receive from the therapist. Both the therapist and the candy, especially the latter, represented the attention and nurturance that she openly craved. In the first session, when the topic of problems was introduced, Gail described many fears including darkness, witches, devils, and dying. In the early sessions Gail spoke quite frequently about the devil, whom she said had died and went to heaven but couldn't behave there so he was sent to hell. She seemed to identify herself with the devil, and on occasion reported that her father had called her a devil. She would then scream, "I'm not bad, I'm not bad," and become extremely agitated, rolling on the floor or jumping up and down. On several occasions during the first four or five sessions Gail's anxiety reached near panic proportions. The therapist felt these reactions stemmed from guilt and fear of punishment and also that Gail seemed to obtain some enjoyment from bringing on these very anxiety-laden states.

Gail also expressed much aggression toward the therapist and frequently attempted to provoke her to anger. Gail would swear, call the therapist dirty names, and imitate her in a mocking fashion. She would also make statements such as "You're stupid, you should be mad at me." During these early therapy sessions she also made manipulative threats to harm herself. These threats were usually associated with throwing herself down the stairs, out the window, or over backwards in the chair. The therapist thought these might have represented being thrown into a grave or hell, which Gail seemed to fear or believe that she deserved. Moreover, these threats and fears appeared to have been reinforced by receiving considerable attention from adults in the past. Recall that for many years Gail had been allowed to get into her parents' bed at night whenever she became frightened. While Gail was threatening to throw herself over backwards in the chair, one day crying out "Help me, help me," the therapist requested that she move the chair so that if she fell she would not hit her head. Gail immediately stuck out her tongue and said, "My mother or my aunt used to come running when I did that." Often she would also remark, "I'm accident prone, you know," as she would put herself into precarious positions.

Occasionally during the first few sessions Gail's anxiety remained low enough to permit her to play out quietly certain past experiences and fantasies. The first of these experiences was watching her father urinate, which she said she had done on occasion. The second was the making of "schoodlepump" out of playdough, clearly representing feces, which she then converted into hot chocolate and tried to eat. On one occasion she managed to get some of this onto the tip of her tongue before the therapist intervened. She then became very upset and tried to vomit.

On several occasions Gail also played out intercourse with the dolls in the therapy room. Although at first she approached the subject with mixed embarrassment and delight, she gradually became less reticent about playing out parental intercourse in great detail. She would accompany this play activity with sighs and grunts and appropriate sexualized movements. The therapist felt that Gail often identified with the male and appeared to be receiving much vicarious gratification from this play activity. On one occasion after the parental dolls had engaged in the sex act five or six times, Gail put them to bed with the infant between them. In the morning she sent the father off to work, which she represented by holding the father doll between her thighs, putting on a great show of delight. Whatever emotion Gail evidenced, she always did so in an unusually exaggerated form, whether it be joy, anger or fear.

In the therapy sessions, Gail frequently exposed her abdominal scar. Once, after she had enacted conception, she again exposed her scar stating that her mother had put her in the hospital when she was very small and that they had operated on her. The therapist asked if Gail was afraid she might not have babies on account of the scar and she said "Yes" and that some of the other girls in her living unit also believed this about her. The therapist said this was not true, and Gail seemed relieved. At this time Gail inquired about whether the therapist had any babies, and she seemed very glad to hear that the therapist did not, since it meant that she could love Gail all the more.

In a subsequent session Gail drew a picture of the therapist as a nurse with a large stomach on which was drawn what appeared to be a face. She said that she was going to remove the therapist's intestinal tract but then, instead of painting a picture of the operation, she daubed her nails with red paint. This probably represented both her own operation and fantasized castration. Toward the end of that session Gail put a bandage around her arm and stated that she had always wanted her arm in a sling, which again could symbolically be regarded as a form of castration and inadequacy.

At the time of this first report, the therapist stated that recently Gail had picked up a roll of playdough that she tried to eat. Gail explained, "That's my problem. I want to eat playdough, I want to eat hot dogs, I want to eat boys' dicks." She then pretended that the playdough was a penis and she was urinating saying "I want a great big dick!" When the therapist inquired whether Gail thought she had one when she was small and now did not have one, Gail hung her head and nodded yes. The therapist tried to explain that boys and girls are different from birth and that the anatomical differences are both necessary and useful. After a few questions, however, Gail replied "let's mash our dicks together!" As the therapist commented in her report, Gail was obviously still rather confused.

In addition to feeling castrated, Gail feared loss of love and impending disaster at any moment. This was probably associated with the fear of punishment that she believed she deserved for her angry anal and sexual fantasies. She saw her father, who had apparently been seductive toward her, as a very punitive figure. It should be recalled that he took over most of the mothering in Gail's infancy, which may well have contributed to her sexual confusion. In the words of Gail's therapist, "She seemed to have identified nurturance with sexual gratification and to have interchanged the penis and the breast, so to speak."

After about six months of seeing Gail twice a week for individual psychotherapy, the therapist reported that although Gail continued to be intensely afraid of death, which she perceived as a form of punishment, she often threatened to kill herself after she expressed hostility toward the therapist. She also continued to be concerned with sexual matters, which were linked with aggression and death on one hand and with nurturance and life on the other. According to the therapist Gail had two wishes, (1) to have a male genital and (2) not to die. However, her dilemma was that the former implied death to her. This appeared to stem from her fantasies surrounding the hernia operation in infancy. She still had the scar from this operation and showed great concern over this mark on her body. On occasion she reported having heard her mother say that when Gail was a little girl she had a long thing sticking out of her stomach and if they hadn't cut it off, she would have died. Thus, in Gail's mind, at one time she had a penis but had it removed because it would have eventually killed her. This continuing confusion involving penis envy, castration anxiety, and fear of death led to inability to function adequately within her social environment or to feel any degree of inner calm.

The therapist reported that Gail on occasion made sexual overtures toward her as a precursor to taking an infantile role in which she was quite content and docile for brief periods. She then became intensely demanding and hostile. She was obviously very ambivalent about the therapist and about becoming dependent on her. After sessions devoted to this type of content Gail would usually try to prove to the therapist how awful she was. However, whenever she was unable to succeed in alienating the therapist she clung to her and did not want to leave the therapy room. It appeared that her hostility was an effort to keep her from getting close to the therapist. At this time in the procedure the therapeutic goal was to help Gail understand the role served by her expressions of hostility and to point up the more basic underlying issues.

Toward the end of this year of psychotherapy, when the therapist was preparing to leave the institution, she reported that Gail's progress had remained generally slow, with occasional setbacks, until it came time to begin to terminate. Gail insisted that she wanted to go with the therapist and began to demonstrate grown-up ladylike behavior in the therapy sessions. However, when the therapist said she could not take Gail with her, she curled up in a ball in the chair and cried. She began to praise the therapist, using a very adult vocabulary, and apologized for being so mean to her in the past. The therapist emphasized that she was not leaving because of anything Gail had done. She also pointed out that no actions on Gail's part could keep them together at this point even though she did not like saying good-bye either.

In the closing session when it was time to go out for a "going away treat," Gail became quite upset saying she didn't look right and that she had to fix her hair, wash up, and change her clothes. It turned out, however, that "not looking right" referred to her being black. She was worried about what people would think if the two of them were seen together. As Gail had often said in the past, "You can't be my mother because you are not Negro." The therapist stated that people would know that she was not Gail's mother and also pointed out that other Negro girls at the hospital had gone out for treats with their therapists when it was time for them to say good-bye. This relieved Gail, and she was then willing to go out into the community.

In describing this final experience together, the therapist said, "When we got to the parking lot at the ice-cream parlor, Gail objected that people were staring at us. I tried to reassure her that this was not the case and that we did not look funny together. I also recommended that if anyone stared at us, Gail should smile and people would smile back at her. In the ice-cream parlor Gail tried this with the waitress, who seemed to be a warm and friendly person, and they got along famously. As we drove back to the institution, Gail opened the gift I had given to her. She seemed very pleasantly surprised that I had wrapped it up so nicely and, when she saw the bracelet, she was delighted and kissed me. But she was disturbed because she had been making a gift for me and had not brought it along with her. As soon as we got back, Gail gave me her gift—a key chain and coin purse that I could say very honestly I needed and appreciated. I reminded Gail that we now each had our gifts and would not forget each other. We then kissed good-bye and Gail ran out to play with the other children."

SUMMARY STATEMENT UPON COMPLETION OF RESIDENTIAL TREATMENT

Toward the end of her three-year stay in the residential treatment center, Gail occasionally went home on weekend visits with her family. She seemed to be getting along better than she had years previously, but she was still far from being a "normal" child. Since she continued to need residential treatment, an application was made for her to be transferred to another treatment center, much like a private-school setting, that could treat her during her adolescence. At the time of discharge it was stated that while she had improved noticeably in social functioning, she needed continued help. Although the staff was beginning to see more of the warm, affectionate, healthy side of Gail's personality, the problem areas that so frequently interfered with her functioning were still far from adequately resolved.

At the time of discharge from the institution Gail was just turning 13 years of age, and her condition was judged to be "improved." She appeared to be moving upward from the extremely infantile and disordered state of personality evidenced in the beginning stages of her institutionalized treatment and headed toward healthy and age-appropriate behavior. However, she was still at the early levels of this development and very immature for her chronological age. It was felt at this time that prognosis was highly dependent on the environment she encountered and the help she continued to receive during the next few years. Although she had made tremendous strides during the last few years, she was still at a young-child level of development with very real potential for regression under stress.

SUBSEQUENT ADJUSTMENT AND LONGER-RANGE OUTCOME

During the second year after Gail's discharge from the institution, a letter was received from the coordinator of pupil services in the public school system in Gail's hometown. The communication said they were involved in planning institutional placement for Gail for the following year and would appreciate a full psychiatric report and evaluation of her progress during treatment. About 26 months after her discharge, another letter was received from a large mental hospital in the state in which Gail lived. This letter stated that Gail was now a patient at this hospital and it requested information about her three years of earlier residential treatment. The social worker who wrote the letter from the state institution mentioned that they were particularly interested in progress made with the parents during Gail's earlier treatment and also wanted to know the therapeutic outcomes obtained with Gail.

At this point Gail was 15 years old, and she had obviously not continued to improve as she proceeded through adolescence. The indications and suggestions of possible psychotic features evidenced at various times throughout her childhood had probably come to fruition. It is not reassuring to realize that a child from an intact family who received psychiatric and psychological treatment from such an early age was unable to be sufficiently helped that she could have been prevented from spending the rest of her life in an institution.

11. THE CASE OF LAURA AND DONNA:
Identical Twins with Elective Mutism

Laura and Donna, attractive, 12-year-old identical twins, had been a source of despair to the school authorities for their entire academic career. Their difficulty was a simple one: they would not talk in school. The symptom began in kindergarten, literally on the first day, and persisted through the years. At first, their mother saw this silence as just another example of their shyness. As twins they had always been very close to each other, forming a unit that held the rest of the world at arm's length, although their mother felt that at the same time they always resented being twins. People "oohed' and "aahed" at them as babies, and they withdrew and disliked this sort of attention from strangers, often hiding or remaining silent when visitors came to the home. In any case, this pattern continued in kindergarten where during the first day they became frightened, wandered away, and stood on a street corner for several hours. They were apparently afraid to go back to school or to go home. When a neighbor recognized them and offered them a ride home, they were terrified of his car, but finally went along.

Returning to school the next day, they were anxious and seemed fearful of punishment for having wandered off the day before. In fact, after they were brought home by the neighbor, their mother had emphasized the difficulties that could come to children who would not go to school, and both girls seemed to expect the worst when they returned to school. The teacher, who was new and young, became exasperated with their previous day's behavior and angered because she could elicit no response from the fearful girls. She made them come to the front of the room and stand together holding hands, ridiculing them before the rest of the class for not talking. Her comment, "They are quiet like mice, we'll call them the mouse twins," brought laughter and teasing from the other children and an even more determined silence from Laura and Donna. The girls continued to talk at home, to the parents and to their older brother and sister. They were also seen talking to some children from the neighborhood and even in the schoolyard when out of earshot of teachers. However, after this incident, they were never observed talking to adults outside the family.

Their kindergarten teacher, at first angry, soon lost interest in the twins. Inexperienced in her first teaching position and overwhelmed by her large group of kindergarten children, she found Laura and Donna to be a relief in comparison to the rest of the class. Since the twins always played quietly together, she had more time to deal with the noisy, active, dependent, and demonstrative members of the class. Even the other children paid little attention to them. Their teasing and the laughter of the first few days soon became indifference, an attitude that persisted for the remainder of the school year.

The twins were promoted to the first grade where they continued their silence. A counselor from the school guidance office was told of their case, became interested and decided to involve himself. He saw the girls separately and together for several interviews, but could not get them to talk. Bringing the situation to the attention of their mother, he finally gained permission to go to their home and from a concealed spot heard them talking, without their knowledge of his presence. However, nothing further came of this home visit.

The first grade teacher, after a great deal of effort mainly consisting of bribery with special privileges, was eventually able to get the girls to whisper to her on a few occasions and was satisfied with this response. She was not too concerned, particularly since the twins progressed in writing, spelling, and arithmetic. Although they would not read aloud, they showed by their progress in other areas that they were learning to read. At this point the girls became very popular with their classmates and were liked by the teachers because they actually created no difficulties in behavior other than their muteness. Just as in kindergarten, the first-grade teacher found them rather welcome when she was faced with the remainder of her noisy, unruly first graders.

When the twins were passed into the second grade, the new teacher did not take their behavior quite so casually and arranged a special conference with the girls' mother.

At the teacher's insistence, mother finally took the girls to a child guidance clinic where a psychiatrist became interested in them, and followed their case for about seven months. He saw them together and also separately, but made no progress in eliciting any verbalization. He did, however, attempt to advise their mother on her handling of the girls. He felt that the children should be allowed to go along without so much stress given to their differences from other children, either because of their twinship or because of their lack of speech, and suggested that they would eventually grow out of the latter. The school had considered placing the girls in separate classrooms, but the psychiatrist felt that this would be undue pressure on them and suggested that they should not be separated at that time. The twins had done well in their written work, and were passed to the third grade on this basis.

In the third grade, the school's reaction became somewhat more intense. Another guidance counselor involved himself in the case, began working with the teachers and, as he put it, attempted "shock therapy." He set up a program with the third-grade teacher in which Donna was shut up in a dark closet because of her refusal to talk. Laura was told that she was the good twin and that she should not listen to Donna. Donna was also hit by the teacher and made to sit under her desk for a long period of time. The theory behind this treatment was that Donna appeared to be the dominant twin and that if the teacher and guidance counselor could break up the pair and induce Donna to talk, Laura would follow. The children did not tell their parents about this treatment for some time, and it only came to mother's attention when a neighbor heard about it from her own daughter. Mother then contacted the superintendent of schools and the school principal, asking them to investigate what was happening. A conference was held, in which the superintendent described the counselor and the teacher as professionals who were only attempting to do their job, and to do what was best for the girls.

By this time, Donna and Laura had become a legend in the school system. A multitude of teachers and guidance personnel were eager to become involved and reacted with varying degrees of interest to the challenge of curing the symptom. Everyone knew of them, but the best efforts made to induce them to talk seemed only to reinforce the difficulty. All efforts were to no avail. Finally, while they were in the third grade, another psychiatrist was consulted. He suggested that they be separated, a tactic that was eventually tried when they began the fifth grade. This produced no change, and they still failed to speak in school, although their written work continued to be adequate.

In the sixth grade, the pattern became more serious because of the increasing importance of oral participation in class. A letter was sent to the girls' mother, requesting her to come to school because her daughters were failing in several subjects. Teachers had previously talked to the mother about the girls' inability to take part in oral work, and at this point mother felt that she was completely helpless. However, she claimed to be willing to try anything to get the children to talk. The teachers and guidance personnel felt that mother was not seriously concerned with the problem except for the pressure from the school and had accepted a clinic referral only to comply with the school's wishes.

The guidance counselor who now became involved made the last serious effort to correct the problem before the twins finally began clinic treatment. As the counselor described it, she tried to get the children to talk, but when they didn't, asked them to write a note stating why they would not. Laura wrote, "Don't read this out loud. When I was small I just did not want to talk for some reason I don't know. Now I am older I still don't know. I am afraid what people will say if I start now." Donna, independently of her sister wrote, "My reason is the same as why my sister doesn't talk. She doesn't talk, so I don't talk. I don't know the reason." The counselor noted that Laura seemed easier to deal with, and described how in a separate interview with her one day she decided to hold out as long as possible in order to get Laura to speak. The dismissal bell rang for the end of the school day and the counselor asked Laura if she walked home with her sister. Laura nodded yes, and the counselor told Laura that she could go with her sister if she would just say the word "yes." Laura responded to this with a silent stare. After waiting for a few minutes, the guidance teacher told Laura that she had all afternoon, was in no hurry to go home, and that Laura herself would not go until she answered the question, "Do you want to go home?" with the word "yes." The two sat staring at each other for about 10 minutes with no result. Then the guidance teacher told Laura that she had some work to do, and would be busy until Laura made up her mind. Turning to the work on her desk, she ignored Laura for a while, and the child became gradually more and more upset, until a few tears appeared. Finally after about half an hour, Laura reportedly said "yes" in a strong, clear voice, and was immediately allowed to go home. This was not followed up because of the busy schedule of the guidance teacher, but it was her impression that Laura was upset mainly because she was afraid that her sister would find out.

The school insisted that the mother involve herself seriously and get psychiatric help for them, since the problem was becoming increasingly difficult from year to year. If they did not start to talk, the result could be a need to repeat grades, or even the termination of their formal schooling at the age of 16.

PRESCHOOL HISTORY AND DEVELOPMENT

The twins' parents were married in their early thirties and the girls were mother's third pregnancy, there being an older brother and sister. Mother had a better education than her husband, having finished high school and worked as a secretary since that time, except for a period of several years after the birth of the twins when she was ill. Father had dropped out of school at the age of 16, and worked as a laborer since that time. Mother seemed to dominate, and she said that the children looked to her for guidance and support, with father very definitely taking a backseat. He was a year or two younger than his wife, a passive, quiet, rather withdrawn man. For several years he had little to do with his family, using the home for eating, sleeping, and little else. He had a drinking problem as well as other medical difficulties, and was described as quite shy.

Mother compared herself to the twins in terms of their silence, relating it to the timidity she had felt herself. She almost admiringly commented that at least the girls, unlike herself, were not afraid *not* to talk. Except when outsiders put pressure on her, such as the referral by the school and occasional calls from the teacher or guidance counselor, mother was not particularly concerned about the twins' refusal to speak. They did talk to her, she got along well with them and, as far as she was concerned, there were few, if any, problems. She did not try to differentiate them, although she was able to tell them apart, a feat that few other people could consistently match. She dressed them alike, and even had them sleep in the same bed until, on the advice of the second psychiatrist, when in the fifth grade, they were separated in school, and stopped sharing a bed at home.

The maternal grandmother came to live with the family after the girls were born, because of mother's need to work and her recurring respiratory illness. Although emotionally this was difficult for the mother, practically it worked out well, since grandmother was very fond of the twins and they became very attached to her. Notice that the mother became ill and was hospitalized just after the twins had begun to talk, about one year of age. Grandmother's care helped tide them over this period, and no difficulties were reported in their development until about age three. At this time, grandmother became ill, and an aunt came to help care for the children. Mother's health again was poor at this time. The aunt was a strict disciplinarian, punitive and harsh, who reacted particularly strongly to the twins' rather inconsistent level of toilet training. When they wet their bed, she scolded them, spanked them, and made them stay in their room for many hours, which led to even more rebellion on their part. They seemed to blame grandmother for their difficulties with aunt, and were overheard saying that they were angry at grandmother because she had left them with their aunt to be spanked.

Shortly after this time, grandmother died and the twins seemed very upset. One could speculate that they attributed grandmother's going away and death to their own rebellion. In any case, they now became noticeably more quiet. Father's mother came for a few days to help out, and although the girls played with her, they did not talk with her. This was the first time that their refusal to speak really became persistent and noticeable. Again mother was not too concerned, attributing the difficulty to the girls' shyness. Comparing this with her own shyness she mention that she sometimes went for days without speaking to her husband and seemed to accept this behavior as a relatively normal thing. In any case, for the next few years, the twins became even less verbal and less spontaneous. When strangers or visitors came to the home, the girls seemed to communicate with each other through a kind of sign language that usually resulted, after a few moments of signaling, in the girls' disappearance from the scene. No one paid much attention to this, and the behavior was generally accepted by the family and others. Indeed, some thought that the behavior was even positive, providing evidence of the girls' closeness, saying "they really stick together."

DIAGNOSTIC EVALUATION

Both girls, as well as their mother, were given a battery of psychological tests. The girls were also seen in initial psychiatric interviews for further assessment. Donna, who was tested first, was found by the psychologist to be a petite, fine-featured girl who appeared slightly younger than her age. She was dressed in typical fashion for the time, in a sweater, skirt, and ponytail. During the testing session, Donna made no effort to communicate except through writing. She would not speak and when asked to nod yes or no, responded with a faint, almost indistinguishable, head movement. When confused by the test material, her expression resembled a smile. Within these limits, however, she was cooperative throughout, seemed to understand most of the instructions, and worked well, although quite slowly.

On the projective tests, which included the Thematic Apperception Test and the Rorschach, she spent a good deal of time but offered only a few written responses that were brief and minimally elaborated. On intelligence testing, Donna was found to function at the average level, but there were some indications of a slightly higher potential. She seemed to work best with the more superficial and impersonal tasks and tended to do poorly on tests related more to deeper feelings and experiences. Concerned with outer appearances, she was quite uncomfortable in more personal interactions and relationships. She appeared to be an extremely fearful and restricted girl, who worked very hard to present an inconspicuous outer picture, almost as if she did not wish to be noticed by others, perhaps to hide her feelings of inadequacy. She was found to employ compulsivelike defenses in controlling her more intimate needs and feelings, and she related to the environment with great care and caution. By making herself inconspicuous, Donna could apparently feel less vulnerable and, therefore, less inadequate.

Although she could not reveal much of herself in everyday situations, she appeared to lead an extremely active and intense fantasy

life. Her mutism, which in some ways showed need for inconspic-
uousness, actually provided her a weapon that could control and
manipulate others. By not talking she could keep everybody at a
distance, was held responsible for little, and had even less demanded of her. The examiner noted that the dynamic reasons for
Donna's symptom were difficult to formulate. There were some
suggestions of angry feelings toward her mother, associated with
rather immature dependency needs, and fear of separation from
mother if she should show her hostility. It appeared that Donna
was a frightened and constricted girl who rigidly maintained her
symptoms and defenses with which she could be comfortable and
which resulted in little distress and anxiety. Since her defenses
constituted a powerful weapon against interpersonal involvement,
they would be difficult to overcome in psychotherapy.

Laura, seen at the same time by another psychologist, was found
to be similarly silent, but very well motivated and quite pleasant.
She paid close attention to instructions, occasionally responded
with a faint smile, and was willing to write out answers to all the
questions, even though the rather long session was obviously tiring
for her. Like her sister, she was found to be functioning with average intelligence and, again, a somewhat higher potential was predicted for her. Her performance was highest in areas that had least
to do with human interaction. Tests involving the recognition and
anticipation of interpersonal events were far below her best scores.
Thus, not only emotionally but cognitively as well, her ability to
function satisfactorily in interpersonal relationships seemed to be
impaired.

The projective tests revealed Laura to be tense, anxious, and
insecure. She seemed emotionally constricted, using obsessive-
compulsive defenses, and attempting to prevent an anxiety-
provoking expression of feelings. She was obviously shy and in
many ways evasive, not only in failing to speak but also in her
written replies. These, all done unwittingly, revealed little beyond
the superficial level. It was felt that her reluctance to communicate
represented a kind of negativism by which she could passively
express some of her anger, and by which she could also control her
relationships with others and resist their influence. Like her sister,
she used her symptom as a weapon. Underlying hostility toward
both parents was seen, although it was expected that Laura would
be unable to express this openly.

Although Laura was by no means insensitive to the feelings of others about her, she attempted to cover up her unhappiness, trying to hide her resentment toward her parents, and generally ignoring any unpleasantness with others. Her approaching puberty seemed to make her even more uncomfortable with people and with herself, and her defenses appeared very unsuitable in helping her deal effectively with the problems of adolescence. Indeed, if anything, the symptom and her defenses were more likely to aggravate the problems of the years ahead rather than to help solve them, particularly since they kept her apart from others. It was felt that both girls were quite vulnerable because of the importance of peer relationships during the period of adolescence and because their symptoms cut them off from communication with all but a few of their age-mates.

Laura seemed to have more anxiety about the approach of adolescence than her sister Donna, and there were feelings of hostility toward *both* parents. Donna, on the other hand, seemed more angry toward her mother and was somewhat more positive toward her father whom she saw as being somewhat seductive. Donna showed more potential for independence and for social sensitivity, and with her more active and intense fantasy life, somewhat better potential for movement. Both girls, however, made great efforts to deny their deeper feelings and to conceal as much as possible about themselves. Both seemed to use their symptom as a means of controlling others, and of manipulating the environment to prevent any occurrence of anxiety-provoking situations.

Mother, when tested, was cooperative and made an effort to be pleasant with the psychologist. Underneath this, however, she was a tense, defensive person, who made strong efforts to control herself. Indeed, at times, she seemed quite overcontrolled. She was very unsure of herself on the tests and very self-deprecating. "I don't have any brains," was a typical comment. She was found, however, to be functioning almost at the superior level of intelligence. This good capacity was not evidenced in other parts of the examination. Thus, on projective tests she showed a lack of imagination, an inability to use her inner resources constructively as a means of coping with problems, and a reliance on outwardly conventional and conforming expectations as guides to behavior. When caught in a situation where the latter were not applicable, she resorted to evasion or blocking. Thus she would say, "I never say anything like that," or "Do people really see something in these things?"

When the situation became too intense, she said, "Funny, how you can blank your mind out," and was unable to respond at all. This behavior pattern was not unlike the twins' mutism and, indeed, much that was found in their behavior as well in the psychological evaluations seemed to follow the mother's own attempts at denial and avoidance of any difficulties.

Mother was found emotionally to be immature and rather impulsive, with a number of wish-fulfilling fantasies that were ineffective in helping her to cope with her reality problems. She was easily stimulated to anxiety, for which she had a low tolerance and that she could handle only through her defenses. Very strong feelings of inadequacy were expressed despite her superior ability. She showed a lack of feelings for other people although she seemed to have some ability to get along well on a superficial social level as evidenced by her test productions. There was a moderate amount of distrust and hostility toward other people, which seemed to be due to her lack of understanding and sensitivity toward them. From this, it was predicted that she would probably show an uncompromising, moralistic outlook toward others.

It appeared that the mother's relationship to her children was probably not actively hostile, punitive, or cold. Instead, she was a concrete, conforming person who seemed well-meaning, if not very sensitive or reflective. Her flight from anxiety and her use of defenses did not seem to set much of an example for the children in learning to deal actively with their own problems. She seemed ready to admit that she was not a "good" mother in helping the children to cope better with their difficulties, but could only express helplessness, retreating from the problem as she did all others. There were indications that she was ready to form a dependent relationship with a therapist in which she would probably accept at least an intellectual, if not an emotional, insight into her problems. In part, this potential for forming a dependent relationship was inferred from her dissatisfaction with her current role in the family. She expressed feelings of stress and unhappiness about having to be the "man in the family." Although there was much repression and avoidance of genuine feelings and relationships, mother's anxiety, her adequate reality testing, and her other personality assets suggested that psychotherapy with her would have a reasonable chance of success.

Both girls were seen shortly after this by a psychiatrist who, after some rather strenuous efforts, was able to induce each girl to accompany him for a brief play interview. In a parallel fashion, both girls independently managed to paint a picture of a house, and both, as could be expected, refused to communicate verbally in any way. The psychiatrist's impression was that these girls were in excellent contact with reality, with absolutely no evidence of any type of psychotic behavior. He felt that much of the difficulty depended on the relationship between the two girls, partly on the expectation and partly on the fear that the other would talk. He found them both to be extremely anxious, but both seemed to gain some self-confidence during the interviews, and on this basis he felt that an attempt at psychotherapy was at least feasible.

PSYCHOTHERAPY

Two different therapists were assigned to the twins with the understanding that no pressure would be placed on them to verbalize during their interviews. It was decided at that time to provide casework with the mother also on a weekly basis, to coincide with the therapy of the girls.

During the first two months, the twins presented much the same behavior in their weekly interviews. At first, the therapists concentrated on forming relationships, each playing games with his own patient. Neither girl showed much initiative, and both remained mute throughout this time, as indeed throughout the length of their treatment. However, each girl gradually relaxed and began to smile and laugh a bit during the sessions. On one occasion, when it was necessary for her to come alone, Donna seemed to enjoy the hour much more than when she came with her sister. An initial relationship seemed to be established, although the girls still refused to talk. It was interesting that each time before separating to go with their different therapists, the girls signaled each other as if to renew the mutual support of their silence. On one occasion this was accompanied by a good deal of smiling and even some muted laughter. The therapists later were strongly suspicious that the girls, for one interview, had traded places with each other. They resembled each other so closely that in any case it was impossible to tell them apart. Interesting differences did occur in their play, however. Donna was eager to win at competitive games while Laura became hostile when the therapist tried to let her win.

Because of the difficulty in eliciting material from the girls and with the relationships with their therapists becoming stronger, it was decided to introduce new material into the interviews. This was done through the use of word-association and thematic-apperception techniques. As before, Donna was concerned with the problems of a growing teenage girl, particularly regarding her attractiveness toward the opposite sex. She was better aware of her needs than Laura and more open in expressing them, although at the same time obviously resistive. She showed negative feelings toward her mother, but more mature heterosexual interests than her sister, Laura, who appeared more repressed and afraid of aggression and of men. Donna seemed to stress her individuality while Laura seemed concerned with maintaining the twinship. Therapy, which had begun in the late spring, continued in this fashion throughout the summer.

At the beginning of autumn, feeling that the relationship was strong enough and in view of the continued resistance of the twins, the therapists initiated a more direct approach. Questions were asked of the girls, and they were encouraged to write answers. Some of these questions were specifically related to their difficulties, such as: Who of the two was the first to begin to refuse to talk? How much of a social handicap was their silence? and How did the school react? The reaction to these questions was negative, as neither girl wished to respond. However, Donna did express her dislike of coming to therapy and her negative feelings toward her sister, but refused to answer questions about her father. Laura expressed considerable resentment of being a twin, of her school, of the woman who drove her to the clinic, of coming for treatment, as well as shame that her friends might find out that she was coming. It was clear that the girls did not like each other very much at this point, and that both shared a dislike of being pressured or pushed. Laura appeared especially concerned regarding what others might think of her, and again less independent than Donna in this respect. Despite a dislike for her sister, Laura nevertheless appeared to be more attached to Donna than Donna was to her.

After a month or so of using this approach, Donna began to increase her communication and for a while appeared more relaxed. However, after beginning to have sessions in her therapist's office instead of in the playroom, she again became tense, writing of her disappointment and renewed resistance to treatment. Her therapist verbalized her anger and suggested that perhaps one of the problems was her fear of expressing hostility. Donna then began to present material about her girlfriends. She had different friends than her sister had and was concerned that these girls might find out that she was seeing a psychiatrist. A little later in this interview, Donna was manipulating some clay in her hand. The therapist verbalized that she might feel like throwing something at him, and she nodded in agreement. While Donna appeared to be making some therapeutic gains, Laura became more depressed, hostile, and refused to write very much. She was resentful and jealous of her sister's getting along better and especially of her sister's friends.

This period marked the beginning of the separation of the twins and an increase in their jealousy of each other. Their relationship seemed to be clarified by the relationships they had with other children, especially their girlfriends. Donna began to express more in writing, particularly about her activities at dances, and with her friends. She wrote of her disappointment and her feelings of rejection from her father. Laura seemed more afraid to be independent and was ambivalent and jealous of her sister. She denied having boyfriends and said that she did not want to do what Donna was doing, although she was well aware that Donna herself had a boyfriend. Laura seemed angry, frustrated, and hostile, expressing this in the playroom through several activities, including on one occasion shooting a toy gun during an entire session. There seemed to be a growing lack of communication between the twins, with Laura being afraid to come to the clinic by herself. She seemed anxious about the separation from her sister, and criticized her sister's boyfriend. Donna, on the other hand, seemed to relax more and seemed to enjoy her social success. However, she was able to write about her boyfriend only after discussing the relationship with her father first.

During this period, work with the girl's mother was increasingly focused on her part in the girls' muteness. For example, she came home from work one day to find that the twins had been fighting and had broken a vase to which she had a great sentimental attachment. She expressed little feeling about this, saying to the girls only that it was disappointing. However, the next time the girls started to argue, mother threatened to separate them "for good." This brought an immediate disappearance of the rivalry between them for the following week, and they insisted on going to school and playing in each other's company only. Mother now recognized that she had frightened them by threatening separation as a punishment. She began to search for other means of disciplining the two, discipline that was less vague and general and more specific for the misbehavior. About this time, mother first heard Donna talking to her boyfriend on the telephone, and anxiously questioned her about this. When he called again, Donna held the receiver without talking into it and eventually hung up. Mother at first saw her own anxiety as a result of her proper concern for Donna's welfare, but then came to realize that she was actually exerting pressure to keep the girls together, urging Donna to include Laura in her activities.

In the spring, Donna seemed to gain security. Thus, when asked whether she thought she was popular, she wrote, "I don't care, it doesn't bother me if I am not." She elaborated further about the lack of interest her father showed in her and about the boyfriend who was interested in her. She seemed to express greater feeling in her writing and to be less anxious about revealing her teenage interests. In spite of her continued complaints about having to come to the clinic, she seemed to enjoy her interviews. Laura, on the other hand, still was resentful, depressed, and appeared to feel left out. She was lonely and expressed several fantasies about teenage activities, for example, showing her therapist her pictures of rock'n roll singers. Donna seemed to consolidate her gains and to enjoy the reality of her situation and her growing success, while Laura began to take greater refuge in fantasy.

At this point, the fears of separation between the girls and mother had lessened a great deal. Their newly achieved sense of identity was ready to be tested and perhaps strengthened by separate experiences, and the therapists decided to attempt this through separate camp placements during the coming summer vacation. The girls had never been separated from each other, their mother, or their home. Mother resisted this plan, stating that she could not afford it and that the twins would be terribly frightened and angry toward her. However, because all of her rationalizations were interpreted according to her need to keep the girls together, she became angry, cried, and stated that as usual everyone was placing all the responsibility on her shoulders. She raged against her husband for his detachment from the family, his irresponsibility, his drinking, and his overspending. However, as her hostility was accepted in the treatment relationship, she began at the same time to accept the twins' anger against her, including even their threats of running away from home should they be forced to attend camp.

Donna in her writing expressed a firm determination not to go. She felt that her mother was sending her to a camp for "crazy people." She was concerned that activities in the camp might be geared for younger children, and "it was her business to decide what to do." She also brought up her fear of remaining alone in the dark. Laura withdrew even more than Donna, showing her passivity by saying that she would rather do nothing at all than go to camp. She avoided the issue of what kind of camp it was, saying that her therapist should know, because he was the one who was sending her there.

With these events, the twins' ambivalence became more open, Donna appearing as the active partner in the twinship, Laura as the passive one. Both expressed open feelings of hostility and disagreement with the mother. As before, and consistently, Laura appeared more attached to the twinship with a greater readiness to use withdrawal as a defense, while Donna was more concerned with her own individuality.

In spite of the girls' resistance, arrangements for camp attendance were completed with mother and, finally, even father became involved in the planning. After the separation became a fact, both girls, particularly Donna, and their parents acted with relief and pleasure to find that they were going their separate ways. Each remained two weeks at camp, and treatment at the clinic was interrupted during the summer months.

When seen later, Laura appeared angry because her sister had been the first to go to camp. Nevertheless, she smiled when her therapist mentioned that she had not been with her sister during this time. Donna expressed criticism of the camp, particularly of the food that she described as "awful." Nevertheless, reports from the camp indicated that she had been quite successful, since she was offered a job as a counselor for the following years. Both girls were well liked at the camp and participated in sports and other activities, and both girls reportedly talked openly to others.

SUBSEQUENT ADJUSTMENT

In the fall, the girls began high school. After consultation with the clinic, the principal, who was aware that the girls were ready to talk publicly, made it clear that he expected them to do so in his school. The girls began to participate orally in class, and as the symptom had now been eliminated, so also was the pressure for treatment. Thus, by agreement, therapy sessions were spaced out progressively less frequently. By Christmas, Laura had obtained a boyfriend of her own, and seemed to be following in Donna's footsteps to a more adequate social adjustment.

Toward the end of therapy, Donna began to differentiate experiences as coming before or after treatment, and recognized her previous behavior as "silly." She stated that she felt "funny" still not being able to talk to some people that she had known for a long time, while she felt quite comfortable talking to people who did not know her. She added that if she were to talk freely to people who had known her, "they would tell me how silly and everything I was before."

At first, the girls spoke as little as possible in school, their grades dropping below the previous level. However, their school participation gradually improved, and by the end of the school year Donna was on the honor role and Laura had passed all her subjects. They were now almost 15, and Donna began to think about her future career as a nurse, hairdresser, or secretary, while Laura thought of general office work. The social life of both girls gradually improved, although along separate lines. Each had her own boyfriend and both talked freely with other people, with the exception of their therapists, with whom they still communicated only in writing and who had never heard the girls speak.

12. THE CASE OF ROY:
An Abandoned Child

Our information about this black male child begins at the time he was found in the basement of a rooming house in a large mid-Western city. He was wrapped in a sopping wet towel with a bottle of curdled milk lying beside him. The police took him to a hospital where he was found to weigh nine pounds and was suffering from malnutrition and a severe cold. He was then placed in a Catholic institution, St. Peter's Infant Home, while attempts were made to find his parents and to learn about his early history. These efforts proved unsuccessful.

Authorities in the institution therefore had to make some arbitrary decisions about this foundling's personal identity. They assigned him an official birthdate approximately six months prior to his abandonment, and decided to consider him a Catholic with the legal name of Roy Peters.

Following a year in this infant home, Roy was placed in another home for neglected children. At age two, he was reported to be fully toilet trained, and was described as playful, mischievous, and quite stubborn. He remained in this second institution for approximately two years, and was then hospitalized for surgery of the left eye to correct strabismus. Roy remained in the custody of the state Child Welfare Division, and when he was four years old, was placed in a foster home. This placement, however, lasted only two days. The foster parents complained that Roy cried continuously, was destructive with toys, and was disobedient. He wandered away from the house several times during this brief stay, looking for the social worker who had brought him there.

Placed once again in a receiving home for children, Roy had temper tantrums, and was disobedient, enuretic, and destructive of his personal belongings. After a short stay in this receiving home, Roy acquired a second set of foster parents with whom he remained for approximately 18 months. However, his adjustment to this family was equally poor, and he was described as destructive, and openly hostile and aggressive with other children. At various times, Roy attempted to smother, choke, and strike another child living with this family. On one occasion he started a fire in the basement and another time he turned on the gas heater, saying he wanted to kill the woman who was left to take care of him in his foster mother's absence. The second foster mother found it impossible to continue to care for Roy and requested that he be removed.

When he was five and a half years old, Roy was placed in a third foster home where two other foster children were already residing. He related very well to the father, who reportedly was fond of Roy, but he still evidenced serious acting-out behavior. Much of his hostility was directed toward the foster mother. During his stay in this third home, Roy was seen for a complete psychological testing at a local child guidance center. The psychologist reported that most of Roy's difficulties stemmed from his profound struggle with oral-dependent, aggressive, and sexual impulses. When he was seven years old, the foster mother requested his removal from their home because she felt that she could no longer cope with his acting-out behavior.

At this point, a fourth foster home placement was attempted, but this arrangement lasted only two weeks. Roy continued to show temper tantrums, severe negativism, and also set fires in the kitchen, basement, and closets of the house. Since at that time there was no place for Roy to go, the third set of foster parents, with whom he had stayed the longest, agreed to take him back temporarily while the Child Welfare Division tried to place him in a residential treatment center. It was generally agreed that a foster home or any ordinary form of family placement could not adequately treat Roy, and that he seriously needed residential psychiatric care.

ADMISSION TO RESIDENTIAL TREATMENT

Roy's estimated age at the time of his admission to the residential treatment center was almost eight years. His general appearance was that of a thin youngster with a dark complexion. A comprehensive physical examination revealed a physically healthy child except for poor vision. An EEG obtained results within normal limits, thus not suggesting any known organic damage.

A battery of psychological tests administered to Roy shortly after his admission revealed an IQ of 91, and showed him to be a severely deprived child, with many dependency needs, and little expectation for gratification. Moreover, he revealed a very negative image of himself and of others. The findings also suggested that although Roy would be able to conform with sufficient guidance, he had little inner stability and few internal resources to guide him without the pressure of immediate punishment or gratification. The tests also revealed that Roy was preoccupied with his own identity, and strongly needed maternal nurturance, and some form of stable therapeutic relationship. Based on this psychological assessment, Roy was assigned to a female psychotherapist during his initial stay in the treatment center.

PSYCHOTHERAPY

To give a more thorough understanding of Roy's psychopathology, and changes that he showed in the course of his five years of residential treatment, we will present certain information obtained from reports of his psychotherapy. For the first two years, Roy was seen by a female therapist, and then for the latter years of his stay by a male therapist.

After the first year of therapeutic interviews, the female therapist stated that for much of this time, Roy's problems and behavior were on the oral and anal levels of psychosexual development. From the start his conflict about being black was obvious. He spent many hours in the play-therapy room mixing paint colors; the result was always a dark brown mixture. Roy spoke of it as a "bad color," and continuously tested the therapist's reaction to it. For the first few months of therapy, he refused all chocolate candies, denying his fondness for them. Then he gradually began offering these candies to the therapist and waited for her verbal expression of satisfaction. At this time, Roy began saying that he felt different from other members of the foster family that he most regarded as his own family. He said that many of them had light brown skin, while he, himself, was very black.

The family of dolls used with the dollhouse in the play therapy room consisted solely of white dolls, and Roy frequently hid the female dolls and spent time poking at their blue eyes. When the therapist assured him that she liked boys, he appeared relieved and soon requested that the therapist obtain a black-boy doll. Upon receiving this doll, Roy immediately dressed it in pants and spent many hours playing the mother's role with this doll. He made "oatmeal" out of sawdust and soda and served it to the doll to "make him grow strong as any good mother would do."

Roy began speaking about wanting to be a one-year-old baby in order to be cared for. He started placing soda in the baby nursing bottle and began to spend time in the crib in the playroom, speaking baby talk. He called the therapist his mother and indicated that he wanted her to take him home, so that she would always take care of him.

During this first year of therapy, Roy frequently arrived for interviews without wearing his glasses. He recognized his self-destructive tendencies when angry, and spoke of wanting to be blind. The therapist perceived this as a final defense from a harmful rejecting world. He talked of feeling safe only within the institutional grounds.

Throughout this period, the therapist tried to help him develop a feeling of self-worth and acceptance as a black child. He continued to play with the dolls, preparing meals and nurturing the child dolls. He assigned the therapist the role of feeding, washing, and loving "the little Roy doll." Roy displayed immense pleasure during these interviews, speaking of the different mothers who had been good to him. The third foster mother symbolized a good mother whose place Roy wanted the therapist to take. He also recalled having set an ironing board on fire to get away from one mean foster mother. Roy was now able to speak of his feelings of anger and the resulting impulsive behavior that led him into difficulty.

In comparing the good foster mother with his therapist, Roy requested that the therapist wear a black dress to the interview, as if he was attempting to obtain her acceptance for a darker appearance. In talking about his experiences with foster parents, he mentioned a younger foster child and openly expressed death wishes for him, verbalizing his desire to be the youngest and most loved of all.

Throughout the latter part of the first year of his therapy, Roy continued to play the role of cook during the sessions making endless brown-colored meals on his toy stove. Then, according to the therapist, Roy's play started to indicate emotional growth. He began to prefer playing cards, shooting guns, and working at model building. He now verbalized hating the father doll who was bigger, and he expressed the desire to eat good food to grow strong. The Oedipal stage was reenacted in Roy's play with the dolls and interactions with the female therapist. He became sexually curious, often trying to get into positions to peek under the therapist's dress. This natural curiosity was discussed with him, and Roy proceeded to admit that he had often done this at home with his foster mother. The therapist assured him that he had the correct information about sex differences, conception, and childbirth.

On one occasion, he used a large ball to strike out again and again at the mother doll, saying that she was "a boy's mother and did not take care of him as she should." This opened up a discussion about his knowledge of his real identity. Roy said that he did not know his real mother, but then, referring to the mother doll, stated that "she never wanted to have the baby come out of her hole because she did not want to bother taking care of him." The therapist openly recognized with Roy his wish to be loved and cherished, and this again brought out his fantasies of wanting to live in the therapist's home. However, by this time Roy had begun to have a better self-image. He would sometimes stand in front of the mirror giving himself a satisfying appraisal, and spoke much more positively about various black adults who worked at the institution. Also, he said another black child patient was his best friend.

During the second year, Roy increasingly expressed interest in the sexual area. He often pretended to be grown-up boy who called for his date in a big car. He made up stories about shooting other men to protect this girl friend. The therapist felt that Roy's frank verbalizations regarding sexual matters probably indicated that he had either received or witnessed much sexual stimulation.

She reported that this nine-year-old boy, supposedly in the latency phase of psychosexual developmental level, vacillated from infantile oral and anal levels to preadolescence. At that time, Roy became very determined to improve his appearance by using vaseline on his hair. He verbalized the desire to be 18, so that he could smoke, drive a car, and have children.

Roy continued to mix paints, and openly expressed a desire to be the best chemist in the world to discover "the right shade of brown." On one occasion, he painted five doll figures representing his foster family, so that they would all be the same shade of brown. He continued to express openly considerable hostility toward the other foster children he had lived with in the various foster homes. The therapist's plan at this point was to enable him to express his resentment in the hope that his feelings of sibling rivalry might be resolved. Moreover, the therapist felt that she had to work very closely and carefully with Roy to help him deal adequately with his sexual concerns.

Throughout the second year of his therapeutic relationship with this female therapist, Roy continued to make gains, although he never fully resolved these deep-seated conflicts. On occasion, following many months of psychotherapy, Roy still expressed concern about being black, and wished that his complexion were much lighter. In fact, during one therapy session, he requested the therapist to obtain toothpowder that he had seen advertised on TV, wanting to put it on his face to lighten his skin. He continued to test the therapist, seeking overt signs of approval and fondness. He spoke of spending the rest of his life with her, either as her child or her husband—whichever would make this permanent relationship possible. Throughout all of this, the therapist reassured Roy that he was valued and loved for his own sake, and also tried to get him to see the fallacies in his thinking about some of these concerns.

A particularly noteworthy episode occurred when the therapist announced that she was about to leave her position at the institution. Roy immediately mentioned that the soda he was drinking was sour and would make him sick. At least symbolically this interchange seems related to the fact that as an infant his mother had abandoned him with a bottle of sour milk that made him sick. Although it may seem like a wide stretch of the imagination, this interpretation certainly fits with clinical observations of the continual preoccupation with early frustrations that Roy evidenced throughout his stay in the treatment center.

A male therapist took over treatment of this child following the initial two-year period with the female therapist. At first Roy was very depressed, blaming himself for the female therapist's having left the institution for a job elsewhere. The new therapist attempted to help him resolve these feelings of depression and then proceeded to follow a therapy plan in which Roy would be encouraged to advance beyond his more infantile strivings. The therapist started setting limits, for example, in regard to the amount of candy and soda Roy was given during therapy sessions, the number of outside trips, and the kinds of play activities he was permitted to engage in. He attempted to focus with Roy on his occasionally expressed wish to grow up and be a "big boy." As he stressed the mature aspects of Roy's behavior, the therapist was quite often the main target of Roy's resentment and hostility.

In one session, Roy brought in a clock the male therapist had given him and was crying because it was broken. However, it soon became clear that Roy had broken this clock himself because he did not want anything from the therapist. He made comments stating that this new therapist had taken the original female therapist away from him and was now taking the fun out of his therapy sessions. He complained bitterly that the therapist was not providing enough candy to eat or things to play with. He inquired if the therapist was too stupid to help him build models. This struggle between the seeking of immediate gratification of infantile desires and tolerating the frustrations involved in growing up was evidenced in most areas of Roy's institutional life. On the one hand, he was saying "You do not give me enough," but on the other, he was asking "Why do you treat me like a baby?" At another level, this conflict in therapy could be viewed as revealing the Oedipal aspects of the transfer of therapists, with the father figure preventing the child from having the desired love relationship with the mother figure. In the present case, the therapist felt that Roy needed to express aggression toward him, and have it accepted within limits, to facilitate the development of his masculine identity.

Roy continued to test the therapist: making demands, sulking, leaving the therapy room, and occasionally trying to see just how much the therapist would take from him without reacting with hostility. For example, Roy would play catch with the therapist and begin throwing the ball harder and harder until he was actually hurting the therapist with the ball. Also, he tended to devalue what they did together. For example, whenever they went on trips, Roy would point out that they were not as good as the trips he used to make with his female therapist. During his calm periods,

however, Roy and the therapist talked about his feelings of bad-
ness and his tendency to alienate people, and they agreed that
they had to work to change these feelings. Roy verbalized that
he wanted to control himself and did not like being so mean with
other people. Gradually Roy began to make some progress and
complied much more with the therapist's requests. At times he
would sulk briefly, but then would brighten up and say that he
was only kidding.

After two years of therapy with the second therapist Roy
demanded much less during his therapy sessions. His frustration
tolerance seemed noticeably improved, coping with disappoint-
ments by verbalization instead of physical destruction. He began
talking more about the future and stated that he would like eventually to become a child-care worker in the institution. He also
discussed other types of vocations that people could engage in
and talked more and more about growing up and going to work.
However, he seemed quite anxious about the possibility of eventually leaving the institution. In all areas of functioning, during
the latter part of his stay at the treatment center, he showed
greater maturity and left many of his infantile concerns further
behind him. He began talking more about what happened outside
of the institution and became very interested in automobiles and
what he might do in the future. He was now getting along very
well both with other children and with staff members, and it was
obvious that his overall adjustment had improved greatly.

The therapist summarized his observations and evaluations up
to then:

"Therapy has attempted to symbolically nurture this boy and
then to wean and help him grow. I believe that from the combined
efforts of all the people who have worked with Roy during his
several years of institutional life, this has been at least partially
achieved. Yet I know that he is still assailed by feelings of self-
doubt, is sensitive to criticism, and not quite sure that people can
be trusted. Roy is worried about his ability to cope with life on
the outside and wonders whether he will need, and receive, continued emotional support after leaving the institution. I share his
concern. He is less anxious, however, and has developed a more
effective defensive structure. In this regard it is noteworthy that
he is no longer enuretic. His self-esteem has increased noticeably,

and I think that Roy now has a good chance of making a successful adjustment in the years ahead."

GENERAL COURSE IN RESIDENTIAL TREATMENT

Initially, Roy was placed with the youngest group of children where he was described as a child with insatiable needs, and unable to cope with even the most minor frustrations. He was very destructive of his own property, as well as that of others. On 17 different occasions Roy broke his eyeglasses, and they had to be replaced. In the beginning, he appeared to be totally bewildered, and some child-care workers wondered if he was actually dull or mentally retarded. There was a general pessimism about his ability to improve with residential treatment. Overall, the major therapeutic goal was to build confidence and self-worth in this youngster.

In time Roy became much more cheerful with noticeably increased frustration tolerance. He was able to use his friendliness and sense of humor to move closer to people, at least within the confines of this therapeutic milieu. Roy did not progress too well in school, although he did somewhat better during the last year or two. However, he remained considerably behind his expected grade level.

For several months prior to leaving the treatment center, Roy worked with the maintenance staff, doing odd jobs and being paid for his labors. He worked well and gained in self-confidence, enjoying the opportunity to learn that there were jobs in the world that he could do successfully. In view of his increased ability to handle his problems maturely, Roy was given permission to leave the institutional grounds on Saturday, going into the city and using his own earnings to see a movie or go shopping. Thus, although the oral-dependent quality was still evident, it was not nearly so pervasive and all-consuming toward the end of Roy's stay as it was when he began treatment.

TREATMENT OUTCOME AND SUBSEQUENT ADJUSTMENT

All staff members agreed that Roy had improved greatly during his residential treatment and, with the right future placement, the prognosis was regarded as quite good. However, there was little likelihood that he would complete much formal schooling, and he seemed destined to encounter many difficulties in making a successful adjustment to life in the community.

After almost five years of residential treatment, Roy was discharged to another institution for adolescent boys in his home state. There he underwent vocational training and continued to make considerable advances in his personal and social adjustment. When he was 17 years of age, he worked at a Job Corps camp and seemed to function very well. This was now four years after his discharge from the residential treatment center, and he still continued to periodically write brief messages to his therapist and certain child-care workers with whom he had spent his days in residential treatment.

We see that this unwanted boy, who had been left to die at an early age, was making a good adjustment to the world. He became neither psychotic nor delinquent, and his neurotic conflicts proved to be helped by psychotherapy and residential treatment. As he progressed toward early adulthood, he appeared to be on his way to becoming a working, self-sufficient member of society. In view of Roy's start in life, this would certainly be a quite remarkable accomplishment.

6

PSYCHOTIC DISORDERS

Psychosis of childhood is an area full of confusion and contradiction. Professionals cannot agree on diagnostic criteria and labels, etiological factors, or preferred modes of treatment. Efforts are being made to clarify some of these unresolved problems, but there remains a great need for increased understanding. Diagnoses in this area utilize such terms as infantile autism, childhood schizophrenia, the atypical child, symbiosis of childhood, and chronic brain syndrome. Some therapists include autism as a subcategory of schizophrenia, and others believe that these are entirely separate entities. Other therapists maintain that these several varieties of severe childhood disorders should be subsumed under the broad category of psychosis.

Psychotic children usually show some, or most, of the following characteristics.

1. Impaired emotional relationships with people.
2. Apparent unawareness of their own identity.
3. Preoccupation with mechanical objects.
4. Resistance to changes in their environment.
5. Abnormal sensations and perceptions.
6. Excessive anxiety.
7. Disordered speech.
8. Strange bodily movements (for example, arm flapping and body whirling).
9. General retardation but often with circumscribed areas of exceptional skill.

A very important prognostic sign (predicting future outcome of a case) is the use of language. If the psychotic child does not possess meaningful speech by the age of five, the outlook is particularly bleak. Even for those cases who do speak, follow-up studies usually show a relatively low rate of significant improvement. Thus, for children who suffer from psychotic disorders at an early age, there is considerable likelihood they will continue to show marked psychopathology in later years.

Treatments have varied at different times in the relatively short period that childhood psychosis has been recognized as a psychiatric diagnostic category. They have included the use of electric shock therapy, lobotomy (brain surgery), drug therapy, long-term residential treatment, intensive psychotherapy and, most recently, behavior therapy. At present, the preferred method of treatment is behavior therapy (also known as "behavior modification"), usually in a residential treatment setting.

An especially controversial issue is the role of parents in "causing" the child's psychosis. Theorists like Bettelheim maintain that maternal rejection and lack of parental love, especially during certain "critical periods" in the child's early development, provide the basis for infantile autism. Consistent with his view of parents as causative agents, Bettelheim recommends long-term psychodynamic child therapy within the confines of a residential treatment center, with the parents being kept away from their child while undergoing intensive psychotherapy themselves. On the other hand, Rimland has presented a strong case for biological causation of infantile autism, with the disorder resulting from neurological impairment occurring prior to birth, which is in no way the fault of the parents. Since the parents are not viewed as culprits, Rimland and others (notably Schopler and Reichler, and Lovaas) have incorporated the parents as cotherapists in their treatment programs for psychotic children. These programs have an educational orientation, using behavior modification techniques to help the children acquire skills and abilities that are particularly difficult for them to master in the course of normal socialization.

In the cases presented in this section, all three children are boys. This is consistent with the general finding of a much higher incidence of childhood psychosis in boys than in girls. In Kevin, we see a boy whose closest companion was the television set. Deprived of normal sibling or peer relations in early childhood, this boy spent countless hours in front of the TV, and soon developed a fixation on TV commercials, reciting them endlessly. In many ways Kevin is a puzzling case, since there is no obvious cause for his psychosis. He was a physically healthy infant and remained so throughout childhood; there were no signs of neurological impairment; and he was an attractive youngster. His mannerisms and speech, however, were most abnormal, and his level of overall functioning was that of a much younger child. This case study traces Kevin's life from birth to age 15, and shows the progress and outcome of almost 10 years of therapeutic treatment.

Although his fixation on TV commercials was only one sign of Kevin's psychopathology, it was a very important one, and any significant improvement in his condition would be reflected in the elimination of this symptom. The obvious question is: Did the several years of psychiatric and psychological therapy succeed in ridding Kevin of his strange preoccupation? Kevin's case study contains the answer to this particular question but, unfortunately, it provides few, if any, answers to the baffling riddle of childhood psychosis.

Jerry showed many of the classic features of childhood psychosis. He was born to parents who were extremely intelligent, academically oriented, and professionally successful. Although they were probably not very warm, outgoing, and comforting, they were also not "pathological" in their personality makeup or in the treatment of their children. In many ways, they could be viewed as a relatively normal, stable, upper middle-class family, with no obvious basis for producing a psychotic child. Their son Jerry showed strange mannerisms and behavioral idiosyncrasies from very early life, and continued to become even more bizarre as he progressed through childhood. Preoccupied with mechanical objects, showing a great need to preserve the sameness of his surroundings, confused about his own personal identity, and using language in a repetitive, unsocialized manner, Jerry was obviously psychotic. The course of his progress is charted in the present case study, and some of the unresolved issues and perplexities of this case are discussed toward the end of the report.

The case of Larry points to important theoretical and practical issues in diagnosis and treatment of childhood psychosis. The problem of differential diagnosis is fundamental to this field, with distinctions having to be made between psychosis and mental retardation, and among the various subtypes of psychosis, including schizophrenia and infantile autism. The role of neurological impairment must also be considered in attempting to evaluate the relative contributions from psychological and biological factors. Highlighting controversial issues, asking crucial questions, but finding no adequate answers, this seems a fitting case with which to end this final section devoted to the most perplexing form of childhood psychopathology.

RECOMMENDED READING

Bettelheim, B. *The empty fortress: Infantile autism and the birth of self.* Glencoe, Ill.: Free Press, 1967.

Des Lauriers, A. M., & Carlson, C. F. *Your child is asleep: Early infantile autism.* Homewood, Ill.: Dorsey Press, 1969.

Goldfarb, W. *Childhood schizophrenia.* Cambridge, Mass.: Harvard University Press, 1961.

Rimland, B. *Infantile autism: The syndrome and its implications for a neural theory of behavior.* New York: Appleton-Century-Crofts, 1964.

Wing, L. *Autistic children: A guide for parents and professionals.* New York: Brunner-Mazel, 1972.

13. THE CASE OF KEVIN:
Fixation on TV Commercials

If permitted to do so, Kevin would spend most of his time reciting TV commercials. From the time this little boy got up in the morning until he finally went to sleep at night, he would contentedly run through his repertoire of commercials, giving a verbatim reproduction of the way he heard them on TV. Many of these were "classic" ads, such as the one referring to "Mr. Clean," but he also had memorized a great many lesser-known commercials. Anyone who had heard the commercial originally on TV could immediately recognize Kevin's replication of it. At times, being in Kevin's company was like being in a room with a TV set turned on, but with all interesting content tuned out, and only an uninterrupted string of commercials emanating from it. Although it is easy to turn off a disturbing TV set, it was unfortunately much more difficult to terminate the commercials coming from this psychotic youngster. Along with this particular preoccupation, Kevin had many other pathological characteristics that led to his being institutionalized in a child psychiatric treatment center at the age of six and one-half.

FAMILY BACKGROUND AND EARLY HISTORY

The information about Kevin's early history was obtained from his mother who was interviewed by a psychiatric social worker prior to his institutionalization. Kevin's mother was a small-framed, attractive, rather girlish woman of 27 years, whose large, almond-shaped eyes were her dominant feature. Well-groomed and tastefully dressed, she responded intelligently with thoughtfulness and deliberation. She seemed motivated to give conscientiously a complete history, but showed some reserve when discussing Kevin's father and her mother—two topics that seemed particularly conflict-ladened for her. In describing her interactions with Kevin, her closeness to him impeded her powers of observation, making it difficult to recall certain details from his early history. She expressed some guilt over her refusal to recognize Kevin's illness at an early stage of his development, but was now determined to secure as much help as possible for him in the years ahead.

Kevin's First Six Years. Kevin's mother met his father while they were attending high school. They had been going together for about two years at the time of his conception. The mother was then 20 years of age and wanted to marry Kevin's father, but he did not share this desire and she did not attempt to force him. After about four months of pregnancy she told him of her condition, and continued to go out with him until the sixth month when she left home and went to live with a friend in another state.

She concluded a normal nine-month pregnancy without complications. The total labor lasted 30 hours and was described as not being difficult, with a minimum amount of anesthesia and a normal delivery. Kevin weighed 8 pounds and 3 ounces at birth and was bottle-fed immediately, since his mother realized she probably would have to leave him with friends while she went to work. A voracious eater, Kevin cried very little and appeared to be an alert, happy baby. When seen by a visiting nurse at 12 days of age, he was said to be "very advanced for his age."

During the subsequent three months, his mother left him with her friend in the hope of making some plans for her life that would be best for both of them. This friend who took care of Kevin was described as a warm person who had raised two children of her own. For a while, Kevin's mother considered the possibility of placing him for adoption, but she was never able to follow through with this consideration. When he was three months old, his mother brought Kevin to live with her, his maternal great-grandmother, and two maternal aunts.

When Kevin was about 20 months old, his mother began weaning him to a cup; this was completed without difficulty before he reached age 3. He held his head up at age 2½ months, sat alone at 4½ months, walked at 19 months, and began to speak single words at about 9 months. Toilet training was initiated at about 1½ years, but was given up because he was rebellious and noncooperative.

Gradually, through increased understanding of his nonverbal signals, his mother was able to help him attain a satisfactory degree of toilet training, which was finally accomplished at age 5½. However, he remained persistently enuretic at night, with only occasional dry spells. Refusal to eat certain foods characterized Kevin's behavior throughout his early childhood. For example, he consistently refused eggs, cereals, all vegetables, and all soups except noodle soup.

Kevin's attention span was extremely short for all activities other than watching TV. Throughout his childhood, Kevin spent numerous hours every day and evening intently watching TV, and a major portion of his intelligible speech consisted of reciting TV commercials. Frequently he played store by himself, repeating a commercial for each product on his shelves.

He could be affectionate and at times would indicate to his mother or his aunts that he wanted to be held and cuddled. He enjoyed sitting on the laps of people he liked and frequently went to his mother for hugs and kisses. When someone read to him, Kevin would follow the spoken words with his fingers or indicate he wanted the reader to do so. He remembered many words that he read and seemed to have a phenomenal memory even without the original printed stimulation. His mother further aided his learning by pointing out simple words, objects, and names. However, unintelligible speech and noises, such as loud humming, occurred far more frequently than words or phrases used for communication. Until the age of three and one-half he communicated most frequently with single words, not using sentences prior to age four. Although Kevin was developing into a precocious reader, and at times could be affectionate, by the time he was four years old, his mother could no longer deny his obvious abnormalities, and she finally sought the help of a pediatrician. When he was enrolled in school, at the age of five, his inability to communicate and his inappropriate behavior were quickly noted by the school authorities, who recommended that the mother take him to a child guidance clinic. Actually, Kevin had been in school only three days before they referred him for psychiatric consultation. On the basis of this evaluation, Kevin was immediately diagnosed an autistic child, and residential treatment was recommended.

Kevin's Parents. Kevin's mother consistently refused to divulge the name of his father. However, she stated that he graduated from college, majoring in business administration and also earned a degree in journalism. At the time that this history was taken, Kevin's mother reported that the father was living in New York with a wife and one child. However, although she believed he was now legally married she was not positive. She described him as "an extremely intelligent, high strung, nervous individual" and also "a warm person." When she first knew him eight years previously, he had a "nervous stomach" that later developed into an ulcer.

Kevin's father had never seen him, nor had he ever expressed a wish to do so, although he asked the mother all sorts of questions about him. In describing her relationship with this father of her child, she said it was "kind of a semi-formal relationship— friendly, but not really romantic." He still telephoned her every two or three months, but she had not told him about Kevin's referral for psychiatric treatment. She was not clear in her own mind why she did not want him to know about this, but said she was afraid it might upset him and she did not want to do so. She added, however, that she no longer felt protective toward him.

Kevin's mother was the only child of a mother of Swedish-Italian descent, and a father of Irish-German descent. Her mother worked for many years as a secretary and her father had been employed by a utility company. She described her childhood as unhappy. Her father, whom she recalled only slightly, died in an auto accident when she was 3, and she and her mother went to live with her maternal grandmother. Her mother remarried when she was 9 years old, and she disliked her stepfather whom she felt rejected and ignored her. She left the new household after four weeks and returned to live with her grandmother whom she described as "a very warm, sweet person." Although she was happy with her grandmother, at the same time she found it difficult living away from her mother. In fact, she reported that the strain of this situation caused her to have an ulcer when she was 13 years old.

She was a good student in high school, making the honor roll, and participating in a variety of extracurricular activities, such as the Glee Club. She recalls this as having been a happy time of her life, enjoying popularity with both sexes and dating several boyfriends while in high school. She then went to a teacher's college, but decided after one year that she did not want to pursue a teaching career. Thus, she returned to her grandmother's home where two widowed aunts also lived and took a position as a nurse's aide in a local hospital. While working there she became pregnant with Kevin.

Kevin's mother kept house for her grandmother and two aunts, while also caring for him, until the grandmother's death. Kevin seemed to have real affection for his great-grandmother. After her death, he and his mother continued to live with the two aunts who worked in a laundry. When Kevin was placed in the residential treatment center, his mother had been seeing a psychiatric social worker for therapeutic interviews at the guidance center where Kevin had the evaluation that led to his institutionalization.

RESIDENTIAL TREATMENT

Kevin was admitted to the treatment center with the following problem behaviors.

1. Inability to communicate verbally.
2. Hyperactivity and short attention span since birth.
3. Inability to attend to personal needs.
4. Lifelong enuresis.
5. Tantrums when frustrated since age two.
6. Noisemaking such as humming and nasal sounds since age three.
7. Headbanging since age four.
8. Refusal to eat numerous foods since age four.

Psychiatric Diagnostic Evaluation. About a month after Kevin's admission to the institution, he was seen by a female staff psychiatrist for two diagnostic sessions in the playroom, separated by about a two-week interval. The following information was excerpted from this psychiatrist's mental status report.

"Kevin went fairly easily with me as he had been somewhat acquainted with me during the time he has been here. He ventured off exploring the laundry room, but most of the time he stayed close to me, often holding my hand or shoulder with a very light touch. He appears to be about the stated age of six and one-half, is quite pale and colorless, has light brown hair, is average size, and slightly built. Most of his movements are slow, somewhat delicate, and almost effeminate. He walks a little slew-footed, but shows no major abnormalities in his gait. His motor activity is highly variable, at times, when excited, jumping about, waving his arms, and showing much facial grimacing. His more usual activity, however, is to walk gingerly and slowly and to move in a seemingly aimless fashion.

"As we walked upstairs, he proceeded very slowly, taking one step at a time, placing both feet on a step before putting the first foot to the next step. He seemed to be looking off into space and was in rather poor contact with me, talking chiefly to himself. Speech was spontaneous, but scarcely in relationship to the situation about us. He was more inclined to repeat things he had heard on television, and his face had a wan smile, at times grimacing as he spoke, enunciating carefully and seemingly enjoying the sound of his voice.

"Once in the playroom, Kevin moved about in his own slow way, and did a little exploring, but most of the time he sat in a rocking chair, holding some of the things he had picked up in his initial exploration of the room. First, he favored the dollhouse bed, but this was a transient interest. He then moved across the room to a cabinet where he found a box of dominoes. As he picked out one or two, many of the others fell on the floor. Kevin seemed unconcerned, indifferent to them, and made no attempt to pick them up until much later in the hour, at which time it was a joint project. After finding the rocking chair, he established it as his headquarters. He sat in it toying with the dominoes.

"From time to time he would get up to look at or pick up something else that caught his eye, and would then return to the rocking chair, toying with what he had picked up. His feet were curled up under him and there was a quiet muttering to himself, again with a fairly happy expression, but vacant in other ways. While playing with marbles that were in the Chinese checkerboard, when some fell on the floor or got away, he looked at them but made no attempt to move or recover them. He simply sat rocking in the rocking chair, holding a domino in each hand, and looking off into space, while spouting about cake mixes, Betty Crocker, General Foods, and so forth. Off and on, throughout the hour, he often quoted advertisements he had seen and heard on TV, one of which went somewhat as follows: 'This great tasting cake mix is now available. They are yours in 16 new improved flavors.'

"At one point, Kevin picked up a book for beginning readers entitled 'Jerry and Dr. Dave.' He was able to read through it with very little help and looked through most of the pictures in the book. In looking at a picture of a boy, Jerry, having his temperature taken, Kevin made some reference to swallowing the thermometer. There was considerable concern that something might get stuck in him and not come out. He seemed to be expressing great fears about the physical examination of his body. Just as he had held the dominoes and sat rocking with them, similarly he held the book to him and hugged it, even trying to tuck it under his shirt, all the while rocking and seeming to drift off into his own fantasies.

"After these periods of rocking and preoccupation, living in his own little world, Kevin would look about, realize my presence, and begin speaking, not necessarily to me, but verbalizing some of his thoughts. Many of these were either too softly spoken or difficult to comprehend for other reasons. He seemed a little distracted by my writing, but made no comment or obvious objection to it. He made no request for things nor to leave. The rocking seemed to be a consolation to him, during which time he frequently drifted into daydreaming and was not verbal. When the time was up and I told Kevin this, he seemed to understand, gradually got up from the rocker, did not want to leave the book, but accepted that it would be on the desk the next time we came, and he left it there.

"Two weeks later when I saw Kevin again, he came along quite easily, showing no difficulty in separating from his child-care worker and the other children in his unit. In this second diagnostic session, there was somewhat more movement and greater use of materials and imperceptibly more contact with me. It was hard to say just in what way this occurred, for there was still very little contact physically or even eye-to-eye or actual conversation. But nonetheless, Kevin was interacting more with me, and seemed more alert and also more involved in the play.

"On entering the room, he picked up two books, the one he had read the week before and another book entitled 'Hurry Surry,' and sat in the rocking chair, hugging the books and rocking with them. Later, in using the doctor's kit, Kevin said, 'Hasbro's doctors' case.' The first part of the hour was occupied with his thoughts on the book about the doctor's office and the doctor kit. He called himself 'Dr. Kevin, boy doctor.' Everything that Kevin picked up to play with (books, clay, pencils, a sheet of paper, and other things) he held in his hand or in his lap as if there were no other place to set them, even though a large center table was close at hand. In this hour he used the rocking chair, two books, and later the Dr. Kildare coloring book, the doctor kit, and a small hammer which he most enjoyed. Halfway through the hour he got up and went to the dollhouse where he played with the furniture, but did little vocalizing about this activity.

"During this time I noticed not only the facial grimacing and some of the previously noted grinding of teeth, but a type of belching gurgling sounds in his throat, and bringing up air from the stomach. Kevin continued his repeating of TV commercials, including 'Send name and address and a quarter to NBC, Box 10, Detroit, Michigan for a useful color portrait.' Similarly he played with a bottle of Jergens Lotion that was in the room, squirting some of it on his hands, rubbing it slowly, delicately, and with obvious enjoyment over his fingers, his hands, his face, and even in his navel, while lying on the floor. He then repeated the commercial 'Jergens Lotion keeps your hands soft, your hands feel soft, soft as satin in seconds.' Almost all of his associations seemed to be repeats of TV commercials that had a connection with the play material or with the pictures or words in the books.

"Kevin's use of his hands is remarkable. At times, he holds or rests his chin on his lightly clenched fist, looking very much like a little old lady, his movements are delicate and careful and slow, almost rhythmic. He uses limited space and limited amount of materials in the room. He seems never hurried or particularly enthused, but goes at a very measured pace. There is an evenness and a monotony in his facial expressions, movements, amount and degree of activity in using materials. There seems to be no hurrying or intruding on his slow and consistent pace. In this hour, as in the previous one, Kevin kept the materials near him in a small sphere and had little difficulty in leaving the room at the end of the session, except for some reluctance to part with the two books and the little hammer.

"My overall psychiatric impression of him is that of an autistic child who has fairly understandable speech but does not use it for effective social communication. He is preoccupied with his own thoughts and particularly with recollection of TV, which is his only real companion. He has deficient contact with reality, shows some anxiety and fears, and tends to be compulsive and withdrawn. Even with long-term treatment of Kevin and his mother, there might well be a very limited prognosis."

Physical and Psychological Evaluations. Yearly physical examinations were performed during Kevin's four-year stay in the treatment center, and all observations and findings were essentially negative. Brain-wave recordings (EEG) also revealed no sign of abnormality. Thus, these medical examinations provided no evidence of physical or neurological impairment in this seriously disturbed youngster.

Soon after his admission, at 6½ years of age, Kevin was administered the Vineland Social Maturity Scale, obtaining an age equivalent of 3 years and 10 months, and a social development quotient of 54. On the Peabody Picture Vocabulary Test (PPVT) administered at that time, he obtained a mental age of 4 years and 1 month, and an IQ of 64. Although he was essentially untestable by standard psychological test procedures, the examining psychologist felt that both socially and intellectually Kevin was functioning at the level of a 3-year-old child.

Eighteen months later, psychological testing was again attempted, but Kevin was either unable or unwilling to perform consistently on the PPVT, and the results obtained suggested an IQ ranging from 57 to 83. On the more formal Stanford-Binet Intelligence Test administered at that time he scored in the severely retarded range, obtaining an IQ of 33. Although these results must be regarded merely as estimates, it is obvious that Kevin, who was then 8 years of age, continued to function at the level of a much younger child.

Psychotherapy. As part of an intensive treatment program, Kevin received individual psychotherapy from 3 to 5 times a week throughout the 4-year period. The following information is excerpted from reports of the female clinical psychologist who was Kevin's therapist for the first 18 months.

"Kevin exhibited all the symptoms for which he was referred, reciting commercials endlessly, waving his arms, tiptoeing, humming noises, apparent indifference to people, fearfulness, inability to interact with other children, and inability to manipulate fine objects, such as pens and pencils.

"The only entrance to Kevin's world in the beginning was through his TV commercials, which I learned and recited faithfully with him for the first five months of our contact. Gradually he became somewhat attached to me, and I was able to make certain demands on him. I started to work very directly with him by making him hold my hands, squeeze my hand, touch the snow, feel the sunlight, or talk about it. I tried to name objects that he would somehow relate to his body experiencing. He responded very well to this, and started to display slightly more self-asserting behaviors. For example, in playing ball initially he would neither throw the ball to me nor catch it, but gradually he learned to do so. However, he still remained basically unreachable.

"In the next phase I treated him like one would treat a deaf-and-dumb child to some extent. I insisted that he talk to me, that he listen to me and, when he did give verbal messages, that he speak in a loud enough tone of voice. I discouraged commercials, making it very clear to him that he was too old for this and that we would no longer indulge in it. At the same time, I also insisted that he walk on his whole foot rather than tiptoeing. I made him stop his aimless arm motions and tried to help him experience his arms as a part of his own body: I insisted that he climb the stairs in a normal fashion, placing only one foot on each step. In a sense, I began to deal more directly with the symptoms.

"When he went into a commercial, I would ask him what he said, and he would tell me, with a big grin, 'It's commercial talk,' and that he would stop doing this. He gradually began telling me what he had for breakfast and other meals, and also related to me what happened when his mother came to visit him on Saturdays. Whenever I thought that he had a particular feeling, I tried to put it into words for him, something that he responded to at least minimally. He appeared to be developing some degree of identifying certain feelings like fear and anger. I also tried to help him with his body image, by having him draw people for me. It was necessary to hold his hand while doing so, and we would identify various parts of the body in this fashion."

After 18 months of treatment, the therapist, who was then leaving the institution, wrote the following summary of progress.

"Although Kevin still shows some of the symptoms that were present when he was admitted, there seem to be a few important changes. He is less frightened and much easier to engage in realistic interpersonal conversations and interactions. He has more awareness of what is going on around him and it is much easier to bring him out of his withdrawal. His tiptoeing and arm twirling have decreased significantly, and he seems more able to respond appropriately when reminded to do so. Kevin needs a great deal of additional therapy, and he is certainly not able to function in a normal social setting. It seems that the kind of therapeutic approach that is most worthwhile with him is a semieducational one, in which he is encouraged to deal more directly with reality, helping him to build his own self-identity. One major aim is to have him obtain more of his gratifications from reality interactions with other people instead of from his own personal world. Thus far, progress has been slow but steady, and I feel that a great deal can be done for Kevin in the years ahead, providing that we integrate all our treatment resources and continue to insist that he behave more like a normal child."

Following a two-month interval without a therapist, Kevin was assigned to a male psychiatric social worker, who saw him several times a week for the remaining two years of his stay in the institution. The mode of therapy employed with Kevin remained quite consistent with that of his former therapist—emphasizing educative techniques that use every opportunity to stimulate Kevin to learn, to react, to feel, and to verbalize. The following material is taken from this therapist's summaries.

"Although Kevin was able to answer simple questions and at times seemed to pay attention, quite often he drifted off chanting commercials or flapping his hands vigorously and seemingly unaware of my presence. However, I soon learned that I could usually stop his chanting of commercials by saying rather firmly, 'No commercial talk.' After I had been seeing him for several sessions, his favorite game became playing 'secret,' which consisted of his whispering secrets in my ear and asking that I do the same to him. Usually, the secrets that he whispered were such statements as 'I want to be a baby,' 'I am a baby,' 'I am a girl,' or 'I am a flower.' When I corrected him and explained that he was not these things, he would usually smile or laugh and one almost had the feeling that he was doing this as a way of testing the reality of his own thoughts.

"On occasions when I took him off the institutional grounds, Kevin was generally quite manageable. I feel that this experience was valuable, providing him with a variety of stimuli that were not ordinarily available within the institution.

"Kevin is extremely affectionate and usually spends part of the hour sitting in my lap, putting his arms around my neck and pressing his cheek against mine. Frequently, he will touch my face, and then identify his own eyes, nose, ears and mouth. Another intense interest during his therapy hours has been reading magazines or looking at the pictures in them. I use the magazine pictures to identify various persons or objects, and try to elicit some kind of comment or reaction from Kevin concerning them. For example, whenever we come across a picture of a boy or a man, I point out to Kevin that he is also a big boy like the one in the picture, and that one day he will grow up to be a man. He seems to have learned something from this, because whenever he picks up the magazine, he usually repeats things that I have said previously about the pictures.

"The promise of candies, soda, and magazines has proved an effective reward for getting Kevin to complete various tasks (for example, printing his name and unlocking the door) and having him recount verbally certain incidents. He still drifts off, but a sharp increase in my voice or a firm tactile stimulation will bring him back to reality. If I show disappointment, he becomes acutely aware of my feeling and will yield to my request or demand with the resigned 'Okay.' He has also increased his demands on me, occasionally getting quite angry, although he follows this with apologies, such as 'I am sorry,' or 'Forget it.' Once, when we visited a store and I would not purchase an expensive toy for him, he became very upset saying, 'I hate you,' and repeating it several times. I see this ability to express negative feeling as one of the most significant changes that have occurred."

Following these lengthy periods of individual treatment with two different therapists, Kevin continued to be an extremely disturbed youngster who still harbored many of the bizarre behaviors and abnormalities that characterized him four years previously. In other words, although he had improved noticeably in certain areas, and had made many advances, he was still abnormal in almost all areas of human functioning.

Group Living and School Progress.   In his living unit composed of psychotic children, Kevin initially required considerable help and supervision from child-care workers in performing relatively simple tasks such as washing and dressing. Through their constant encouragement, however, he developed more self-help skills and gradually assumed greater responsibility for himself.

Temper tantrums, which were very prevalent in the beginning, diminished almost completely, and toward the end of his stay there was little, or no, head banging or other self-abuse when he became upset. All child-care workers who were assigned to Kevin's group reported that his frustration tolerance was noticeably higher than it had been earlier, and that he seemed to derive more enjoyment from participation in group activities, especially in the swimming pool. He became more friendly toward peers and adults, and no longer displayed excessive fears when interacting with other children. However, his peer relationships continued to lack any true spontaneity, and he never reached the level of engaging in competitive games or activities requiring cooperation and mutual participation.

In the dining room, Kevin began to eat a greater variety of foods, especially vegetables, which he formerly avoided completely. The tiptoeing and arm flapping that were so prevalent during the first year or so of his stay gradually decreased, although they were still displayed whenever he became excited. And "the commercial talk" that he showed upon admission still constituted a large part of his behavioral repertoire at the time of his discharge.

Several different psychotropic medications were tried with Kevin at various times during his four-year stay at the treatment center, in an attempt to decrease anxiety and control his bizarre symptoms. In general, however, drug therapy did not appreciably alter Kevin's psychotic behavior.

Throughout his stay in the treatment center, Kevin was enrolled in a special educational program for psychotic children, receiving both individual and group instruction geared to children with severe learning disabilities. Much of the initial work by the teacher was devoted to establishing a relationship with Kevin, and eventually he became able to spend 30 minutes each day in this nursery school program working on structured activities such as drawing pictures, building blocks, or cutting pictures. At times Kevin resisted any attempts to get him to focus on the material in front of him, and he would react with temper tantrums and emotional outbursts. Eventually, however, some positive changes were noted. He began to scribble more meaningful lines and pictures, his chanting of commercials diminished somewhat, and his verbalization of feelings and emotions increased. But his attention span and concentration remained very short, and he was easily distracted by external and internal stimuli. After he had been in this special education setting for about three years, Kevin appeared noticeably more controlled and could more often be found sitting quietly in the classroom. When doing so, however, he seemed in a daze, often muttering commercials in a barely audible fashion, almost as if he were saying them to himself. Thus, using Kevin's school performance as an indicator, improvement in his personal, intellectual, and social development was very limited.

Psychiatric Casework with Kevin's Mother.   Kevin's mother was seen each Saturday on a weekly basis throughout Kevin's treatment by a male psychiatric social worker. Initially, she appeared as a depressed, angry, highly defensive woman beset by many guilt feelings about her child's illness and her involvement in it. She frequently related that she had kept Kevin at home with her for six years, not seeking help for him, although she recognized that he was disturbed. At first she approached this institution suspiciously, inquiring in specific detail into the routine of Kevin's daily activities and treatment. She also continued to have casework interviews with a social worker at the referring agency, and attempted to control the present interviews by remarking that she had already discussed these matters with the other social worker, implying that immoderate demands were being made by asking her to repeat confidential things that she had discussed in the other setting. After several phone calls and a meeting with the social worker at the other institution, it was decided that Kevin's mother would cease her contact with that guidance center and depend solely on this instiution for her casework.

She then became better able to use these therapeutic sessions to increase her understanding of Kevin, and also to feel less guilty and depressed about his plight in life. She frequently mentioned feeling drained after her visits with Kevin. Unrealistically expecting great changes each week, she became frustrated and annoyed whenever Kevin did not achieve or perform up to her expectations, and often when she returned home on Saturday she would sleep all day Sunday, barely managing to recover from her visit by Tuesday. Then, once again, she repeated the cycle of building her hopes and anticipations for the next visit.

The mother also used casework to help herself understand her tremendous dependency and inability to support herself. Several months after Kevin's institutionalization, with the social worker's encouragement, his mother accepted employment near her home in a small restaurant. This was the first time she had been employed since her pregnancy with Kevin. Although continuing with this job, she felt frustrated by it and expressed the need for more of a challenge, but did not yet have sufficient psychological strength to move on to bigger and better things. One can notice a perceptible masochistic core in her behavior, with her recognizing that she is worth more, but having a need to punish herself. For over seven years, she accepted $40 monthly payments from Kevin's father, but recently she informed him to stop sending this money because she did not need or want it. There was obviously an element of anger in this refusal, as she seemed to still have considerable feeling for this man who was now married with a family of his own. By rejecting his assistance, she was hurting herself as well as psychologically punishing the father. In some distorted way, it may also have served to keep alive her hope that someday this man who had wronged her would return and make things right.

Mother's inability to accept limitations in others and her perfectionistic approach to people were revealed in her remarks about her own mother whom she blamed for abandoning her when she was a child. While admitting that she had been unwilling to accept the stepfather her mother had chosen, she now maintained she should have been forced to stay in her mother's home, and should have been punished for resisting. Thus, the need for punishment and desire for strong maternal control appears to go all the way back to childhood, indicative perhaps of unresolved conflicts deriving from her father's death when she was in the midst of the Oedipal struggles described by Freud.

Toward the end of this lengthy period of casework treatment, her self-concept was much more positive, with increased independence and ability to make her own decisions. In fact, she began attending night school to attain secretarial skills that she hoped would eventually enable her to secure more satisfying employment. She still questioned her ability to be an adequate mother, and wondered if underneath Kevin's strange behavior there might be a suppressed rage similar to that which she harbored toward her mother. At the time of his discharge, she realized that he would have to be institutionalized elsewhere, since she could not possibly provide the kind of care and constant supervision that he still needed.

Discharge Diagnosis and Prognosis. The etiology of Kevin's difficulties remained baffling even after years of intensive study and treatment. Neurological components do not appear as major determinants, and his life history reveals no clues other than inconsistent mothering and possible separation trauma in infancy. Uncertain that she wanted to keep him, Kevin's mother was emotionally unresponsive during his early years of life. It could be speculated that Kevin's autistic denial of the world symbolically reflects his mother's denial of his existence.

Regardless of the original "cause" of this childhood psychopathology, Kevin remained a severely disturbed boy in need of continued individual psychotherapy and therapeutic group living, hopefully preventing further withdrawal and isolation from his environment. His formal psychiatric diagnosis at the time of discharge from the treatment center was "schizophrenic reaction, childhood type," and the prognosis, even with further intensive care, was "guarded." Thus, in spite of the best efforts of a host of mental health professionals, this psychotic youngster faced rather dim prospects for the years ahead.

SUBSEQUENT ADJUSTMENT AND
LONGER-RANGE OUTCOME

Following 4 years at the residential treatment center, and now 10½ years of age, Kevin was discharged to another private child treatment center. He remained there for approximately one year, and showed relatively little improvement in that setting. The following year, he was transferred to the children's unit in a large state mental hospital and, at the age of 15, he was still in that institution. A college senior who spent a summer working in Kevin's unit, supplied us with additional information based on hospital records.

On admission, Kevin showed a good vocabulary and was able to read difficult material, although he was unable to answer questions about the content of the passages he read. He had adequate self-help skills, although occasionally he was nocturnally enuretic. His affect was very flat, and he was placed in the autistic unit with the diagnosis "schizophrenia, childhood type, with autism."

Two years after his admission, he was transferred to a cottage for seriously disturbed boys. Kevin did not like his new environment and showed his displeasure by urinating on the rugs, and purposely dropping his meal tray. He did not talk to the other children or to staff members, but recited TV commercials and bits of TV cartoons to himself. He carried a small paper bag around with him, hitting it gently on walls and furniture. Kevin isolated himself from the other boys and did not challenge them when they took his bag or hit him. He had to be forced to engage in any form of group activity. For several months, he was administered psychotropic drugs, but with little beneficial effects.

At the age of 14, after being in this state hospital for about 2½ years, Kevin took to carrying around "a red thing," a three-dimensional piece of red plastic that was part of a toy-building set. The other boys enjoyed stealing or hiding the red thing, to which Kevin sometimes reacted with appropriate anger, but more often with passivity or quiet tears. The red things, of which his therapist had a large supply, were of different sizes, and each had a tiny number inside that would easily escape notice. But Kevin had memorized the numbers on each red thing, and would ask for each when required to do so in order to obtain it, by saying, for example, "May I have number 20 red thing please?"

At the time of the most recent follow-up evaluation, Kevin was just turning 15 years of age, and had grown into a very large boy (5 feet 10 inches, 170 pounds), although he gave an impression of extreme flabbiness and lethargy. He walked in a disorganized and uncoordinated manner with his arms and legs very loose. When forced to run or when excited, he flapped his arms and hands at head level, increasing stimulation from his body. He was receiving no medication, and a recent EEG recording again showed all patterns within normal limits.

Much of Kevin's time was spent by himself, sleeping, sitting and staring, or holding the red thing. His favorite activity was still watching TV. If left alone, he would watch quietly until a commercial came on, and then recite along with the TV in a loud voice, jumping and flapping in excitement. If bothered by the other boys who often said, "Kevin is crazy!," he would watch the TV from a distance. He would also recite commercials when not actually watching TV, and imitate Bugs Bunny ("What's up Doc?") and Tweedy Bird ("I taught I taw a puddy tat.") These recitations made him very happy and excited, accompanied by smiles, jumping and wild flapping.

Kevin continued to have a very good vocabulary, but only engaged in interpersonal conversations when spoken to first, usually responding with a flat tone and dull expression. He hummed in a monotone constantly as if to block out the world. A typical conversation with Kevin might go as follows:

> *Staff Member:* "How do you feel, Kevin?"
> *Kevin:* "Mmm . . ."
> *Staff Member:* "How do you feel, Kevin?"
> *Kevin:* "Fine thank you. Mmm. What's up, Doc? Mmm . . ."
> *Staff Member:* "Where is the red thing? (He produces it from under shirt) What red thing is it?"
> *Kevin:* "Mmm . . . Jim Gibbs, wethead, Jim Gibbs, the dry look, Mmm. . . ."
> *Staff Member:* "No, Kevin, what red thing is it?"
> *Kevin:* "Mmm . . . Number 8. Mmm. . . ."

Thus, it was still much easier for Kevin to absorb passively information from the TV rather than actively engaging in interpersonal conversation. And even when he did converse, his verbalizations were often stock phrases or repetitions, and not original speech expressing thought.

When deprived of something he wanted, Kevin would bang his head against the wall or hit himself in the temples with the back of his wrist, while crying and asking for what he wanted. On one occasion, some of the boys were being taken to the Dairy Queen and Kevin said he did not want to go but, as soon as they had left, he wanted to go. When told that he could not go because he had already said that he did not want to, Kevin began a tantrum, yelling "I want a D.Q.," and "I want my mommy," while hitting himself on the head. These outbursts were dealt with by putting Kevin in the isolation room, under watch, removing the possibility that social reinforcement for his behavior might occur, and he usually quieted down within a few minutes.

Although Kevin usually avoided interacting with the other boys, his constant humming and recitation of commercials annoyed them, and his passivity and bizarre behavior made him a favorite target for their mischief and aggression. They frequently hit him and took his red thing, but he rarely retaliated. It was pitiful to see a huge 15-year-old boy being bullied by a tiny 8-year-old. Whenever Kevin did fight back, the staff members rewarded him with praise and encouragement.

In school Kevin withdrew from the situation into mumbling if not given individual attention. He could read any material presented to him when encouraged, but without comprehension. He had no number concepts and, with the exception of vocabulary development, he functioned on a nursery-school level. Kevin received individual psychotherapy, with a male psychologist, twice a week in the playroom. At first, he was conditioned to perform some interpersonal tasks to obtain a soap dish, which he liked to hold because, according to Kevin, it made him feel strong. M & M's were used as rewards to establish quiet sitting and eye-to-eye contact. After the sitting behavior had been strongly established, it became possible to stop Kevin's tantrums by telling him to sit down and fold his hands. Rewarding successively longer commercial-free intervals with presentation of a red thing greatly diminished that behavior. The red thing also was used as a reinforcer to teach Kevin left and right, and as a reward for doing exercises to enhance his body image.

In view of the minimal therapeutic gains realized at this stage of Kevin's existence, now a psychotic adolescent, he will probably require some form of supervision the rest of his life. If his bizarre behaviors can be further eliminated, with the proper training, he might possibly become capable of working and living under supervision in a sheltered environment. At this point, however, the likelihood of even this degree of further improvement does not seem probable. It is most depressing to realize that in spite of his early and continued treatment, using the best psychiatric facilities and treatment methods currently available, it was impossible to effect sufficient positive changes that would enable Kevin to function as a contributing member of society.

14. THE CASE OF JERRY:
Schizophrenia of Childhood

"To whom it may concern: Have you replaced the elevator in the main building or is it still the same one? If it is the same one, when will you replace it? If it is still the same one, I would like you to replace it. Love, Jerry."

The above note was written when Jerry was 22 years of age, a resident of a state hospital in the Midwest.

BACKGROUND AND EARLY HISTORY

When Jerry's parents were married, his mother had just graduated from college, and his father was working on his doctorate in comparative linguistics, in a prominent ivy league university. Both parents, then, were intelligent and well educated. Mother, who was the youngest of two, had been a conforming girl until her senior year in college, at which time apparently she became somewhat more rebellious, resisted attendance at classes, and so on. She was given psychological counseling, calmed down, and completed not only college but subsequently obtained a master's degree in education. Father's family background was somewhat less serene, in that his parents had been separated for quite some time, and he stayed with his mother through adolescence. His educational career was interrupted by having to work several years, and having to spend some time in military service.

Both parents were quite verbally articulate. Father, a rather tall, thin, very "collegiate" looking person, appeared somewhat detached and impersonal, but certainly well-versed in psychiatric terminology and knowledge of residential treatment centers when the parents referred Jerry for inpatient consideration. By that time, when Jerry was almost nine, mother had, as a result of consultation with a psychology instructor, decided to seek psychotherapy for personal problems. She seemed to be having conflict with her role as a wife and mother, and some difficulty with her husband. She also seemed to convey to her therapist a relative lack of acceptance of Jerry, with greater acceptance of his two younger sisters.

Jerry was born slightly one year after his parents' marriage. The prenatal, perinatal, and neonatal period of his life were unremarkable. His developmental schedule was normal as far as is known, except for some delay in the onset of speech. No difficulty was reported in feeding or toilet training.

By the age of one, his parents noted that Jerry tended to ignore people. He never looked others in the face. Friends of the family at one point asked whether he might have some difficulty in hearing. In retrospect, mother and father thought that Jerry was a very placid baby, and they referred to baby pictures of him as showing an unhappy, withdrawn child with "a haunting look."

Interestingly, the parents look back on Jerry's earliest years as being happy ones for them. Father had not only completed his doctoral program, but had moved to a full-time faculty position in the Midwest. There was now a greater degree of economic stability for the family.

Not until age three did the parents become genuinely concerned that something might be wrong and that Jerry might require some kind of treatment. He had continued to ignore people, including his parents, and his new sister who was born when he was three and one-half. Although Jerry began speaking around age three, he did not use meaningful sentences until he was about four. The main concern, however, was his hyperactivity and increasingly inappropriate behavior. Jerry was preoccupied with fans, elevators, sliding and revolving doors, and other mechanical objects, all of this to the exclusion of the normally expected interest in people. When taken downtown, he would readily slip away from his parents, searching madly for new fans and elevators, running off to visit a favorite elevator in a building. With the development of speech, Jerry showed somewhat more interest in people, especially his parents, but his focus continued to be on the mechanical objects that had been his interest since he had been about six months of age. He engaged in repetitive questioning on the details, for example, of whether a particular elevator in a particular store had a gate as well as doors, whether it was operated by hand or by buttons.

During his fifth year, Jerry began twice weekly outpatient psychotherapy that continued for about two years. His therapist considered him "autistic." Some improvement in his ability to relate to others was noted, but he still seemed to be markedly deficient in this regard.

By the age of six, it was clear that Jerry could not attend public school because of his inappropriateness and hyperactivity. He received schooling at home for an hour a day, five days a week, and appeared to be making fairly good progress. He seemed to be bright, but it was questioned whether he was comprehending what he was studying or merely memorizing it.

In view of their continuing difficulty in managing Jerry, despite his having received intensive psychotherapy, and on the advice of a psychiatrist, the parents made referral for residential treatment early in Jerry's ninth year.

EVALUATIONS, TREATMENT, AND OUTCOME

When the parents brought Jerry for admission to residential treatment, they had by now, through their general education, through their specific concerns about their son, and through discussions with mental health professionals, developed a considerable repertoire of knowledge about the field. It was noticed that while mother appeared to be warm, intelligent, and highly sophisticated, and was cooperative, she tended not to volunteer very much to the intake social worker. She had dwelled on her son's difficulties for so long that her verbal facilities and conceptualizing abilities permitted her to present material in very abstract terms. Father was also described as "impressive in his psychiatric vocabulary, knowledge of residential treatment centers, and acquaintance with the literature on childhood schizophrenia. His speech was animated, but presented in an impersonal, detached way, on a theoretical, almost professional level."

At the time of admission, at this particular institution, mothers of patients were routinely administered a battery of psychological tests. Jerry's mother scored intellectually in the superior range. In terms of personality dynamics, she generally attempted to avoid emotional expression. "Under this defensiveness, there was much hostility, especially in relation to unresolved conflicts with parents, and in this regard her own mother in particular." She employed the defenses of intellectualization and denial, and sublimated her strivings for independence and achievement through impersonal, intellectual pursuits. There was a conflict between aggression versus submission, and she exerted rigid control over her feelings. It appeared that she had not fully accepted her role as a woman and as a mother, but she did have some capacity for affective relationships. When her Rorschach inkblot test responses were scored according to a scheme to predict whether the subject would be capable of positive gains through psychiatric casework, Mother was rated in the positive movement category.

Because of the distance from their home, parents were not seen actively in intensive casework at the treatment center. They did have monthly contacts with a local social worker with the aim of helping them accept the idea of long-term treatment for Jerry. They visited for about a week at a time each summer during the four years that Jerry was in treatment.

Officially, the chief complaints concerning Jerry at the time of referral were:

1. Indifference to people since birth.
2. Preoccupation with mechanical objects since the age of six months.
3. Hyperactivity in public places from about three years of age.
4. Inappropriate behavior in the community, such as collecting all the doormats in the neighborhood, since about the age of three.

When Jerry arrived at the residential treatment center, he was a withdrawn boy who was extremely preoccupied with fans, elevators, locks, music boxes, and women's purses, for example. He generally related to adults by getting them to draw pictures of the above-mentioned objects. He would repeat over and over again questions about inanimate objects, and would become clinging, whining, and upset when the adult could not give an answer. Ultimately, Jerry might resort to jumping up and down, spinning in circles, or trying to bite the hand of the adult. He would ask whether he was good or bad, a boy or a girl, and why the adult did not like him.

Jerry was unable to tie his shoes or make his bed when he

arrived. He was distracted and preoccupied, and needed constant direction to dress himself. In the course of treatment his self-care skills improved greatly, so that he was able to wash, make his bed, dress himself, and tie his shoes with less need for reminders. Initially, he was very compulsive about cleaning himself. If he spilled something on his shirt, he would take off the shirt altogether. After a year, Jerry became completely the opposite; indeed, he became impossible to keep clean. Eventually, there was more of a "happy medium." Actually, Jerry really never seemed to care how he looked in the eyes of others.

He was completely toilet trained when he arrived, but he became terribly anxious and confused when he needed to make a bowel movement and to urinate at the same time. He would run to the adult in a panic, crying, asking if he were a boy or a girl. His reasoning was that a boy urinates standing up, a girl sitting down. Therefore, if he sat down for a bowel movement and urinated at the same time, he might be a girl. From the outset, while Jerry generally accepted reassurance that he was a boy, this had to be repeated again and again.

Socially, Jerry had very limited interaction. His play experiences were minimal and repetitious. He preferred adults, and those who were familiar rather than strangers. He frequently would ask adults to draw pictures of locks or elevators. He liked to have a considerable degree of sameness in everything—schedules not to be changed, appointments not to be missed—and would become highly anxious if these things would happen.

When Jerry was first tested psychologically, he had on the Wechsler Intelligence Scale for Children (WISC) a verbal IQ of 95, a performance IQ of 89, and a full scale IQ of 91, which indicated that his intellectual level was generally average, but that he was quite inconsistent. However, that he was able to score even average indicated some ego strength, and suggested a greater potential for improvement than if he had been completely untestable.

The psychologist at the time noted Jerry's extreme distractability, his opening of every drawer in the desk, turning light switches on and off, and his particular fascination with the electric fan. The examiner had to bring Jerry back to the office and hold him in his lap with one arm while trying to test him with the other. Jerry was very anxious in dealing with the personality projective tests. He showed a severe problem in testing reality, and had a very high level of anxiety, and defective socialization. The psychologist noted that Jerry "seems to have a relatively good prognosis for children of this type, in that he can function as well as he does intellectually and in certain behavioral areas."

Jerry was tested four other times during his inpatient treatment, showing great variability in his results intellectually. Actually, at the time of his last testing, in his last year of residency, Jerry obtained a full-scale IQ of 83 on the WISC, which shows a drop from earlier levels. In each of the intervening testings, Jerry showed improvements in being less distractable, less anxious, and more able to accept the requirements of staying in the situation and responding more appropriately. During the second evaluation, Jerry did not seem to be as threatened by the unstructured material presented to him, but he still had a tremendous problem in reality testing, and gave inappropriate, bizarre responses, typical of schizophrenic contamination. He was, however, beginning to become more relaxed and showed better awareness, and did not seem to have as much need for compulsive control.

On the third occasion of testing, again less anxiety was evident in Jerry, and less direct support was needed to get into the testing. He was beginning to show the inkling of real concern with other people, and a more realistic awareness of the world.

At the time of the last testing, it appeared that while his IQ scores were lower, Jerry seemed to understand and find more meaningful that which he could do. Socially he appeared immature and dependent and operated mainly on an individual level and mostly with the people most meaningful to him. Overtly, he still was rather rigid and compulsive in his approach to demands. There was a decrease noted in the idiosyncratic ideation, and he appeared less fearful and preseverative. The psychologist summarized, "One must say that Jerry remains basically with the same problems he had on admission, but with a difference in that he can overcome, or bypass, them to some extent, and begin to relate more adequately to the world around him. Although his prognosis must necessarily remain guarded, one can foresee some possibility of Jerry's eventually being able to relate, if only marginally, to a limited but noninstitutional environment."

In treatment, within the therapeutic milieu and small group living, as mentioned above, Jerry did have a good deal of help and showed improvement in the area of self-care. Various psychotropic medications were tried at different times, but no benefit appeared to accrue from these and, ultimately, they were discontinued altogether. Jerry also received education, but from the beginning was unable to adapt to a classroom situation with other children. He was usually taught through hourly individual sessions. When he arrived he was able to read, and he continued to be fairly active in reading. His problem, however, was in comprehension. It took several years for Jerry to be able to comprehend what he had been reading and memorizing so literally. By the time of his discharge, when he was 12½ years old, and chronologically might have been completing the seventh grade, he scored an overall battery medium on the Stanford Achievement Test of 4.7. His word-meaning score was 1½ years higher than his paragraph meaning score, and his spelling, at 6.5, was highest of all.

Jerry was seen by a staff psychiatrist approximately three times per week for the entire hospitalization. In his first year of treatment, Jerry seemed to be very anxious from the outset. He engaged in many compulsive mechanisms, such as naming objects over and over, spelling the names of objects over and over, and opening and closing doors and drawers. He was preoccupied with toilets, and would take his therapist with him to check on the status of toilets throughout the building. He continued his preoccupation with fans, radiators, and elevators.

Ultimately, Jerry began asking his therapist to draw objects in which he was interested, and this activity, the therapist drawing, persisted during every session even up to the time of discharge. By that time, Jerry's therapist felt that "Will you draw for me?," had come to mean, "Do you love me?" Drawing became, in the early months, the main means of communication between Jerry and the therapist. Jerry would not converse. His therapist, partly to relieve the monotony of repetitively drawing the same things hour after hour, began to invent new kinds of locks, doors, elevators, for example, to draw.

Jerry also began to indicate his concern about what went on in the bathroom. He insisted that, as far as he was concerned, the only bathroom activity he engaged in was brushing his teeth. He needed much reassurance that it was all right to be curious about behavior in the bathroom and about differences between male and female. He also had to be reassured that his interest in electric fans would not lead to getting his fingers chopped off. Gradually, Jerry formed a strong dependent relationship with the therapist, so that cancelled appointments greatly increased Jerry's anxiety.

In subsequent months, Jerry occasionally appeared to be close to dropping his compulsive defense of repetitious drawings through the therapist. Occasionally, he would ask the therapist to draw something else other than locks and doors. When the therapist drew a coat or a bathing suit, Jerry frequently became too frightened, and in a panic he would ask the therapist to erase those drawings.

During the second year of treatment, several months passed during which Jerry appeared to be more anxious and began resisting appointments, and if he did come to the appointment, he spent most of the time in the adjoining bathroom. He talked about "eating up" his therapist, wondered if he were a boy or a girl, and asked, regarding all the other children in the institution, whether they were boys or girls. Reassured that he, himself, was a boy, he still seemed anxious. Eventually, the therapist recognized that Jerry's wish was to be a girl and after this was voiced by the therapist and acknowledged by Jerry, Jerry sat in the therapist's lap "drinking soda from a bottle warmed on the radiator." He then expressed interest in the therapist's family, children, and home. The therapist recognized Jerry's fantasies and pointed out that Jerry could not be the therapist's son, even though they did like each other.

As months passed into years, Jerry became very close to his therapist, very dependent, and somewhat less anxious. Requests for compulsive drawings almost disappeared, but generally the therapist had to draw a few things at the beginning of each hour. Jerry's interest shifted somewhat from fans and elevators to more oral items, such as tarts, sweet rolls, maple syrup, all to be drawn by the therapist. Occasionally, Jerry could inquire about the principles behind the operation of gadgets, but this reality interest was infrequent. The therapist noted, "Slightly increased tension will easily throw Jerry back into asking compulsive, repetitious questions about fans, record players, door locks, etc." Eventually, in the sessions the therapist was able to point out that Jerry would resort to these compulsive questions because he was upset, and it was often possible for Jerry to tell what it was he was upset about. It was noted that Jerry's "awareness of other people and social situations had greatly increased." Although he was still extremely fearful interpersonally, there was slow turning toward reality and the formation of object relations.

Adults gradually were able to discourage Jerry's requests that they all draw and he accepted this, perhaps because his therapist took over this function for him. Although Jerry could engage in some play, such as with blocks, and some group games such as bingo, he was not really interested in arts or crafts nor in other children. He generally preferred to stay alone, outdoors, curled up with a Sears-Roebuck catalog. He would play no games that involved physical contact.

Jerry would approach strangers by asking "What is your name?" but he preferred to stay with familiar adults to whom he could cling and seek dependent-need gratification. He generally remained more fearful of physically large and strong-looking adults, as if he expected to be hurt. He would seek less threatening-looking adults for protection. When Jerry knew that the adult understood him and could control him, he felt more at ease. He even became able to accept constructive criticism when it was offered in a non-threatening way.

Each time his parents visited, they seemed very pleased with the greater reality orientation that Jerry showed. On one of these visits, during the third summer in treatment, while on a visit to town, Jerry ran away, ran into a store and got on an elevator. He was ultimately found by the police, and taken to police head-quarters where he, typically, became preoccupied with the elevator in the station. When visitors came to the institution, he would always try to go through women's pocketbooks. Whenever there were community activities, such as trick-or-treating at Halloween, Jerry would take the open door as an invitation to come in and inspect kitchen fans, locks on doors, and so forth.

In the last year of treatment, during a visit, Jerry's younger sister said, apropos of his request for a ride on the elevator, "Jerry, don't act that way any more, because you are 11 now." And Jerry responded by acting more appropriately.

At his first staff conference, the diagnosis made was "schizo-phrenia, childhood type." This diagnosis was never changed. In trying to determine the etiology of Jerry's disorder, the possibility of hereditary or organic components was raised, but with little to support it. On the other hand, it seemed more reasonable to suspect that Jerry's disability was related to environmental variables; consequently, the role of his parents was examined in detail. For some people on the staff, these parents appeared to be of the "Kanner-type," that is, both intellectual and relatively lacking in affective expression. Father had been struggling to pursue an academic career, mother had indicated she had not had a warm relationship with her own mother, and she had reported that as an infant Jerry was restricted because they lived in an apartment where he was not allowed to make noise. However, the view of these parents was inconsistent, because other people noted that when mother was seen at the institution, she seemed to be a much warmer and more likable person, who was well-intentioned, and who on departure was moved to tears in leaving her son behind. Also, in the first year of Jerry's life both parents described themselves as being happy, economically secure, and sociable with friends. In addition, the parents were the ones who first recognized that something was wrong with their child. Although mother felt she did not get much from her mother, she nonetheless was able to give of herself to her daughters, who appeared quite normal. In contrast to any feelings they had of rejecting Jerry, the question arose concerning the impact of a basically unresponsive child on his parents, leading to their withdrawal of unrewarded affective overtures. Indeed, it was difficult to recognize severe disturbance in these parents that could account for such a profound problem in their child.

In subsequent staff conferences the question of etiology again arose, and ultimately elicited the statement, "In the final analysis, we must frankly admit we don't know."

In each year of treatment Jerry's progress was slow. He was less socially withdrawn and showed greater awareness of his surroundings in all areas. However, there was guarded optimism about future improvement. Notable was the extreme interest in and amount of effort of staff at all levels in trying to help Jerry.

As Jerry's time at the hospital drew to a close, it was clear that he would need further placement, and by now his parents recognized the need for continuing placement away from home. At the last staff conference, it was expected that "Jerry will be able to live in a protected environment outside an institution, but not as a self-sufficient member of society."

Jerry's therapist summed up, "After four years of psychother-apy, Jerry is still psychotic, but less bizarre and withdrawn." On his last day in the hospital, Jerry, "in a very appropriate way promised to write and promised to visit."

FOLLOW-UP NOTES

Jerry left the institution at the age of 12½. He was immediately enrolled in a residential center which worked with adolescents, where he visited home twice a year. At the age of 16, approximately 4 years after he had left the first residential treatment center, Jerry returned for a visit. It had been determined that Jerry was functioning at a fourth-grade level academically, and that his reading and English were considered to be very good. He seemed to be more verbal, and more eager to visit his home. Jerry spent about 1½ hours checking all the fans from the service building right up to the third floor of the main building and also checking all the record players in the children's living units. He had his dinner with the "Golden Eagles", his old living group and, before he sat down, he wanted to know whether, if he ate at their table, he would become a "Golden Eagle." The adult reassured him that he would not become a "Golden Eagle" again. Jerry appeared to remember many of the staff, but he did not seem to be interested in people overall. He moved quickly and, as mentioned, was espe-cially interested in checking some of his former preoccupations. Father, who had brought him for the visit, was very pleased at the way Jerry was coming along.

Jerry's gains at the second treatment center were insufficient to enable him to return to community living. In addition, he had now reached the age limit in terms of support for special educa-tional placement for emotionally disturbed children, according to the rules of his state. His parents reluctantly recognized that they could not provide for him or his needs in the home, nor did they have sufficient financial means to place him in a private institution. Consequently, he was admitted to a state hospital, from which, at the encouragement of a psychiatric aide, Jerry printed in childish form the letter that introduces this report.

COMMENTARY

Whenever the concept of schizophrenia of childhood is employed, questions of causality inevitably arise. In Jerry's case, the staff of mental health professionals were in some disagreement on etiology, and ultimately felt that they really did not have the answer. One might consider a biogenetic agent as creating a dysfunctional infant, since there were early attempts on the part of the parents to attempt to cope with this puzzling and unresponsive child, and in view of the presence of two apparently healthy siblings. However, at the time, there were no data that could support such a hypothesis. The people who seek to find the answer in terms of child-rearing practices might consider whether these were really schizophrenogenic parents. Although in some ways they appear to resemble the "Kanner-type" of parents, with their high intelligence, and high level of education and sophistication, they did not impress everyone so convincingly as being cold and unable to give emotionally. Even if they were somewhat resentful and unemotional with Jerry, the years in which they might have reached out to him, with no rewarding response in return, could well have accounted for their subsequent attitudes and behavior toward him. In the course of treatment, the parents never attempted in any way to undermine, undo, or interfere with treatment efforts or recommendations. They were generally pleased with his progress.

Jerry himself certainly demonstrated some of the frequently mentioned hallmarks of the schizophrenic child. A typical characteristic is the withdrawal from social interaction, although Jerry's behavior did not approach the extreme of that withdrawal as seen in the mute, "autistic" child. Jerry's bizarre preoccupations, especially his preoccupation with inanimate, mechanical objects is also common in this disorder. Jerry employed compulsive, repetitive, stereotyped behaviors, which appeared to come into play when he became anxious. He also had a great need for sameness, and unexpected changes caused him to experience considerable anxiety.

Jerry's functioning revealed many primitive elements. His anxiety was not that of a neurotic, but was "primary anxiety," because he lacked ego boundaries, felt greatly threatened by the world around him, feared his own impulses, and was confused about his identity, not only in terms of male and female, but in terms of animate versus inanimate. In the course of therapy, Jerry's confusions about his identity were pronounced, and he also displayed anxiety over his primitive, infantile wish to incorporate orally his therapist.

Despite all of these pathological symptoms, Jerry was likable, and elicited affection and perseverance from all levels of a very devoted staff. Still, despite the intensive and comprehensive treatment afforded, and what must be considered remarkable progress relative to his condition when first brought to our attention, Jerry remained a severely disturbed and psychotic individual. This is an not uncommon result in the treatment of schizophrenia of childhood. This does raise questions concerning the commitment of precious professional time and effort to this kind of individual treatment, and the allocation of limited financial resources. It might be argued that out of such efforts and expenditures comes greater understanding but, all too often, as in Jerry's case, we are left with more questions than answers. Although schizophrenia in children may be fascinating to study, attempting to treat this disorder can be extremely frustrating in the long run.

15. THE CASE OF LARRY:
Psychogenesis Versus Biogenesis

The purpose of this case study is not primarily to provide clarification concerning Larry's condition but rather to exemplify fundamental aspects of a current controversy pertaining to psychotic children. More specifically, this case provides an empirical basis for discussing certain theoretical issues relevant to the etiology and diagnosis of childhood psychosis. In this report there is some inconsistency in the use of various diagnostic terms, since they are used in keeping with conflicting etiological positions that are advanced at different points in the presentation.

PRESENTING SYMPTOMS AND DIAGNOSIS

Larry was a 5½-year-old boy who had been in residential treatment, in a special program for autistic children, for approximately one year. The chief complaints at the time of his admission were:

1. Inability to relate appropriately to adults and children since age 2 or even younger (he ignores people, shuts out what they say, and appears nonreactive to social stimuli).
2. Delayed speech development noted since 2 years of age (vocabulary of single words, a few short phrases, and jibberish jargon).
3. Odd behaviors noted since 14 months of age (twirling, hand flicking, preseverative interests and activities.)

Thus, this boy evidenced the kinds of abnormalities that are often characteristic of psychotic children. During the first 4 years of life Larry was examined by various psychologists, psychiatrists, pediatricians, and neurologists. On occasion he was diagnosed as an autistic child, but some examiners also noted that he seemed to have some form of organic handicap.

In reviewing this case at a staff conference, it seemed as though the diagnostic material could lend itself quite easily to either a psychodynamic interpretation or an organic interpretation depending on the theoretical preference of the clinician. Here we will view the case from two different perspectives: first, making a case for psychogenic causation and, second, attempting to establish a case for biogenic causation. The aim of this intellectual exercise is to demonstrate how easy it would be to derive conflicting interpretations from the same factual body of case material.

LARRY FROM THE PSYCHOGENIC VIEWPOINT

This boy had shown numerous psychoticlike features since he was two years old. His twirling, hand flicking, preoccupation with sameness, inappropriate use of language, and withdrawal from social contacts, are major symptoms found frequently in psychotic children.

Parents of schizophrenic children are often highly intelligent, and this is certainly the case with Larry's parents. On the Wechsler Adult Intelligence Scale, Larry's mother obtained an IQ of 130 and his father obtained an even higher IQ of 144. Thus, both parents test intellectually in the very superior range. Moreover, both of them are well-educated. The mother is a college graduate, and the father holds a master's degree in physics. Kanner, Bettelheim, and other authorities in this field of childhood psychosis have noted that not only are the parents usually very bright, but also the fathers are often scientists of a variety similar to Larry's father. Thus, on the basis of IQ, education, and occupation, this family seems ideally suited to exemplify parents of a schizophrenic child.

Several social workers have noted that these parents, especially the mother, seem cold and aloof. Statements contained in the case record indicate that this mother seemed to feel more comfortable not having Larry around, and that she found it very difficult to relate to him. This description of her as a distant, cold, reserved woman fits exactly with descriptions of the so-called "schizophrenogenic mother" that appeared in the literature some years ago. Consistent with this interpretation is the observation that Larry seemed to relate much better to males than to females. When his mental status was assessed by a female psychiatrist, he appeared particularly disturbed. However, when he was administered psychological tests by a male examiner, he appeared to be much more comfortable and less anxious, and performed at a noticeably higher level. Similarly, throughout his institutionalization he seemed to form better relations with male child-care workers than with female workers. These clinical observations provide considerable support for the hypothesis that a strained unhappy relationship probably existed between Larry and his mother during his early formative years.

Further supporting evidence is obtained from the Parental Attitude Research Instrument (PARI), which provides objective measures of hostility and control in maternal childrearing attitudes. In response to this questionnaire, Larry's mother received an extremely high score on the hostility factor and a very low score on the control factor. In fact, of the many mothers of psychotic children studied in recent years at this institution, Larry's mother obtained the highest hostility score seen thus far. These findings further indicate that she felt very uncomfortable in her marital relationship and maternal role and felt held down by child-rearing tasks. The low score on control probably indicates that she was not concerned about being involved with the child and would rather avoid him than worry about controlling him.

Both parents were administered the Rimland Diagnostic Checklist (DCL) and while Larry obtained fairly high scores on the autistic items, he received unusually high scores on the items indicative of childhood schizophrenia. Based on the mother's responses, Larry received a schizophrenia score of 16 and from the father's responses a comparable score of 12. Overall the A:S ratio (autism/schizophrenia) is about 2.5, which does not qualify as indicating infantile autism. However, it does indicate relatively high standing on the syndrome of childhood schizophrenia.

Thus, this family constellation generally fits very harmoniously with theoretical statements in the literature concerning schizophrenic children and their families. The parents are sufficiently bright, the mother sufficiently hostile and rejecting, and the child sufficiently disturbed for this case to be viewed as an example of childhood psychosis caused by psychogenic factors.

LARRY FROM THE BIOGENIC VIEWPOINT

This boy's abnormalities could be regarded as resulting from some form of central nervous system disorder, although the evidence is ambiguous. After a thorough examination at a leading medical center, it was concluded that Larry suffered from a "developmental expressive language disorder; that is, congenital motor aphasia." However, a later report from the pediatric-neurologist at the medical center stated that his examination showed no specific neurological signs and that Larry appeared to have adequate intellectual ability, but gave "the basic picture of autistic behavior."

The mother's pregnancy with Larry lasted somewhat longer than nine months. Labor lasted about 12 hours, and was described by the mother as being "very rough" because it was extremely painful. She reported that delivery was prolonged and difficult, with Larry's head subjected to a great deal of battering because of poor dilation. She was of the impression that this difficult delivery must have caused some type of brain damage. However, Larry was described by his mother as having been a healthy newborn, weighing 8 pounds and 3 ounces at birth with no need for oxygen or special care. Mother and child were discharged from the hospital after three days.

Larry was somewhat colicky until 3 months of age, but generally ate and slept well during his first year. The mother was unable to breast-feed Larry and he was, therefore, bottle-fed from the first week of life until being weaned at 14 months of age. Throughout his first year, Larry was described as very quiet and sweet. He played with toys and was "a very good baby." However, while he did not strenuously object to being held, he was not very cuddly.

When he was four months old, Larry was riding with his parents when they had an automobile accident, with their car striking a guard rail. Larry was thrown out of his carbed, but remained in the car. Hospital examination noted a bruise on the left side of his forehead. He was not x-rayed or treated for this, and since no symptoms developed, the family considers this incident unimportant.

During the second year of life, Larry seemed to be physically normal, but the parents became concerned about his lack of speech and the fact that emotionally he did not compare favorably with other children whom they observed. He did not utter his first words until he was three years and one month old, and the parents feel that they "forced him" to do so by ignoring his nonverbal demands. About two years of age, toilet training was attempted but with little success. The mother believed that this difficulty was because Larry was nonverbal and thus did not understand what she was attempting to get him to do. Until age five, bowel control remained a problem with Larry.

When Larry was two years of age, a brother was born following an uneventful and comfortable pregnancy and delivery. The child is said to be normal, healthy, and happy. The emotional well-being of this younger brother provides rather compelling evidence to contradict the notion that these parents were responsible for Larry's psychotic adjustment. This is the position taken by theorists like Rimland and others with a biogenic orientation. According to this view, since parents with a seriously disturbed child like Larry are so often found to have other perfectly normal children within their family, it does not seem plausible that they would show selective psychopathology toward one child to a degree that would lead to psychosis.

Returning now to the diagnostic process with Larry, beginning at two years of age he was examined by pediatricians and neurologists in various settings where the parents sought help for his delayed speech development. In general, it was felt that Larry was not mentally retarded, but was slow in development, and showed some autistic features. The parents even attempted to obtain some special language training for Larry at a school for deaf children. When he was not quite three years of age, he was accepted for the program at a day-care center for physically and neurologically handicapped youngsters. Psychological evaluation at the time showed potential for at least average intellectual functioning but also revealed development delays in several areas, particularly language and motor skills. The language difficulties included problems in both comprehension and expression, with receptive ability the more seriously impaired. Moreover, there was diminished ability to integrate aural material.

In view of the emotional component in Larry's abnormal functioning, it was recommended that he be institutionalized at a children's psychiatric hospital. In this residential treatment setting, Larry was enrolled in a behavior modification program for "autistic" children where, at the time of the present study, he was completing a year of treatment. As evidence of cerebral dysfunction in this case, Larry had a febrile convulsion at 20 months of age. At that time the EEG was mildly abnormal, and although the findings were not prominent or specific, they lend support to an organic basis for the convulsion. An EEG done at the psychiatric hospital, some months after Larry's admission, showed "no significant abnormality." However, a comprehensive staff conference devoted the Larry's case, approximately six months after his institutionalization, led to the formal psychiatric diagnosis of "chronic brain syndrome" and "immature personality."

In other words, in this particular psychiatric hospital setting it was decided that the most prominent aspect of this case, for diagnostic purposes, was the organic disorder. This diagnostic decision was made in spite of the absence of convincing evidence of brain dysfunction. In this regard, note that Larry is a very attractive boy who appears physically normal and healthy. Also, what may seem an irrelevant observation, both of Larry's parents are Jewish. However, these physical and ethnic features have been described by Rimland as being characteristic of autistic children whom he believes suffer from a difficult to detect neurological abnormality.

OVERVIEW AND CONCLUSIONS

Here we see a boy who clearly exhibits abnormal development. Results of psychological evaluations make it evident that he cannot be classified as mentally retarded even though his abilities in some areas are well below normal. Actually, he was found to perform many tasks at a better than average level for his age, even though his verbal skills are deficient. The most recent psychological examiner stated that Larry's pattern of abilities in the verbal area suggest a central auditory disorder that has affected his ability to encode language. This clinical psychologist also felt that Larry had developed well in many areas despite serious handicaps, which provides some encouragement for his future outlook.

However, this boy remains far from normal. He continues to be shy, anxious, and withdrawn in the presence of adults. He still evidences a few odd mannerisms and does not use language in keeping with his chronological age or his estimated intellectual ability. These serious abnormalities are found in a boy who is the offspring of very bright, well-educated, and seemingly successful parents who are presently rearing a "normal" younger brother. Does it then seem likely that this "refrigerator mother" and rather detached scientifically oriented father caused the strange behavior evidenced by this son? Or does it seem more likely that some form of brain dysfunction or central nervous system deficiency had led to his inadequate development and abnormal behavior?

It is not our intention to attempt to provide answers for these questions or clarification of these issues. The main purpose of this presentation is to show how it is possible to view the same case from different viewpoints and to make it all fit rather neatly. If a theorist or clinician preferred to view this case from a psychogenic viewpoint, and to minimize the organic aspects, the material could quite easily be made to fit with psychodynamic interpretations. On the other hand, if one had a predilection to approach this case material from the biogenic viewpoint, it would also seem to make good sense, with little necessity of calling on psychological explanations. In view of the problems we have emphasized in this one case, is it any wonder that differing schools of thought find it so difficult to reconcile their theoretical and clinical differences?

7

CONCLUDING COMMENTS

The reader should now be well aware of the many unresolved issues in this field. Among the most important of these are the roles of heredity and environment in producing childhood psychopathology. Most behavioral scientists agree that these contributing factors interact and rarely, if ever, can severe psychological disorder be attributed solely to constitutional *or* environmental causes. It seems more likely that in many instances of childhood disorder traumatic life experiences meet a vulnerable child. For example, many children with learning disabilities are believed to have various forms of neurological and sensory impairments. Certain types of psychosomatic disorders are said to be partially attributable to "organ weakness" or physical susceptibility. And the controversy regarding psychological versus biological causation is seen most vividly in the conflicting views of childhood psychosis. Leading workers in the field have assumed diametric positions, with some attributing this severely disabling condition to psychological interactions between parent and child, and others maintaining that the disorder is entirely due to a constitutional defect in the child.

Psychotic children, who are the most seriously disturbed of all, do not usually come from the worst backgrounds. A child like Roy, who underwent early experiences that must have been extremely traumatic, might well be expected to become psychotic, yet he did not. Starting from the most horrible beginnings imaginable, he was less emotionally disturbed than the psychotic children whose early life experiences certainly seem much better than his. Moreover, Roy was able to benefit from psychotherapeutic treatment and eventually to return to society, while Kevin and Jerry appear destined to spend the rest of their days in closed institutions. Obviously, we have much to learn about causes of these varied forms of child disorders. Hardly anyone would deny that society's ills can quite easily make a physically healthy infant into a psychologically disordered child. And most would agree that the majority of childhood emotional and behavioral problems could be greatly alleviated with a lessening of the social pathology that is so rampant today.

Another interesting observation is that this casebook contains more boys than girls. In the introduction to the section on psychosis we mentioned that the incidence of this particular disorder is much higher in boys. This finding is not limited to psychosis but is true for most types of childhood psychopathology, with a general incidence of about four to one in favor of boys. At the adult level, however, this ratio changes dramatically, with more females than males undergoing treatment in psychiatric institutions. Sociocultural factors could be strongly influencing these findings. In childhood, girls do not get into the kinds of trouble that come to the attention of authorities; they are more apt to be quietly neurotic, with less acting-out or participation in delinquent activities. That is, their emotional difficulties and psychopathology may be expressed quite differently from boys. By adulthood, the more serious emotional difficulties of females come to the fore, requiring psychiatric treatment. Also, certain biophysical changes that accompany increasing age seem to have more detrimental effects on the psychological adjustment of women in adult life.

In view of the prevalence of childhood disorders, there is great need for effective methods of treatment. We have seen from the present cases that marked success is not the usual outcome of child therapy. Some available treatments seem to work better than others, and there is much greater likelihood of therapeutic success with certain types of disturbed children than with others. From the cases described here, one should gain a realistic awareness of the complexities involved and the great many obstacles that must be overcome in any successful therapeutic venture.

It is essential to conduct follow-up studies of individuals who have undergone various kinds of psychiatric, psychological, and special educational treatments in childhood, and to evaluate the effectiveness of these procedures. These traditional "therapeutic" practices are extremely expensive, and should not be perpetuated routinely without a demonstration of their worth. If adequate follow-up studies were conducted with former child patients who had been treated in different settings throughout the country, there would be much more objective evidence to help decide which kinds of "therapy" are obviously ineffective and should be replaced with newer therapeutic approaches that might prove more successful.

Grappling with these issues can be a most frustrating and depressing enterprise, and many people would prefer to avoid thinking about them. However, it is imperative that society does not turn away from its troubled children. For it is the nature of the human race that adults must devote much of their energies to nurturing their offspring if society is to survive. If the kinds of childhood disturbances described in this casebook are allowed to occur with increasing frequency, our society will become ever more pathological. The reaction is that of a vicious cycle, with emotionally disturbed children growing into troubled adults who then have a crippling effect on the succeeding generation. Children may try, but rarely do they develop to their fullest potential in pathological social surroundings. There must be better ways to ease the conflicts of children, and all people who care should search to find them.

INDEX